From the Volcano
to the Gorge

Getting the Job Done on Iwo Jima

Howard N. McLaughlin, Jr.
Raymond C. Miller

TOWER
PUBLISHING

For permission to use any material from this book or product, submit a request to: Tower Publishing, 588 Saco Rd., Standish, ME 04084
http://www.towerpub.com

Acknowledgments:
The authors of the two memoirs contained in this book have done their best to capture on paper accurately and comprehensively what they experienced, felt, and thought as they took part in the invasion of Iwo Jima. With the passage of more than half a century, some details, particularly names of individuals, may have been lost or misremembered, but the book is true to the authors' recollection of events.

The maps shown on pages 201-204 are reprinted with the kind permission of historyofwar.org, a website whose account of the Iwo Jima campaign at http://www.historyofwar.org/articles/battles_iwojima.html is highly recommended.

Information about sunset and sunrise times on Iwo Jima during the invasion was provided by the Web site sunposition.com.

Cover Designed by: Mitchell Fernie Design & Production, Cumberland, ME

Cover Photos used courtesy of the National Archives, Washington, DC

ISBN-13: 978-0-9827955-4-5

PRINTED IN THE UNITED STATES OF AMERICA

TABLE OF CONTENTS

TABLE OF CONTENTS

Publisher's Preface

No moment in American military history is more deeply stamped into our national memory than the flag-raising that marked the capture by U.S. Marines of Mount Suribachi, on the tiny Pacific island of Iwo Jima, in February 1945. The famous photograph of that moment, widely reproduced in magazines, books, films, and statuary, has for nearly two-thirds of a century stood as the quintessential symbol of American patriotism and Marine valor.

This is as it should be. The battle of Iwo Jima, whatever the historians eventually decide its strategic importance to have been, was a monumental clash that demanded near-superhuman effort and sacrifice on the part of both the American attackers and the Japanese defenders. Suribachi, a dead volcano at the island's southern tip, was a heavily fortified artillery platform and all-seeing observation post. As long as it remained in Japanese hands, it threatened the entire U.S. operation. The gallantry of the small band of Marines who first made it to the top and raised the flag was undeniably crucial to the success of the invasion.

But that moment, which came on the fourth day after the initial landing, was far from the end of the battle. It would take another month of fierce fighting, covering 5,000 rocky acres and claiming the lives of 17,000 more Japanese soldiers and 6,000 more Marines, before full victory was achieved. The capture of Suribachi, militarily and psychologically important though it was, was only the end of the beginning.

This book combines autobiographical narratives by two Marines who landed on the beaches on the first day of the invasion, cheered the flag-raising, and went on to take part in the grinding combat to the bitter end. Howard McLaughlin, nineteen years old on that first day, became a civil engineer after the war and had a forty-year career in California highway construction as well as many years as an entrepreneur and a volunteer in community service. Ray Miller, who was twenty on the first day, returned from the war to his native Midwest and eventually settled in Maine, along the way becoming, among other things, a designer of machine tools, a psychologist, an inventor, and a musician. These two men lived through the most intense weeks of their lives within a mile of each other, but never knew of each other's existence until this book began to take shape six decades later. Neither is a professional author, but each writes vividly and memorably about his role in the historic victory and about traumatic experiences that made him into a man different from the one he would have without the war.

Tower Publishing Company is proud to have the opportunity to give a wider readership to what began as private memoirs written by Howard and Ray for their families and friends. No attempt has been made to "homogenize" the book by blending passages where the two accounts overlap each other or where the authors' recollections differ. We have also chosen, after much consideration, not to try to "sterilize" the often profane and arguably racist language attributed to Marines engaged in prolonged mortal combat. We realize that this risks offending some readers, but we believe it is important that these authentic voices be preserved.

Hundreds of books have been published about Iwo Jima, some by historians taking broad views, some by historians compiling the recollections of battle participants, and some—like this one—by the participants themselves, recounting what it felt like to be in the midst of the action they experienced. We are convinced, though, that more stories remain to be told. With the passage of years, the ranks of those who can tell us those untold stories are dwindling. We hope that the example of this book will encourage other Iwo Jima veterans and their families to take steps to preserve for posterity their memories of what can justly be called America's finest hour.

IWO JIMA
or
Thirty-Five Days in
HELL

As experienced by
Howard N. McLaughlin, Jr.
PFC USMCR

Chapter 1

A WAR STORY

The harsh notes of the bugle sounding over the USS *Darke*'s P.A. system, accompanied by the shrill notes of the bosun's pipe, announced to all hands aboard that a new day had officially started: Monday, February 19, 1945.

Few if any of the men packed like sardines into the belowdecks compartments were awakened by this raucous noise. Occupants of my 400-man compartment, after cleaning and oiling their weapons for the fourth or fifth time, had found themselves with little to do but wander nervously all night long. They drifted to the adjacent heads (toilets) for a smoke, or out on deck to line the rail and gaze silently into the dark, or back to the compartment to lie down and stare at the bottom of the bunk inches above, wishing for sleep that would not come.

Simultaneously with the bugle's blare the compartment lights were turned on, replacing the eerie red battle nightlights with a harsh white glare that clearly showed the tension on the men's faces. Their somber mood was accentuated by the jumbled piles of equipment and field packs stacked in the aisles and passageways. The compartment clock showed the time to be 0330 hours.

Beginning with the previous evening's meal a pall had settled like a wet blanket over everyone, replacing the usual small talk and banter among the troops with rising levels of irritation. Even best friends snapped at each other, and here and there men who had gotten on each other's nerves for weeks now broke into open arguments and yelling. The usual games of craps and pinochle were going on in the heads and gangways, but the usual liveliness was gone. The players went through the motions mechanically and almost silently, as though they hoped to pass the dragging time a little faster.

Uppermost in every man's thoughts was fear—partly fear of facing the enemy in combat but partly a new fear, that after months of pretended indifference to danger, when the final test came you might not measure up to being a Marine in the eyes of your buddies. For every man, no matter how tough he tried to be, this past night had been a time for private thoughts, reflections on what it might be like to die, and lots of prayer. Every man had reasons for his God to let him be among those who lived through this landing.

The tension was far too great for anyone to have slept.

These sleepless men belonged to the Fifth Marine Division, part of a force of 32,000 Marines being delivered by the USS *Darke* and forty-two other troop transports, plus hundreds of warships and cargo ships, to invade and secure the tiny but important Japanese island called Iwo Jima. The master plan for the invasion didn't call for anybody on this ship to go ashore in any of the first three assault waves. Some were scheduled to land in succeeding waves later on this first day, though, and all of us knew that we could be called at any time to leave the ship and reinforce those already on the landing beaches.

We were psyched up and ready. All of us had trained for well over a year and a half for this day, and we understood the stakes: U.S. Air Corps B-29 bombers were now bombing the Japanese homeland daily from bases on the recently captured islands of Saipan and Tinian. According to all reports, the bombing was causing considerable damage, but more was needed to clear the way for our final assault against Japan. Daily broadcasts from "Tokyo Rose" were telling all Americans in the Pacific that even the women and children were being trained to defend their country to the death. Capturing Iwo Jima would move our line of bases closer to the target, as well as knocking out two airfields (and a third under construction) from which enemy fighter aircraft could intercept our bombers enroute to and from their missions.

Not everybody was ready in the same way. I was a heavy equipment mechanic with the Fifth Division's Engineer Battalion. We were specialists, whose job was to repair damaged heavy engineer equipment, bulldozers, cranes, and all kinds of heavy trucks. Like all Marines, we had gone through basic infantry training when we joined the Corps. Instead of going on to serve in the "Infantry" occupational category, though, we were assigned to the "Combat Engineer" category, which required technical training in construction, demolition, and related fields. After that training, some combat engineers were assigned to "line" infantry companies (which did the actual fighting). Others, like me, were selected for transfer to the Engineer Battalion's Headquarters & Service (H&S) Company (which did all of the service work and maintenance for all of the battalion heavy equipment; it was considered a rear-echelon support element).

The master invasion plan did not call for us H&S Company mechanics to go ashore on Iwo at all, unless there was damaged engineer equipment to repair after the battle—which was officially expected to take a few days at most. With our specialized training, it was considered best to save us as a resource to support the upcoming assault on Okinawa and then the invasion of Kyushu, the southernmost island of mainland Japan. The Iwo Jima plan assigned two of the Fifth Division's three regiments, the 27th and 28th Marines, to carry out the assault; the three battalions of the other regiment, the 26th Marines, were designated as Landing Teams 1/26, 2/26, and 3/26 and held in reserve for emergencies. If my unit, the 25-man Repair Section, did get called ashore, it would be split into three fully equipped machine-gun crews and attached to Landing Team 3/26.

We knew that in a combat emergency any Marine could be sent to fill a gap in an infantry unit, and that service troops had proved their worth as emergency infantry replacements more than once in previous Pacific landings. We also knew, though, that untrained newcomers placed in active combat units suffer higher casualties than the veterans alongside them, and we knew that in addition to lacking advanced infantry training we were seriously out of shape.

In the eyes of "real" Marines, H&S Company engineers—and mechanics in particular—were in a category even lower than cooks and bakers. Cooks and bakers and musicians would serve as stretcher bearers for the wounded. Clerks and typists would land and fight as infantry. Even the division and regimental command post people would land ahead of us.

Although I had joined the Marines wanting to win some medals, now that I was actually this close to combat this idea of landing after the fighting was all over sounded just fine to me. With my newfound "maturity" I preferred to learn about combat a little at a time, not just be dumped onto the beach in the middle of the battle.

At 0400 the bosun's pipe sounded again, announcing that breakfast was beginning in the ship's galley. D-Day breakfast was something like a condemned man's last supper—they actually served real steaks and fresh eggs, cooked any way you wanted, as much as you wanted.

I don't think many people really chowed down on this morning, but in the next few days many of us would sure wish we had.

The only food the combat troops making the landing would carry off the ship with them were Assault Rations—small round hard candies, practically all sugar, for energy—and some D-rations, a small hard chocolate bar in a waterproof container. These bars were so hard that unless you had a knife to cut off slices with, all you could do was gnaw on them, leaving rat-like teeth marks. After a few days supplies started coming ashore, including the old stand-by K-rations. Each K-ration packet contained a small can of meat or cheese and some graham crackers, along with four cigarettes and a small packet of powder to make a cup of coffee.

At 0530 the earsplitting "General Quarters" gong sounded over the P.A. system, ending meal service and calling all members of the ship's crew to man their battle stations. The gong was followed immediately by an announcement that this was to be a modified G.Q., with us passengers helping the crew break open the cargo hatches, bring up pallets of artillery ammunition from the holds, and put the hatch covers back in place. One of those holds lay under the mess hall, which (on every troop transport) would be used as a hospital area when needed. Other storage holds lay under the troop compartments; while we had been eating our breakfast, our bunks had been dismantled and stacked to one side so that those hatch covers could be removed.

Out on the weather decks, other members of the crew had begun unleashing the landing craft that each troop transport and cargo ship carried. The *Darke*, like other ships built to the same design, carried twenty of these little LCVPs ("Landing Craft, Vehicle and Personnel"). Each had a crew of three and was just big enough to carry thirty-six combat Marines, or one Jeep and a small trailer plus a handful of troops. The front was hinged to drop flat, so troops and supplies could easily be unloaded onto the beach while the craft was still afloat. Since there were no first-wave troops aboard the *Darke*, all of its LCVPs headed for other ships as soon as they were in the water.

Jeeps and light trucks were stored in the holds below our bunk area. Once those holds were open, we mechanics did our thing—checking vehicles and equipment to make sure they would start, and releasing tie-downs. As soon as the checks were completed, the ship's cranes began hoisting the equipment out of the holds and onto LCMs ("Landing Craft, Mechanized") that were beginning to come alongside. The LCMs were about one and a half times the size of the LCVPs; they, too, had a hinged front ramp that would allow the equipment, at least in theory, to be driven directly off onto the dry beach.

Chapter 2

BEFORE THE BATTLE

I was born and raised in Northern California and attended schools in Sacramento. My sixteenth birthday was two days after Pearl Harbor.

Even before Pearl Harbor there were enough boys in our high school junior and senior years interested in improving our chances of getting into the Canadian armed forces that some special classes were offered.

December seventh changed all that. The focus of the special classes was changed to preparing students for entry into the United States armed forces upon graduation, and the classes were instantly filled to overflowing as students requested transfer into them. ROTC classes also quickly filled to capacity. (There were six full Junior ROTC Battalions in the four high schools in Sacramento. By the end of high school I had advanced to become one of the Battalion Commanders, so I graduated with the rank of Major.)

All most boys could talk about in their free time was the U.S. military service and which of its various branches were really the best. In the middle of our senior year, recruitment testing was begun by the Army, Navy and Army Air Corps.

Just about everyone, including me, wanted to join the Army Air Corps and become a fighter pilot. But when I took the Air Corps examinations, what they offered me was a chance to go to college and become a bombardier/navigator. I wasn't thrilled enough with that offer to pursue it.

I had already decided that I didn't want to join the Army. I was actually more interested in what the Marines were doing on the Guadalcanal.

I took the Navy's general test when they held it, and I was one of several students from the four high schools who were called back to take some more tests. These tests established that my IQ score was easily more than high enough to qualify me as officer material and that my mechanical aptitude was also way above normal. The Navy quickly offered to put me through college, and they sent me to San Francisco to appear before a selection board of Navy officers. During this oral interview I learned about the Navy's "V-12" program, from which I could graduate as either a Navy ensign or a Marine second lieutenant. I quickly accepted that offer. I was sworn into the U.S. Marines on March 15, 1943, with my reporting for duty deferred until I graduated from high school in June.

By the time we graduated, at least a quarter to a third of the boys in my high school class were already enlisted in some branch of the service. Four of us from the Sacramento area schools were selected for the V-12 program, and sent to approved colleges where, upon graduation, we would be commissioned as Marine second lieutenants.

The school I was sent to was a four-year college in Flagstaff, Arizona, which is now known as Northern Arizona University. I was one of two hundred Marine cadets and two hundred Naval Cadets. The discipline and military training were great. But at the end of the first semester, although all my other grades were good, my English classes were all failures; and like all other "non-hackers" (both Navy and Marines) I was dropped from the V-12 program and transferred to the Fleet.

The only really good thing about school was that I met a local girl named Helen Ulrey. We kept in very close contact for the next thirty months.

I reported to the Marine Corps Recruit Depot San Diego as one of around 750 to 800 men (boys, really) who showed up that week from Navy V-12 schools across the country. Marine boot camp has a fearsome reputation, but for us with one semester of the V-12 program under our belts, it was like going to Boy Scout camp. I graduated from MCRD San Diego on December 25, 1943 as a PFC.

My first assignment after boot camp was with the Marine Raiders at Camp Pendleton, California. I got there just as the Raiders were being disbanded and used as the nucleus of the new Fifth Marine Division, so I was sent to Camp Elliott, just north of San Diego, to attend infantry school. Upon completion of that course I was transferred back to Camp Pendleton to be part of the just-arriving Fifth Engineer Battalion of the new Fifth Marine Division. That was great, although it was an all east-coast outfit; I quickly found out there were only four of us in the whole battalion from the west coast.

In the first week of September 1944 the whole Fifth Marine Division set sail for overseas. We went first to Hawaii, for more training. Then right at the end of 1944 we again set sail, this time for combat on an unknown island in the Pacific.

Chapter 3

THE CHOSEN FEW

Because the Landing Team we mechanics were assigned to was in reserve and not scheduled to land any time before the third day, we had some free time when we had finished our work down in the holds for the time being. Several of us went topside and found seats along the bulkheads, out of the way of the unloading operations, to watch the "show."

It was still dark, but all the troop transports around us had turned on their deck lights to enable the sailors to see what they were doing. There were ships on all sides of us as far as the eye could see—four or five times as many as had been in our convoy out from Hawaii.

About ten miles off the starboard bow was the dark hulk of Iwo Jima. We knew from our training on the way here that it was only a little porkchop-shaped island, less than five miles from south to north and two and a half miles wide at the northern end. The southern end of the island was dominated by Mount Suribachi, an extinct volcano 550 feet high. Just north of Suribachi was the narrowest part of the island, only 700 yards wide. A plain of black volcanic sand stretched northward from there for a couple of miles, giving way by the mid-point of the island to a craggy 350-foot-high plateau of volcanic rock full of ridges and gorges that had been eroded by wind and rain into fantastic shapes perpendicular to our line of advance. There was no fresh water on the island, and in some areas steam still rose from fissures in the earth.

All we could see of the island was a continuous sparkling of naval artillery shells bursting on its surface, fired by U.S. Navy ships that lay between us and the shore. In the cold morning air the gunfire came to our ears as a steady rumble.

In all our briefings on the landing, the Navy had predicted that this pre-invasion shelling from all of these warships would pulverize every man-made structure on the island, allowing the Marines to walk ashore without having to fire a shot. We Marines had reason to be doubtful: Similar naval boasts before our amphibious landings on Tarawa, Saipan, Guam, and Peleliu had been terribly wrong, and each time many Marines had paid a terrible price.

As dawn broke and visibility began improving, some of the Navy warships moved in even closer to shore, firing almost point-blank at the area overlooking the landing beaches. Looking through field glasses, we agreed that the shells were exploding among shapes that looked like pillboxes and gun emplacements, but we couldn't be sure—the beach area mostly looked like one big cloud of smoke.

It was also quite a show to watch as Navy and Marine planes dive-bombed and strafed the lower slopes of Mount Suribachi, but the real crowd-pleasers were big LSTs ("Landing Ship, Tank") that had been specially modified to serve as floating rocket launchers. They drove in really close to shore and poured thousands of fiery-tailed 4.5-inch rockets in volleys onto the landing beaches.

There was no return fire from the island. The cordon of warships tightened around it, and the troop ships all moved in closer as well—this would shorten the time it took for the LCVPs to get from them to shore. A couple of destroyers moved in and poured high-volume gunfire into the area around the beaches. Their work was easy to see because of the streams of tracer bullets, which were like fiery fingers probing the smoky shores of the island.

As the Navy had said all along, it just didn't seem possible that there could be anybody alive on that island after all the shelling.

By 0815, as the transports moved still closer to the island, it looked like you could walk from one transport to another on all the little landing craft in the water between them. I would guess that the LCVPs alone must have totaled almost a thousand. Besides them there were LCMs, LSTS, LSMs ("Landing Ship, Medium"), amtracs (amphibious tractors), amtanks (amphibious tanks), DUKWs (type

DKW amphibious Utility trucks), and Control Boats. The whole ocean was covered with little circles of landing craft waiting for the order to move into attack formation.

Soon signal flares of various colors were fired into the air from the command ship, and the little craft began lining up into three waves.

The first wave would be all amtanks, each armed with a 75-mm cannon and a 50-caliber machine gun. Their mission was to stay on the beach till the first three waves were all ashore, then move inland providing fire support to the advancing troops, like regular tanks, until the island was secured.

The second wave would be all amtracs, each delivering about twenty-four Marines to join the assault. Amtracs were armed with two machine guns, one 50-caliber and one 30-caliber; unlike the LCVPs that would land later, they were also armored with a steel hull, and their exit ramp opened to the rear. These features gave the Marines inside some protection against small-arms fire as they exited and moved onto the beach. Once the amtracs had unloaded, they were to return to the transport ships for more troops or supplies. On later trips the amtracs would also be responsible for returning any wounded to the ships.

The third wave would be all LCVPs; all the waves that followed later would be LCVPs, mingled with amtracs on their repeat runs.

Finally we were able to see three distinct waves, moving very slowly toward the shore.

At 0845 the shelling was increased to include every naval gun that could possibly fire at the landing beaches. This raised so much smoke and dust that the landing beaches were obscured—the whole island, in fact, became invisible from where we were.

In the midst of this barrage, a single green star shell was fired. This was the signal for the first three waves to start their mad dash towards the beach.

Our ship's loudspeaker system had been set on the command radio frequency being used by the landing units of the 27th and 28th Marines. At 0902 the units exiting the amtracs onto the beach began calling back to their commanders still on board ship, reporting that there was no small-arms fire from the Japanese and only very light artillery shelling. Similar reports began coming in from more and more units as they landed.

Everybody breathed a sigh of relief. It sounded like this was going to be a fairly easy landing for a change, meeting resistance only from a few scattered small groups of Jap troops. Maybe the Navy's optimism was finally right.

As soon as the LCVPs had landed the third wave, they raced back to the troop transports for more Marines. The fourth wave was already lined up, ready to start towards the beach as soon as the third-wave landing craft were out of the way. The object, naturally, was to put as many people as possible ashore as quickly as possible in order to steamroller over any enemy soldiers who might choose to fight.

As the fifth wave landed, the euphoria aboard the ships began to evaporate. The units newly coming ashore were radioing back that there was a lot of mortar and artillery fire now on the landing beaches; a lot of the unit radios that had been reporting earlier had now gone silent.

At first we all assumed that the earlier waves were just so busy moving inland that they didn't have time to report back about their progress. Soon, though, it began to become clear that nobody was moving inland. Most of the troops were still on the first hundred yards of the beach, being cut to ribbons by Jap shellfire, and they were reporting that if they couldn't be reinforced right away, they would shortly be pushed back into the water.

We listened intently to the loudspeakers as the commanders aboard ship talked with those ashore, urgently trying to piece together a picture of what was happening and why the first units to land hadn't reported it. Finally they understood the terrible truth: The incoming enemy fire was extremely accurate, and while all the units ashore were taking heavy casualties, the Japs were singling out officers and radio operators. There was now no communication with many of the units on the beach. Even as we listened, radios on the beach would go silent in mid-conversation.

Frantic calls for help came from the officers ashore who still survived and had working radios. Besides replacements for the heavy casualties they were taking, they needed tanks and demolition explosives if they were to stay alive. Too many Jap pillboxes and bunkers had escaped damage in the pre-assault shelling; until they were destroyed, it would be impossible for the Marines to get off the landing beaches.

By the time the sixth wave began landing, the Navy's Beachmaster unit was ashore and functioning. Their radio reports added more grim details to the picture. Most of the LCVPs were being destroyed by deadly accurate Jap artillery fire as they dropped their ramps to unload troops. More than half of the fourth- and fifth-wave LCVPs were lost, as were more than two-thirds of those in the sixth wave. The amtanks and amtracs had made it ashore all right, but were bogging down in loose volcanic sand unlike any sand they had encountered before. Once bogged down, they were being systematically destroyed by accurate Jap shellfire.

Now that the naval shelling was over, the pall of smoke and dust was beginning to lift. Even at our distance, we could see concrete pillboxes—many more of them than the planners had estimated— firing down on the landing beaches. The units ashore reported that there were still more that we couldn't see because they were superbly camouflaged. Most of the pillboxes were firing 20-mm cannon or 50-caliber machine guns, the reports said, and a few were armed with tank-killing 47-mm cannon. Very few had been damaged enough to prevent them from firing on the landing Marines.

Deadly as the pillboxes and bunkers were, they fired flat-trajectory, line-of-sight weapons, so our units could spot them and send infantrymen and engineers to destroy them. Our troops were helpless, though, against the high-trajectory artillery and mortar shells raining in on them from out-of-sight firing positions elsewhere on the island.

In an effort to take some of the enemy pressure off, the Navy moved several ships in very close to shore, where their gun batteries could provide direct support to our operations. I guess the Navy felt guilty about the amtanks and amtracs that were now only expensive scrap metal on the beaches, and thought they would do this to replace the lost firepower. It turned out, though, that there weren't many targets the ships could fire at without endangering nearby Marines.

Meanwhile, the seventh, eighth, and ninth waves of LCVPs were landing and being decimated on the beaches. It was quite apparent that this landing was not going well at all, and that the people already ashore were in danger of being pushed off the island if something wasn't done right away.

A little after 1100, Landing Team 3/26 was ordered to report to its debarkation stations on the double. Very soon there were enough troops at each station for at least two LCVP loads, and in most cases four.

As we engineers stood there with the rest of 3/26, we figured we were being mustered as work details to load more cargo from the ship's holds. After all, the invasion was less than three hours old, and although it was going sour fast, there should be plenty of combat-trained infantry available to send into the battle before they called us. Besides, the original plan called for Landing Team 2/26 to be sent in ahead of us, and we assumed that the sequence would remain as planned.

We were naïve. Marine officers began walking quickly down through the assembled ranks of troops, selecting individual men and having them step to the front. When they had picked some 300 of us from my side of the ship—about eight LCVP loads—they ordered those of us in front to go get all our combat gear on the double and be back in ranks in five minutes. The men in back were to stay where they were. Eight of us engineers, who according to the invasion plan were to serve as a single gun crew, were split into two gun crews and assigned to one of the boats.

We had packed our backpacks and all our combat gear the night before, and they were still piled around the edges of the compartment where our bunks had been. All we had to do was find them, saddle up, and hurry back to our boat stations, stopping only for a last-minute visit to the heads.

By the time we got back to our stations, the men who had been left at the railing had already lowered piles of boxes, plus my crew's machine gun and extra ammo, into the eight landing craft floating along our side of the ship. Officers took our names and then we climbed over the railing and started the long climb down the cargo nets to the boats below.

We were heavily loaded.

Most of us had donned "long johns" because of the cold, and I wore a wool shirt besides. We all wore dungaree pants, but replaced our dungaree jackets with wool-lined field jackets. Under our pants we wore leggings, strapped tightly for better ankle support.

We all wore steel helmets, too, of course, but we engineers were not issued the distinctive camouflage covers that marked Marines in the Pacific theater from the "doggies" (the Army). I don't know whether there just weren't enough covers for every Marine, or whether our officers didn't know how the rest of the Corps was equipped. Based on other things that happened, I suspect that ignorance was the reason.

As I remember, we were supposed to leave the chin straps of our helmets unbuckled as we climbed down the nets, so that if we fell in the drink the weight of the helmet wouldn't pull us under. Once on land, we were supposed to buckle the straps, so that we wouldn't lose our helmets when we ran.

Nobody explained to us how to avoid being dragged under water by the rest of our gear, or what to say to some poor soul already in the boat if your unsecured helmet got knocked loose during your descent and fell on him. As I guess you can imagine, we all buckled our helmets and other gear as we descended the cargo nets. (On land we didn't buckle our helmets under our chins, because a nearby shell burst that tried to lift your helmet off your head could break your jaw. Besides, most men soon learned to run in a crouch, with all body movement from the hips down and no jiggling of the helmet. If you had to jump or dive into a shell hole, you simply held your helmet on your head with whichever hand wasn't carrying your weapon.)

On our shoulders each of us wore a "light" version of the Field Transport Pack, which every enlisted Marine was issued for all of his clothing and equipment. The detachable lower half of the FTP, containing important but not-immediately-needed items (like spare boots), we left behind for delivery to us later. We turned the upper half of the FTP into a combat pack by strapping on attachments: an entrenching tool (small folding shovel) on the back and a bedroll (blankets and poncho) in a horseshoe shape around the top and sides.

Each man carried a rifle and a bayonet, and wore a cartridge belt full of rifle clips, plus two extra bandoliers of clips. Attached to the belt and its suspenders were four canteens of water, three or four canvas first-aid pouches, two combat field dressings, two hand grenades, and a K-Bar combat knife. The rifle was slung over one shoulder, with the bottom part of the sling slipped under one of the canteens to keep the weapon in place. Also slung over one shoulder was the strap of a canvas gas-mask carrier that he tucked under his other arm.

The standard first-aid pouch was a three by six inch rectangle about an inch thick. It contained a small packet of Sulfa powder (a disinfectant that wounds were to be sprinkled with if possible) and a field dressing (a gauze pad with gauze strips attached on the sides to tie it in place). Some wounds, particularly from shrapnel, were far too big to be covered by the gauze pad, which was only six inches square.

But the pad and strips could be stuffed into a wound to stabilize it until a Corpsman got there. We also carried a couple of "special" first-aid pouches. These were about two inches thick and six inches square, divided into three compartments, one on top of another. For the life of me I can't remember what was in them, outside of some burn ointment and some water purification pills.

An annoying part of our load was a life preserver that "safety" rules required us to wear around our waists from the time we boarded the ship until the last minute before the ramp went down at the beach. These inflatable rubber belts, about six inches wide when flat, could be inflated in an emergency by little CO_2 cartridges to about the size of a pair of bicycle tires. They might have helped you float if you abandoned ship in just your dungarees, but if you had combat equipment on they were worthless and in the way. None of the Navy officers who made the rules could figure that out, so we wore them with our heavy packs as we started toward the beach.

To top all this off, I had "won" a coin toss which gave me the title of first gunner and the honor of carrying the tripod for the machine gun. That made a total of 100-120 pounds of stuff to run with. But then I was only three months past nineteen, young and strong (and dumb).

The sun was out, but the air was cold. A brisk wind was causing heavy swells and making travel in the small boats a rough ride.

Boarding was a challenge, too. Going down the cargo nets toward the LCVPs, you stepped on the horizontal ropes and kept your hands on the vertical risers, so the guy above you didn't step on your fingers. (He might step on your head, but not on your fingers.)

From up on the side of the ship we saw plainly how bad the swells were. Between the top of each one and the bottom of the trough that followed there was a sudden 15- to 20-foot drop for the little boats. Several of us at a time would climb down the net to the highest point the gunwale of a boat reached at the top of one swell. We'd hang on as it receded to the bottom of the next trough and began rising again; then, just as it neared the top of the swell, we'd all jump off the rungs and pray. With or without the mandatory lifebelt, any of us who missed that jump would have been all the way to the bottom of the ocean before we could get all our gear unbuckled.

We were lucky enough to get ourselves, our boxes of supplies, and our weapons and other gear aboard pretty smoothly, so we left the ship right away and headed out to join one of the circles of boats already forming up.

The three-man crew of the LCVP we were on consisted of a coxswain, a bosun's mate, and a gunner. The cox'n, who steered the boat, was in charge. The job of the bosun's mate was to get the front ramp down and unload the troops and gear as fast as possible the moment the boat touched the beach. The gunner, from a partly armored turret alongside the cox'n, would fire his 50-caliber machine gun over the heads of the landing troops.

With all of the boxes of materials in the back of the craft, there were only about twenty-five men on board. The eight of us who were engineers were being sent in as a couple of machine-gun crews, but I'm sure we had been asked for in hopes that we could help the line companies with combat demolition work. Although several of us had some demolition experience, we were primarily mechanics (like me), carpenters, and bridge builders.

I don't know who the other people in the boat were or what units they came from, but a lot of them seemed to be officers accompanied by radiomen. We were being called in from Division reserve to fill holes in the ranks of units that had already landed. I found out later that this piecemeal method of replacement was used because the Division command did not want to cannibalize the other combat units still trying to land.

These little landing craft really gave you a roller coaster ride in the heavy swells. There were a lot of green-looking faces, but—thank God for small favors—our boat didn't circle very long before another small boat came alongside us to give us our orders. (The earliest waves had not been so lucky. Although the invasion planners must have known how badly seasickness could affect men's fighting ability, they had called for the boats to be loaded before 0600 and to circle for hours before heading for shore.)

I can still remember almost the exact words the Navy officer in the control boat told our cox'n, by bullhorn: "You will be the number [something] boat from the right. Form up on boat number [something], the one flying the yellow pendant from its aerial. You are to land on Red Beach 1, just to the left of Futatsu Rock. This is wave number thirteen. When you see the signal flare go off, start for the beach at full power. Don't lag behind the boats alongside of you, and don't stay at the beach. Unload and get out. The beach is still hot. Good luck."

Although I was bewildered at the time by being thrust into combat so suddenly, it was for the best. The hardest part of any attack or advance is the sitting around waiting beforehand. If you have time to stop and think about all the bad things that might happen to you, you can easily work yourself into a nervous breakdown. Some people had known for three or four weeks that they would land in a certain wave. Not having time to think of all of these possibilities was far better. We had been busy since we were told to board the LCVPs, and the uncertainty of where we were going hadn't had time to register on my brain. I didn't have any time to get scared—everything was moving too fast.

Then there was a flare in the air, the motor revved up, and we were off on a bouncing and bone-shaking boat trip to a "beautiful Pacific island."

Chapter 4

THE BEAUTIFUL PACIFIC ISLAND

It was about a three-mile dash to the beach—a "dash" only in that these little boats were traveling as fast as they could. I'm not sure how fast that was, but they were far from being speedboats.

A cold wind was blowing, and the sea was so rough that it was easy to lose sight of the boats on either side of us—so rough that you couldn't even get seasick.

The roar of the engine drowned out other sounds—almost. The salvos of naval shells passing overhead were deafening, enough to rattle your teeth, so in the LCVP we could communicate only by hand signal or by yelling in each other's ear.

The Marine officer in charge of the troops in this boat passed word back: When we landed we were to go the high-water line and leave our packs, weapons and loose gear. Each of us was to return to the boat at least twice, remove all the boxes of ammunition, grenades, and explosives, and pile them with our gear at the high-water line. When we were finished, we were to wait next to our gear for further instructions.

This was not the kind of cargo handling I had expected.

Then the old call was passed: "Lock and load." It was time to load your weapon, check the gear of the man ahead of you, and remember your training. "The beach is very hot," we were told, meaning that it was under enemy fire. (That sounded just like a John Wayne movie.)

Next came the order to crouch on one knee, keep our heads down till the boat hit the beach and the ramp dropped, then run like hell, keeping our asses down.

Water began splashing into the boat. Those of us getting wet bitched about the cox'n's poor steering until we realized that it wasn't his fault—we were already under enemy shell fire. One nearby explosion really rocked the boat, soaking everybody and making it evident to even the dumbest of us that the shit was about to hit the fan.

We had been issued cellophane sleeves to slip over the muzzles of our rifles in order to keep water from entering the barrels during our boat ride and possibly ruining the weapons. But the old-timers from previous landings had told us that if you forgot to remove the sleeve before pulling the trigger your weapon wouldn't fire. Instead, they told us to cover the muzzle with a condom, which would be blown away as soon as the rifle was fired. If I remember right, we followed their advice, and as we landed those sleeves were still in with our gas masks. (Condoms, by the way, were a generally useful item of equipment—anything you wanted to keep dry you could put inside one and tuck it inside your helmet liner.)

After several more nearby explosions, we got the order to brace ourselves for impact on the beach. As I did so I instinctively looked at my watch. It was 1305, and somebody in the back of the boat was calling for a Corpsman (one of the Navy Medical Corps paramedics that serve with all Marine units). The boat's gunner had been wounded by shrapnel from one of the near misses.

Everything I saw for the next few hours is still plainly visible if I close my eyes, as clear to me after sixty years as it was at the instant it happened. In those exhilarating first few seconds, with the adrenalin really flowing, suddenly the realization that you were in danger was brought home to you. You are in combat. People are actually trying to kill you. This is no longer a game—it's for real. Time seemed to take on a surrealistic quality. Everything happened in slow motion. Small sounds were amplified, and the din of battle was silence. Your eyes saw everything. Your mind noted and remembered it all in minute detail. Time will never dull these scenes, nor will I ever be able to erase them from my mind's eye.

The boat struck the beach, stopping abruptly, and everybody was thrown towards the front.

It was not unusual at this point for landing-craft ramp mechanisms to jam, forcing the troops to climb up the sides, jump into the water, and wade ashore. Even worse was when the boat hit an underwater obstacle far from shore and the troops stepped off the end of the ramp into water that was still several feet deep (as in the terrible landing at Tarawa in 1943).

We escaped both of those possible disasters. Our boat's ramp went down as soon as our forward movement stopped, and we stood up and adjusted our loads. I carried the tripod for the machine gun in my left hand and with my right hand I tried to keep my rifle slung over my right shoulder and hooked around my canteen. This turned out to be too clumsy, and I soon shifted the rifle to my right hand as a counterbalance to the tripod. (If we had been "real" machine gunners in an infantry unit, our personal weapons would have been 45-caliber pistols instead of bulky rifles.)

In the intense excitement of the moment, the vastness of the area and the amount of destruction around us were beyond comprehension. It is still amazing to me how much I saw and how permanently it is registered in my brain.

The bow of the landing craft was hard aground, with a partly sunken ship on our right. Later I found out that we had landed on Red Beach 2, the northernmost of the Fifth Division beaches. North of us, on our right, was the Fourth Division's zone, the Blue beaches. Red Beach 1, where the control boat officer had directed us, was on our left (south), between us and Mount Suribachi, but our cox'n had apparently been unable to find any open space along the shoreline there.

The beach ahead of us sloped upward gently for 150-200 feet, then rose steeply into a sandbank, some twenty feet high in places, that was evidently the high-water line. (No pictures of the landing beaches that I've seen in later years make them look as wide as that beach did to me when the ramp went down.) Along the base of the sandbank, Marines crowded shoulder to shoulder in shallow holes, all hunched down as far as they could get.

The beach stretched northward on our right for almost as far as I could see, still wide and flat but without so high or steep a sandbank on its inland edge. To our left the beach seemed to narrow quickly toward the rocky base of Mount Suribachi, which loomed like a giant over us.

Strewn at weird angles around us on the flat beach was combat equipment of every kind—amtracs, amtanks, Sherman tanks, artillery pieces and their tractors—all wrecked, torn apart, some with their tracks off, some of them burning. All kinds of supply boxes lay scattered around where they had been dropped or blown. Amongst all this debris were numerous shell holes, many of them evidently hastily deepened. Inside, we could see the tops of camouflaged helmets.

Sudden geysers of sand told us that heavy shell fire was coming in. The scream of the artillery shells in their last seconds of flight was terribly unnerving, but the thunder of the explosions that followed was so deafening that the beach seemed silent. All this shelling seemed to be aimed at the ramp of our landing craft.

After what seemed like hours, we started to move forward, down the ramp and into the unknown. We ran down the ramp and off the boat in three lines, with me near the back of the left line. Just as I took my first step onto the sand, a man slightly ahead of me in the middle line stumbled and fell. Even though he was a fellow engineer, I could not stop to help him. All our training had drilled it into us that we had to keep moving and not stop for any reason, because one person stopping might cause the people behind to bunch up and become prime targets for more enemy fire. The wounded would be taken care of as soon as possible, by others, after the landing craft was empty.

The first few steps out of the boat were on packed wet sand, easy to run on. Then came dry sand that made it almost impossible to run with all the weight we were carrying. The shock waves from exploding shells and the constant peppering of sand made me think of

Hollywood movies showing soldiers running through No Man's Land in 1918. No matter which way I looked, there seemed to be as many shells bursting as where I was. I found myself instinctively looking for holes to duck into for protection. Most shell holes seemed too shallow to be of much use, but you could at least kneel for a moment and try to catch your breath as you decided where to run next, and when.

The shelling was so heavy that there was really no safe time to run. But run forward you did, scared shitless and hoping to find a better hiding place up ahead. I ran up the beach, sliding in and out of shell holes. In one fairly large hole I found a Marine who looked like he was gathering strength to make his sprint onward to the next hole—resting on his elbows, head bowed, holding his rifle up out of the sand, one leg cocked. His name, stenciled on the back of his field jacket, was PATTERSON, and he wore no field pack (lucky him, I thought). He was still there when I got ready to move, and we'd been taught not to let ourselves get bogged down, so I grabbed him by the shoulder and yelled, "Let's go, Mac!" (All Marines and sailors called each other "Mac.") But as soon as I started to shake him I knew he was dead.

When I reached the sandbank, I got a closer look at the mass of Marines huddled there in closely packed lines of shell holes and newly dug foxholes. That look told the story of the landing so far. They were all wounded, waiting to be taken off the island. All around them were dead Marines wrapped in their ponchos, piled up as "sandbags" to protect the wounded from the blizzard of shrapnel.

And more Marines were being hit all the time. Our boat's cox'n was not the only one in the latest wave who had been forced by the debris at water's edge to put people ashore wherever he could find a space. This meant that instead of arriving in a nice tight group at a designated spot, our Landing Team was spread along a thousand yards of beach. We were mixed with hundreds and hundreds of men who had landed earlier but were still looking for their units and hadn't found anybody to tell them what to do. Everything was confused and unorganized, like the "Chinese fire drill" I had always heard about, or like crowds wandering up and down the midway at a state fair. Naturally, the Jap artillery kept pounding the beach, and people were being wounded faster than the Corpsmen could treat them. Even after they had been treated and were awaiting evacuation, many were wounded again, often fatally this time, by shrapnel from new incoming shells.

Our boatload had been instructed to come ashore, drop our packs and equipment, and hurry back to unload the remaining supplies from the LCVP. Since we were among the latest to arrive, there was no shelter for us anyplace on the beach. We had to crouch unprotected there in the sand as we took off our gear and dumped it in scattered little piles. Somebody did have the presence of mind to strip a blanket from a nearby pack to cover our rifles and the machine gun against the falling sand.

Relieved of all gear except my cartridge belt, I knelt for a minute scanning the shoreline, but was unable to spot the right LCVP among the wreckage littering the beach. I finally just chose a boat with live people on it and got ready to run, looking both ways as if I was about to cross a busy street. I had just gotten to my feet and started moving when a nearby shell explosion knocked me flat on my ass. As I lay there on my back in the sand, I thought I was already a casualty, but some quick checking convinced me that luckily none of the shrapnel had hit me.

Up again and running back toward the water, I found the right landing craft. A Corpsman was working on the kid who had stumbled next to me coming off the ramp. Thank goodness, he seemed to be alive. (I found out later that he had been hit by shrapnel in the buttocks.)

I picked up two 30-pound pouches of composition C (plastic demolition explosives) and took off up the beach again. This load was lighter than my pack, rifle and machine-gun tripod, so I was better able to run and duck in and out of convenient shell holes. I'm sure I looked like a scared rabbit as I ran up the beach toward the sandbank.

At this point one of the most embarrassing things in my life happened. Without my pack on, there were no longer any suspenders to hold up my cartridge belt, and it began to slip down over my hips as I ran. Before I could find a place to stop and hitch the belt up, it slipped down around my ankles and I tripped on it—with both hands full. I fell face-first into the sand.

I didn't hear anybody laughing, so either nobody realized what had happened, or maybe they thought I had been knocked down by a concussion, just like a few minutes earlier. Anyway, only my ego was bruised.

At our assembly area near the sandbank I dumped the explosives, along with the offending cartridge belt, next to our packs. I took a deep breath, turned, and started back for another load.

As I was about halfway back down to the water's edge, our landing craft disappeared in a cloud of smoke and debris. It had taken a direct hit, setting off all the explosives still on board. The smoke cleared and all that was left was the bottom of the hull. It would have floated away in the surf if the landing ramp had not kept it anchored to the beach.

(Later, back in Hawaii, the kid who had stumbled told me that when the Jap shell had hit our boat, our Corpsman had been loading him onto another landing craft further down the beach that was taking on wounded to transport out to a hospital ship. Luckily, neither he nor the Corpsman helping him was hit. The kid had one cheek of his ass cut off by a piece of shrapnel, and he figured his total time on the island was less than ten minutes.)

I returned empty-handed this time to the high-water line and the little piles of all our earthly goods. There were now seven of the original eight engineers from our landing craft left. None of the officers and their radiomen who had landed with us were anywhere nearby. I assume that they had already been led away to where they were most needed. Leaderless and bewildered, we gathered on the beach near our packs, trying to figure what we should do. "Gathered" may be a misleading word—we were flat on our faces, yelling at each other, trying to decide where we should go to at least find a place to start digging holes to crawl into. I took advantage of this brief halt to find and secure a pair of cartridge belt suspenders for myself.

The sand, I realized now that my face was buried in it, wasn't regular beach sand. It was very dark gray, almost black—a coarse yet almost slippery volcanic ash. Every grain of it been worn smooth and round, so that there was no cohesiveness to it. It was like thousands of little ball bearings, finer near the water, coarser elsewhere. After what I would guess was maybe ten minutes in combat, we, our rifles, and our equipment were already fully covered with sand.

While we were still "deliberating," an officer slid down the steep sand bank ahead of us, saying that he was sure glad to see us. (I'll talk more about our identification system later in the story. For now, all you need to know is that each man had a four-digit number stenciled on his right jacket pocket. The first of these digits denoted his rank. Any man who received an order from somebody with a higher rank had to comply, regardless of whether he belonged to the same unit as the order-giver. Anybody with a number higher than 4–XXX was an officer.) This officer commandeered the first thirteen able-bodied Marines he could find: the seven of us plus six others who I assume were from boats on either side of ours. He told us to leave our gear and follow a man he pointed to. Each of us was to bring just his rifle, cartridge belt, gas mask, and any extra rifle ammo he could find, plus two pouches of high explosives (composition C, about five times the explosive power of dynamite) or as many bandoliers as he could carry. We were on our way to the front lines.

Our guide was bandaged and turned out to be a wounded infantryman from the 28th Marines. He told us we had to climb to the top of the sandbank in front of us, and urged us all to pick up suspenders and hurry. He said it was better up on the front lines than back here on the beach.

Going up the steep slopes was real work. You sank into the loose sand up almost to your knees, and seemed to slide back a step for every two you climbed. The unwieldiness of the packs of explosives swinging on their shoulder straps added to the difficulty, and trying to hold our rifles up out of the sand left us with no hands to help us pull ourselves up. The temptation was great to stop and rest, but the beach area below us was still being shelled by artillery and mortars so that kept us moving. There were no holes to hide in on these slopes.

Ahead of us was really up. Climbing as fast as we could in the loose sand, we passed three or four terraces, each about twenty feet wide and twenty feet above the previous one, and each reachable only by climbing these steep sand slopes. (My recollection is that the slopes we climbed were still virgin territory, unmarred by a single footprint—maybe that's why none of us thought to look for land mines.)

We paused at each terrace to get our breath, but the stops were not long. We were completely winded by the time we reached the top of the long climb, and everybody collapsed to recover.

Chapter 5

A SIGHTSEEING TRIP

Looking back down on the landing beaches from the highest terrace, we saw an absolute junkyard, extending some twelve hundred yards northward (the Fourth Division landing beaches on the Fifth Division's right) and eight hundred yards southward (through the Fifth Division's beaches to the foot of Mount Suribachi).

The mass of destroyed equipment and ordnance was a sobering sight. Wrecked landing craft were wallowing in the surf, three and four deep out from the shore in most places, and I wondered how our cox'n had managed to find anywhere at all to land his LCVP. Clogging the beach, from the water's edge to the high-water mark, were wrecked Jeeps, small trucks, Sherman tanks, amtracs, and just about every other kind of equipment, as well as piles of materials.

Hundreds of Marines scrambled and dug holes among the wreckage, trying to find cover from the constant shellfire. It still reminded me of a World War I scene in a Hollywood movie—except that this "scene" had already been going for hours, and there was no end in sight.

Suribachi towered over the landing beaches, very impressive and forbidding. Obviously, the Jap artillery spotters up there had a perfect view of every move any Marine made. Any grouping of men or any movement of equipment could easily be, and was, immediately shelled.

As we watched, two U.S. battleships moved in very close behind the landing beaches of the 28th Marines, and their starboard gun batteries began firing at Jap guns on the mountain. Those guns were very well concealed, but when they fired at the Marines the muzzle flashes gave away their positions and allowed the battleships to return deadly fire back at them. This was welcome, but knocking out the guns on Suribachi took a long time. We later found out that they were mounted on tracks inside concrete-reinforced tunnels and were pulled back behind mammoth steel doors after each time they fired. Nothing smaller than the fourteen- and sixteen-inch guns of our battleships could damage those doors. Some of those heavy Jap guns were still firing at the Marines well into the second day.

After several days, the guns on the mountain were all silenced at last. But the landing beaches continued to be shelled, from further north on the island, by mortars and artillery pieces that still had eyes up on the mountain looking down on us.

While we rested from our climb, our guide told us that the unit he was taking us to join was at the foot of Mount Suribachi, south of the southernmost of Iwo's three airfields and about halfway across the island. The artillery fire was not so bad up there, he said, but there was plenty of rifle and machine-gun fire from pillboxes protecting the base of the mountain. He also told us to keep our eyes open, because there were still lots of live Japs behind our lines that were sniping at any target that presented itself.

We started our trek again, moving up a shallow sandy draw that protected us from shrapnel and from rifle bullets that snapped and cracked as they passed over our heads. At the head of the draw we passed what was left of a concrete pillbox. It had been carefully blended into the surrounding landscape, with small shrubs and plants growing in the sand that covered it. Now it was scorched by flame-throwers and partly blown apart by explosives.

Six or eight Japs had tried to escape through the blasted back of the pillbox, and their bodies were scattered along our route. One of them lay sprawled on his back across the trail, wide-eyed and grinning, completely naked except for his split-toed "tabi" cloth shoes that the flamethrower had left untouched. His seemingly intact corpse saluted each passing Marine with an erection, swollen somehow by the violence of his death to monstrous size.

I'm sure every man who passed that way had the same thought I did. Among the troops in my time, the worst fate you could wish for somebody you were angry at was, "I hope you die with a hard on!" The meaning was presumably that death would be even worse if it took him suddenly from the most enjoyable act in the world. In the face of this mind-boggling sight, girls were the furthest thing in the world from my mind. All I could hope was that I wouldn't become a similar object lesson for somebody else before the day was over.

Just past this pillbox, we emerged from the little draw and faced a slight incline up toward Suribachi. The ground was very uneven, consisting of undulating volcanic rock partly covered with blown sand and scrub brush that looked like the kind of vegetation you might find on the sand dunes along our ocean beaches. Here and there humps of rock and mounds of brush stuck up as much as a few feet, but there was really nothing to hide behind. Luckily, we were relatively safe from shelling. Shrapnel from the beach couldn't reach us up on the plateau, and as long as we didn't bunch up, the Jap big guns probably wouldn't consider us worth shooting at. We were not protected, though, against stray rifle and machine-gun bullets from the front lines ahead. It was relatively silent, and the snapping of passing bullets, even though not directly aimed at us, was sobering to contemplate.

It was an eerie hike up there. Ever since we had started up the sand terraces from the impossibly crowded beaches, we had not seen a single live person. In fact, other than the dead Japs we had seen at the pillbox, and an occasional bomb crater, there were not even any signs that the Marines had been through here. I shudder to remember now how nonchalantly we walked through this area. Part of our job as engineers was going to be finding and clearing mines and then marking with white tape the areas where it was safe to move. Ninety-nine percent of this area had not yet been checked or marked. We later cleared great numbers of antipersonnel mines from the Third Division beaches on the west side of the island. It's amazing that there were no mines on the eastern beaches and slopes, where the Fifth and Fourth Divisions came ashore.

The 28th Marines, the regiment our little band was delivering explosives and ammunition to, had landed on the left of the 27th Marines and were closest to Suribachi. It was their job to take the mountain, from the heights of which all the Japanese mortar and artillery fire was being directed. Whoever controlled this mountain could see all of the island, so the Japs were defending it heavily—how heavily, we didn't learn until later. The mountain was honeycombed with underground passages that linked the bunkers, pillboxes and gun emplacements protecting it.

Our guide told us that the 28th Marines had partially encircled the base of the mountain, but had been stopped cold in their efforts to climb even the lower slopes because of the rings of pillboxes and the myriad of "spider holes" (concealed firing positions for individual riflemen) protecting them.

As we got closer to the mountain, we had to angle further out into the uneven flatlands that stretched north from it. This made us more visible to the enemy observers above and increased our chances of being deliberately shot at, not just hit by stray rounds. This terrain was increasingly covered with clumps of a leafless scrub brush that looked like manzanita and grew into nearly impenetrable clumps as much as six feet high. We were heading generally southwestward toward the base of the mountain, following a zigzag road that one of our bulldozers had cut through the scrub.

Our guide warned us to keep well spread out, because we were now within easy range of the machine guns in the pillboxes. We followed his example, crouching low and zigzagging ahead in short dashes as we had been taught in infantry school. At the end of each dash forward we ducked down among the scrub brush along the sides of the road, hoping that we were making ourselves invisible to the enemy. That was really impossible, though, because of the pillboxes looking down on us. They were about two hundred feet apart, forming a staggered line that was three tiers deep in places so that the pillboxes above could cover any approach to the ones below.

The road ended right at the base of the mountain. Here I didn't see anyplace at all to hide from the pillboxes that loomed above us, with the muzzle flashes of the machine guns clearly visible in their firing apertures. Yet several of the people at the regimental command post located there were standing or kneeling in the open, seemingly indifferent to the possibility of being shot. Somebody casually waved us into some shell holes and told us to hunker down, but these holes offered no protection at all against the machine guns we could see or the riflemen we couldn't.

The naval gunfire shells bursting right ahead of us drowned out any sounds of small-arms fire, and I saw no little spurts of dust near me, so I assumed I was not being shot at. From what I learned in the next few days, though, I'm sure I was too scared and dumb to be able to tell. In fact, I was going to get a sharp first lesson within the next couple of hours.

The 28th Marines command post people were glad to see us. Their lieutenant colonel interviewed us, asking what we could do for them. When we told him that although we were engineers we didn't have any demolition experience yet, he got on the land line, gave somebody a few choice words, then hung up in disgust. Then, in a softer voice, he placed a call to somebody else. He told them we did not have enough training to be up here, and he asked what he should do with us.

In the meantime we were beginning to learn what was what. Dirty and with their clothing already ripped, line company engineers and infantrymen showed up out of nowhere to take the valuable pouches we were bringing them. One of the engineers, a man I knew by sight, dropped into my hole for a minute to bum a cigarette. He told me how quickly things had gone bad after the seemingly easy initial landing. All our shelling and aerial bombings hadn't hurt the Japs at all, he said. Their artillery was hidden and silent during our blitz and the landing of our first few waves. When our shelling stopped, the enemy big guns came out of their tunnels and began saturating the landing beaches with murderous fire.

Any area the Marines moved into could be bombarded immediately, because the Jap mortars and artillery had been zeroed in ahead of time. Along with the big guns, Jap machine gunners and riflemen were firing from almost completely destroyed pillboxes and block-houses, and even from behind tiny clusters of shrubs. They were well camouflaged and took a real toll on the Marines. Whenever Marine and Naval artillery opened up to counter the fire, the enemy artillery would disappear until our guns shifted to other targets; then the Jap guns would quickly emerge and begin blasting away at the Marines again. This happened over and over for the next thirty days.

Another Jap tactic the man told about was the use of suicide bombers—soldiers who popped up out of nowhere and ran towards the advancing Marines, detonating explosive charges in their back-packs when they got in among them. Several Marines were lost before we learned to spot these bombers quickly and shoot them before they got close enough for their self-sacrifice to damage us.

I asked the man for any news of Sergeant Wolover, a friend of mine who had been an instructor back in our Engineer Training School days. I knew he had come ashore with the engineer company attached to the 28th Marines. The man nodded toward an adjacent shell hole where ten or more dead Marines, wrapped in their pon-chos, were already stacked up. Sergeant Wolover was in one of those ponchos.

On that sobering note, our job as pack animals having been completed, we were sent back to our units on the beach.

Our guide had been right: The Japs were not shelling the Marine lines up here at the front anywhere near as heavily as they were pounding the beaches. In fact, there was almost no shelling up here. We were a little reluctant to leave, but we worked our way back to the edge of the level area, and found our beach by sighting in on Futatsu Rock and a beached Jap destroyer nearby. Then we climbed and slid down the sand terraces, aiming for an amtrac that was lying on its side in the middle of the beach. We knew we had left our little pile of backpacks and the machine gun about thirty yards from it, and we eventually found them. Everything was covered with sand, and a couple of the packs had been damaged by the shelling in our absence.

Seeing us still up and moving, an NCO (noncommissioned officer) asked what unit we belonged to. Landing Team 3/26, we told him. He told us to move all the gear we could salvage up the terraces to the top of the sandbank, which was apparently an assembly area for all the units coming in with the 26th Marines Landing Teams.

We dragged ourselves back up the steep sand slopes, much more fatigued this time. The packs and machine-gun parts felt very heavy. It was during this second D-Day afternoon climb that I nearly got hit by a bullet. (I may have had other narrow escapes, even on that first day, but if so I don't want to know about them.) I was wearing my backpack with my blankets attached as prescribed, tightly rolled and bent in a horseshoe shape on the top and sides of the pack. I felt a sharp impact as the blanket roll above my left shoulder, right beside my head, was slapped by a bullet that must have traveled from Mount Suribachi. The distance was too far for accurate aiming, but it was well within killing range if it had hit me. (I still have those blankets today, punctured by several neat little holes.)

We reached the top and followed the edge of the plateau to an area which I believe was just about on the line between Green Beach 1 and Red Beach 1, almost back to the 28th Marines area. We were joined there by several other engineers from H&S Company, who had come ashore from two different ships. They were as bewildered as we were about why we had been chosen to land early.

There were now probably twenty of us in all, about enough for three machine-gun crews, but we had all the parts for four machine guns. We were told to dig in and get the guns set up to fire westward across the island this evening.

We tried to dig standard two-man foxholes in the sand, five or six feet long by four feet wide by two feet deep, but the sides kept caving in. The holes we wound up with were eight feet wide and about twelve feet long down the slope behind us.

As we dug in and set the guns up for the night we had a front-row seat to watch the havoc on the landing beaches below. It was easy to spot people who were lost, or had lost their leaders during the landings, drifting together into groups to cope with the terror of their situation. This was only natural, but it was deadly: The groups visible to us were also visible to the spotters up on Mount Suribachi, who called in artillery fire missions on them. Even sadder, wounded Marines who had been returned to the beaches for evacuation were placed in groups and attended by Corpsmen, and they too were prime targets for the Jap spotters.

Officers were trying frantically to get all the able-bodied men off the beaches and up to positions where they would be able to fight tonight. Then only the wounded would still be trapped down there.

Around 1530 or 1600, as we were still settling in, about thirty of us—engineers, pioneers, and artillerymen, all from the H&S companies—were sent down to report to the Beachmaster of the 28th Marines landing area.

When we got there, for safety's sake the Beachmaster broke us into small groups, scattered among nearby shell holes, and visited each group in turn. His message was grim. The wave we had landed in, over three hours earlier, was the last one that had been able to put any large amount of men and equipment ashore. The Jap shelling all afternoon had been so accurate and heavy, he told us, that it had been impossible to get boats to the water's edge long enough to unload them before they were hit. Nothing was coming in, and we were fast running out of supplies. It was hoped that we could be re-supplied in the morning, but the commanders expected that tonight the Japs intended to launch their famous "Banzai!" charges until we were pushed off the island. With no boats, our only way off now would be to swim.

The Beachmaster assigned us to pick up all the weapons we could find on the beach so that the Japs who would infiltrate tonight couldn't use them against us. We were also to salvage any rifle and machine-gun ammo, any first-aid gear, and any drinking water we could find and take them from the tide-washed beach to higher ground. It was particularly important to salvage enough 30- and 50-caliber ammo to fend off tonight's expected banzai charges. We were to search all boats, vehicles, and dead Marines for these things. He stressed that this unpleasant task was necessary to ensure the survival of the living at least until the next morning.

We fanned out toward the water in our small groups and worked as swiftly as possible to collect the required items and carry them back to the assembly point. From there, other Marines would carry them to their units up on the front lines.

Occasional artillery shells were still falling among the wrecked craft along the water's edge, but the volume was considerably lighter than earlier in the day. Now that our landing craft had stopped trying to get to shore, the Jap artillery seemed to have shifted its focus to the beach and slopes around the high-water mark, where most of the stranded equipment and people were.

The tide was out now, making the beach about thirty feet wider than it had been when we landed. The newly exposed sand dropped off fairly sharply to the current edge of the water. This was good for those of us doing salvage work among the wrecked boats, because even if shrapnel from the shells hitting up in the crowded area reached us, it had mostly lost its momentum. The landing craft and big equipment we were going through also provided us some cover.

All of us on the work detail armed ourselves with weapons we found that looked useful. Some of the wrecked landing craft even had pump shotguns. In one boat I found a Thompson submachine gun for myself (the military model with a straight hand stock—not like the ones in the "G-man" movies, with a forward pistol grip and drum magazine). I also picked up a 45-caliber automatic pistol.

The most distasteful part of the salvage work was having to remove gear from dead Marines, but I guess that when you feel your life depends on it you can do all kinds of "unnatural" things. Seeing the dead infantrymen made me realize again how out of touch our engineer officers were with how the rest of the Corps was equipped. Every infantryman had on a pair of web suspenders to hold up his cartridge belt once he took off his pack. My lack of that item when I came ashore had seriously hampered my movements until I managed to scrounge one for myself.

We spent about two hours on this task, until the gathering darkness made it unsafe to be moving around. Returning to our machine-gun positions up on the edge of the plateau, we brought back a couple of bundles of empty sandbags. There sure was no shortage of sand to fill them with.

While we were gone, those who had stayed to finish digging in had field-stripped the guns and cleaned the firing mechanisms. The guns were now draped with blankets and jackets in an effort to keep the flying sand from getting back in.

We put final touches on the positions by making little sandbag parapets in front of each gun to provide some protection to the gunners. Then we lay on our backs in our foxholes and field-stripped and thoroughly cleaned our rifles for the first time since we had landed. This would become an urgent necessity many times a day, because of the sand and dust from the incessant shelling. Weapons with sand in the mechanism will always jam when most needed.

Our area wasn't being shelled anywhere near as much as the beach below us, but we were certainly not neglected. By now, though, we were beginning to "get our sea legs" and could pick up the sound of incoming shells soon enough to get down out of the way of the shrapnel.

Finally we got a chance to rest and eat our evening meal. The D-ration chocolate bars took some hard gnawing, but they sure tasted good to us! We would learn later that almost forty percent of the Marines who had landed that first day were killed or wounded. This was the most costly D-Day landing in the Pacific war.

Chapter 6

'TWAS A FULL MOON, AND THE NATIVES WERE RESTLESS

D-Day (Monday) Night

It had been a long and exhausting day. On the advice of the old-timers we divided the night up into two-hour watches, so that we could take turns sleeping.

But there was to be no rest for anyone.

We all expected—maybe because of Hollywood movies showing battlefields quiet at night—that darkness would bring some relief from the shelling. Instead, our area received a steady sprinkling of random individual shell bursts all night long, interspersed at odd times with very intense combined artillery and mortar barrages. Even if nothing hit you, the continual shelling was just often enough and random enough to jar you awake (if you had been lucky enough to begin to doze).

In addition to explosive shells, both sides fired parachute flares all night long, trying to see what was going on. At times there were so many flares in the air that it looked like daylight—but they had a greenish cast which gave a very eerie look to an already chaotic landscape.

All night long the Marine units in front of us were also taking Jap small-arms fire, which increased at times till it sounded as if the expected banzai charge had finally started. We learned when morning came that there had been a charge, but it had never reached where we were.

The most nerve-wracking part of this night for us was a Jap 81-mm mortar that fired forty-nine-round patterns in our area from dusk till dawn. Yes, forty-nine. I counted them, and so did everybody else. First one round would hit, then couple of minutes later a second round would hit, say, fifty yards due north of the first, then a third fifty yards north of that, and so on until the shooter had fired seven rounds in a straight north-south line. (He could do this easily by adjusting the aiming screws on his mortar some set number of clicks each time.) Then he would put an eighth round fifty yards due west of the seventh, a ninth round fifty yards south of that, and so on to complete a second seven-round line just west of the first seven, then a third line just west of the first two, and so on. When he had finished a seven-by-seven square that way he would pick a new starting point and make a new seven-by-seven square overlapping the first, then another square, and so on.

Working that way, he was able to hit every piece of ground in our area several times before the night was out, including several rounds that landed very close to our foxhole. After several hours of this pattern shelling, you subconsciously knew (without counting rounds) when the next one would hit close enough that a fatal direct hit on your hole was a possibility.

When you are being mortared, you have to decide whether to hunker down where you are or run for someplace better. Where we were, any other hole near enough to reach was probably already full of Marines. Also, by getting up from the safety of your foxhole to start running you took the chance of being hit with shrapnel or enemy small-arms fire or, even worse, being shot by some Marine who in the darkness thought you were a Jap. Your only choice, really, was to stay put and pray that this was not your time.

Nobody was supposed to be moving at night, or making any noise; anybody who did was presumed to be a Jap and Marines were supposed to shoot at them. But you had to keep the Marines around you informed of what was going on in the area, so there was lots of talking between foxholes, each one relaying information to the adjoining holes up and down the line.

Being in the center of the area, our machine-gun position received and passed on all kinds of news. This included reports of many Jap infantry probes and feelers against the line in front of us, as well as word that the Japs were swimming out from Mount Suribachi, drifting ashore, and hiding among the wrecked equipment on the landing beaches.

Before long, the beaches were alive with Jap snipers. This was bad, because the wrecked equipment near the water's edge had to be cleared if there was to be room for supply boats to land in the morning.

In the light of the flares, it seemed as if there were almost as many Marines up and moving about down there as if it was daytime. The pioneers and some of the engineers were trying to salvage damaged equipment and otherwise get it off the beach. They worked determinedly, ignoring the incoming artillery and sniper fire. Bulldozers were dragging and pushing wrecked landing craft and other unsalvageable equipment up onto the beach, out of the way, and then further pushing this debris into big piles. The dozers also developed the helpful habit of pushing those piles around a little every time they passed them. This was a quick and easy way of silencing any snipers hiding inside.

The dozers, lighter than the tanks and with much wider tracks, were the only things able to move on the beaches. Every other piece of equipment that came ashore became stuck in the sand and had to be towed off the beach by a dozer belonging to the engineers, the pioneers, or the artillery. Only the engineer dozers had armor plating—specially installed by the repair section at the insistence of the line companies—protecting the operator. Tonight those armored dozers were proving to be worth their weight in gold.

None of our dozer operators was even injured while working throughout the night under sometimes heavy shell fire. (Later in the invasion the Japs hit a Fifth Division ammunition dump. Putting out the resulting fires took several of our armored dozers almost eight hours of work among the exploding ammo; again, the engineers driving them were unhurt.)

Several times during the long night, the infantry out on the flat area ahead of us passed back word that the Japs were on their way.

Our job was to fire our machine guns in the general direction of the Japs from dusk to dawn, just over the barely visible heads of the thin line of infantry ahead of us. That way the infantry didn't have to give away their positions with muzzle flashes from their weapons, and the Japs could come within throwing range of Marine hand grenades before realizing it. Once our infantry started firing we were to stop firing. This was so we wouldn't hit any of them if they had to leave their holes for any reason.

We were firing so much that, even though we alternated with the guns on either side of us, every so often we had to stop to let our barrels cool off. Stopping also let us clear some moving-around space by scooping empty shell casings out of our hole. Even with these rests, we began to run out of ammo toward morning. Other machine guns along our line were also running low on ammo, so we had the people around us reloading the empty canvas ammo belts with individual cartridges from the rifle clips that had been salvaged from dead Marines.

Loading individual cartridges into a canvas belt isn't easy under the best of conditions, but in the semi-darkness, with shell bursts intermittently showering us with sand, it bordered on the impossible. The best the reloaders behind us could do was to work under ponchos and hope not to get hit by shrapnel.

I never even saw anything that looked like a Jap all night long, but the sandbags that had been so carefully piled in front of us for protection were being hit by bullets every so often. Each hit was announced by a sharp crack and by sand that was sprayed over us.

So the Japs were out there somewhere. In the morning the pile of bags was six to eight inches shorter than when we piled them up the night before (a night that had seemed to last about twenty hours).

There was no sleep for anyone that I know of. The guy with the traversing mortar fire came close several times—too close—but there was still no nearby hole to move to that wasn't already full of Marines.

D+1 (Tuesday) Morning

It was wonderful to see the skies beginning to lighten. We were jubilant—we had made it through the night. We began to perk up and there was talking and kidding between foxholes. The main topic of conversation was what had happened to the banzai charge that had always come the first night. The expected drive to wipe us off the island had not materialized.

But we had congratulated ourselves too soon.

With the return of visibility we stopped our defensive firing over the infantry, and the Jap artillery spotters up on Suribachi all came back to work. The intensity and accuracy of the enemy shelling increased rapidly; our old friend dropping the mortar shells now had all kinds of help. The Jap rifle and machine-gun fire passing through our area became heavy enough that nobody was fool enough to stand up any more, let alone to be out moving between shell holes.

Then we got a new twist: In addition to the H.E. (high explosive) shells landing among us and down on the beach, the enemy's artillery harassment began to include a mixture of H.E. and phosphorus shells exploding some 200 feet above the ground.

The aerial bursts looked pretty from a distance. The phosphorus shells went off like big multi-legged white spiders in a Fourth of July fireworks display, interspersed with puffs of dirty gray smoke from the H.E. But when they burst over our heads there was nothing pleasant about either kind of ammunition. The H.E. shells rained shrapnel on us at speeds greater than gravity. Mingled with the shrapnel were myriads of small pieces of phosphorus, which burns at a temperature so high that it will eat through clothing, skin, flesh, and even bone. Burning phosphorus can't be extinguished with water; it must be dug out or allowed to burn itself out. If there were two of you in a fox-hole, it was your job to use the point of your combat knife to dig out any piece of phosphorus that fell on your partner before it could burn too deeply into him; and he had to do the same for you. Neither of you could leave your foxhole to avoid a falling piece of phosphorus—the regular shelling was too heavy for that. It was pure hell.

We found out later that both kinds of shells were being fired at us by the many antiaircraft batteries surrounding the airfields up on the flat part of the island. They were joining every other artillery piece and mortar in shelling the troops inside our little area in an effort to annihilate us first thing this morning, before we could be reinforced or advance any further.

In the midst of all of this phosphorus shelling my fellow gunner Benny and I lay facing each other, knives in hand, when our friend finally dropped a mortar round into our foxhole. I was lying on my left side, right leg flexed, left leg almost straight. The shell hit only inches away from the bottom of my left foot. The force of the explosion jammed my left knee up almost to my waist, and the sound of it in my steel helmet made my ears ring for quite a while. Luckily for us, the round buried itself in the sand before going off, and the shrapnel was thrown up in a cone that missed both of us. It sure covered us with lots of sand, though.

I will always remember the moment when that mortar shell landed in our foxhole. I will always believe I could hear the spring disengage the safety pin and arm the shell at the top of its trajectory, although that happened probably a thousand feet in the air over us. In the midst of the noise of the battle, everything went totally silent and there was no sound but the air passing around the shell as it fell toward me.

I didn't hear the explosion till long after it hit, but I could hear the shell breaking apart from the explosion as it hit the sand. There was total silence for what seemed like two or three minutes and then I heard the crash of thunder inside my helmet, along with the wave of air and heat of the concussion. In that instant I knew for sure that there is a God, and that I had been saved this time for some reason. I knew instantly—this wasn't just something I felt in my scared condition—that I would get off that island alive. (I have always wondered in later years if Benny, who shared that hole with me, felt the same. He only lived two more days.)

After the intensity of the shelling that morning, any other shelling I was in, no matter how bad it seemed at the time, never came close to being so terrifying once I had a chance to think about it. Sure, I was scared a lot after that, but never again in the same way.

I have wondered lots of times, then and later, just how much I or any human being could take of this pummeling and still hold onto some kind of sanity. I was sure that this was just part of the trial; that the verdict was in, and that I would live to get off of the island. Any time I was shelled, though, I worried about how badly I might be wounded. The thought of being a cripple for the rest of my life was uppermost in my mind—in everybody's mind, really. I'm talking about praying to God for clean wounds, for arms or legs cleanly lost—none of the terrible internal wounds, or the multiple maiming wounds, or the horribly disfiguring head wounds, or the thought of living out your life in a hospital bed. As the old infantryman's axiom says, "God has smiled on those who die instantly."

It seemed like hours before our Navy's shelling of the Jap mortars and artillery on the north end of the island began to take effect. Slowly the Jap shelling began to slacken some, and their heavy small-arms fire gradually dwindled to sporadic shots at specific targets. Such shelling that continued seemed to be shifting back onto the landing beaches, where our LSTs were trying to land tanks and other armored vehicles through the gaps that had been dozed clear during the night. For whatever reason, some time around now we got a breather.

I don't have any idea of what time these things were happening, even though I had a watch. Time either raced or it dragged. This, I guess, is more proof that time is really relative. I know that when you are enjoying something, time really flies. But here there were lots of moments of intense action when time seemed to just stand still, with everything passing in my mind in slow motion.

The units down on the beach were frantically calling for more engineers. I had taken my turn dodging shrapnel on the detail to the beach the afternoon before, so I was left with the machine gun this time. But from now on, our gun crew was to be permanently reduced from the original half-dozen or so men down to three. At times there were only two.

Chapter 7

SETTING UP HOUSEKEEPING

D+1 (Tuesday), continued

Later in the morning, probably around 0800 or 0900, we were ordered to move the machine guns to new positions about five hundred yards westward—still along the northerly edge of the 28th Marines area, but now close to the middle of the narrow, relatively flat stretch that connected Suribachi to the rest of the island.

The sand slope where we had spent the night was going to become a parking area for salvageable trucks, tanks and other equipment that could be towed or dragged there from the landing beaches. Clearing the beaches was important—salvageable but inoperative equipment down there was a real obstacle to landing troops and equipment and evacuating casualties.

The only cover in our new location was some shrubs about two feet tall among the sand hillocks. Again there were only a few bomb craters and big shell holes to disturb the little plants that were holding the sand from blowing away.

When you stood up, it looked to be less than a thousand yards to the front lines of the 27th Marines to the north. They were part way up the south end of the main Jap airfield. To the south of us, it was about five hundred yards to the lines of the 28th Marines along the foot of Suribachi. The west beach was directly ahead of us, also about five hundred yards away. We were told that it still mostly belonged to the Japs.

Our new foxholes were in big shell craters. We were plainly visible to the Japs on Suribachi, but we avoided bunching up enough to become inviting targets for artillery and mortar fire. We were almost out of range for aimed small-arms fire—at five hundred yards, only the best shots could hit what they aimed at. There was still a lot of stray small-arms fire coming from the front lines on either side of us, though, and enough falling shrapnel to make you keep down when it wasn't absolutely necessary to be up and moving.

While some of us were still picking out foxhole positions where our machine guns would have the best fields of fire, others started on the numerous trips required to move gear up from the previous night's positions. We had to move all of our own gear plus the gear of the riflemen who were working down on the landing beaches. But the riflemen would protect our backs at night.

It was now overcast and quite cold. Those of us who had been smart enough to wear long johns and field jackets were able to lord it over everybody else.

We weren't even half dug into our new positions when the dozers from artillery started dozing out gun pits right next to us. A few Marine artillery pieces had been salvaged from the beaches, we learned, and here was where they were going to be placed—right in the middle of the island, less than a hundred yards from us.

The dozers went back down to the beach and soon returned towing 105-mm howitzers and some sleds of shells. They immediately began drawing enemy artillery fire, but they kept bringing more ammunition up from the beach. The many Jap spotters up on Suribachi saw all this activity and directed shellfire onto anything that moved, but our people continued setting up the gun batteries. Soon they were able to start counter-battery fire against the Jap artillery to the north of us. Once our guns started firing, the whole area around them, clouded in hazy smoke, became a prime target. Anything, even one or two men, would draw shelling of some kind.

While this was going on, we set up machine-gun positions facing toward the reportedly Jap-controlled west beach. We laid out our guns with interlocking fields of fire, so that the area in front of each gun could also be covered by the gun on either side of it, leaving no hole in the line if one gun was knocked out. This crossfire pattern covered down to about a hundred feet in front of us. If any Japs advanced that close, the riflemen in the holes behind us were to shoot over or through us to stop them.

One of the boundary markers for my gun's field of fire was a poncho-covered dead Marine whose rifle was stuck in the sand next to him with his helmet placed on the stock. This dead Marine, I was told, was Master Gunnery Sergeant John Basilone, who had won the Congressional Medal of Honor for heroism during the Guadalcanal campaign in 1942.

Our leaders expected the Japs west of us to try to infiltrate our lines during the night, or even launch banzai attacks. Our machine-gun teams were combined with some other troops to form a protective force for the artillery batteries. This included conducting night probes out into enemy territory. As soon as it was dark, ten of us were sent out on a patrol aimed at preventing any Japs, particularly messengers, from moving between the north and south ends of the island.

Because I was single, I was chosen for more than my share of hazardous jobs like this. Most of the men in H&S Company were journeymen in their trades, therefore older on average than the people in the line companies and more likely to be married. ("Older" is relative, of course—the oldest man in the company was only thirty-one, and the average age of the married men was between twenty-four and twenty-eight.) Of the 450 or so men in H&S Company probably fifty at most—including the three of us in the Repair section—were single; my partner Benny was twenty-two years old and had two small children at home. When night patrols and probable danger came up, it seemed only right that the singles went before the married guys. Sergeants would go through the company taking single men from different sections to fill the requirement.

Our patrol left the perimeter in a cold drizzle and slithered down a steep sandy slope onto the west beach, which we found to be about thirty yards wide, nice and level. The base of the slope was out of sight of anybody up on the top, making the beach a good route for covert movement by the Japs. We climbed part way back up the slope and scooped out some shallow foxholes from which we could cover quite an area of beach without being seen or attacked from behind.

In our downhill slide, I had managed to get the breech mechanism of my trusty M-1 rifle full of sand. As soon as I got a chance, I lay down on my back in the temporary foxhole, completely disassembled the weapon, and laid the parts on my chest. Then I wiped each piece clean with my shirt tail and put them back together. Over on this side of the island the flares were few and far between, so I worked in pitch blackness.

Every Marine recruit going through boot camp is required, repeatedly, to field strip his weapon and clean it blindfolded. Like just about all my fellow recruits, I had always looked on this as just more of the usual harassment. It had seemed inconceivable that you would need to clean your weapon as often as the boot camp instructors seemed to think. Yet here in the falling and blowing sand of Iwo Jima, it seemed like we were always taking the weapons apart—not to clean the barrel, but to get the sand out of the operating assembly so that the bolt would seat and the rifle would fire. My drill instructor from boot camp would have been proud of me that night.

I had brought the M-1 with me tonight because with it you could hit something further away than fifty feet, the maximum range of the Thompson. Now I was doubly glad that I hadn't brought that sub-machine gun on this patrol. I wasn't that well versed in dismantling, cleaning, and reassembling it, and out here a jammed weapon could cost you your life.

Once we were settled in our holes, several of the guys began seeing occasional passers-by and sniping at them. I never saw any of these shadowy targets, so I never fired my weapon. If they were real Japs, though, they must have been stragglers. After a few shots, suddenly the place would be quiet for a while. We were never once challenged, and during the cold and wet six hours we were on the beach, no one ever saw any large groups of Japs. Maybe they were smart enough to stay in out of the rain.

It was still dark when we returned to our shell holes up on the plateau, meeting another patrol of engineers who were leaving the perimeter as we came in. But there was no rest for us. The Japs shelled the vicinity of our artillery positions all night long; and according to repeated word-of-mouth reports, there were Jap infiltrators in front of us, behind us, moving in among us. In addition, what started as a light mist turned into a drizzle that didn't stop. This made the cold even colder, and it was getting harder and harder to stay dry. So we passed another sleepless night

D+2 (Wednesday) Morning

I don't remember there being any command structure within our little group, or any outside chain of command that we belonged to. Some officer or NCO would come by, ask what we were doing, and send some of us off on some look-busy project.

When morning came, another work party was sent back down to work on the landing beaches, and a few men were left to guard our machine guns. The rest of us were sent out on a short patrol, once again covering the area ahead of us and toward the west beach, looking for stragglers. We did spot several people moving out ahead of us, and I finally got to fire my rifle. But they disappeared in the distance. We were not being rushed into making foolish moves, so we suffered no causalities on our patrol. I don't remember that we ever received any serious answering fire.

We got back from this patrol in mid-morning and learned that our machine guns were to move again. More and more artillery pieces were being successfully landed on the island, and the whole artillery area next to us was rapidly being expanded.

We were happy to move. The new gun batteries were being heavily shelled every time the smoke and dust around them cleared enough for the Jap observers on Suribachi to spot even small targets. The

Marine artillerymen who were setting up the batteries never seemed to flinch, but the pounding was getting on our nerves.

The new position we and the other odd units protecting the artillery were to move into was similar to where we had been the night before, but further west. Once again we set up our machine guns to cover the west beaches with interlocking fields of fire, and we again prepared to go out on patrols.

Our infantry had been through this area once, in the first day's mad dash to cut the island in half. They didn't completely succeed, and it wasn't truly cut in half even now. The west beaches still belonged mostly to the Japs, so this was where we were positioned. Some of the Jap troops had withdrawn during our sweeps of the last two days and were now infiltrating back into the area. There were also a few stragglers who had stayed in the area and gone into hiding. All these Japs were out there now, looking for chances to snipe at unsuspecting targets, but mostly staying hidden when our patrols were nearby.

It was cold, and almost everybody now had on their long johns plus a flannel shirt; some had on dungaree jackets over their field jackets. During the afternoon, the mist and drizzle that had fallen since the night before changed to a light rain. By mid-afternoon, all of our clothes were soaking wet, and the cold wind made it even more uncomfortable.

Our rubberized ponchos were one of the most valuable pieces of gear we had in that kind of weather. After a few days most of the infantrymen had lost their packs and with them, their blankets; but almost everybody carried their ponchos folded at the small of their backs, under their cartridge belts, throughout the campaign. You couldn't wear one with the hood over your head during a rainy day, or wrap one around you when you slept, because it could restrict your ability to move at an instant's notice. But you could sleep under them (rather than in them), and they offered some protection from the elements.

Although most of us were already soaked, in our spare time we began devising ways to use the ponchos to improve our protection from the rain. It all started with somebody using some of the manzanita-like sticks to hold up the center of the poncho, while staking down the outer edges like a tent. Soon tents like these became covers over foxholes, and then the race was on to improve these little shelters as the rain continued.

The shelters worked well for those of us in the rear areas, where the danger of infiltrators and snipers was reduced because so many of us were up and moving around. Unlike the poor infantrymen, we had no need to be able to see in a 360-degree circle all the time.

Within a couple of days the whole south end of the island was beginning to look like a giant shantytown. From above it must have looked like the island was covered, wall to wall, with ponchos. And although the idea of the camouflaged poncho was to conceal your position, there were people flying small United States and Confederate flags from the tents even before Suribachi was secured.

Like the foxholes they covered, the ponchos were scattered unevenly over the landscape. In some places the holes were so close to each other that their poncho covers were tied together; elsewhere the gaps were a little wider. Overall, the area had a helter-skelter, patchwork look.

All afternoon and evening it continued to rain, still not hard but steady. The rain dampened the sounds of the shelling some, but the shelling itself never stopped.

The rain obstructed the vision of the Jap artillery spotters considerably. So even though we had moved farther away from the Marine artillery batteries behind us, we got hit by occasional stray shells intended for our big guns.

Chapter 8

Hurry Up and Wait

D+2 (Wednesday) Afternoon and Evening

In the afternoon, we went for a little walk down on the landing beaches to keep warm. Well, actually, we were sent down there.

And this was actually three long walks. We went back through the western area where we had patrolled in the morning, then through the new truck and material storage area that had been set up where we had spent the first night, and finally down almost to the waterline of the east beach.

I didn't feel very chipper when we started out, but by the end of the third trip, I was really beat. I convinced myself that it was the lack of sleep that was catching up with me.

What with all the shelling, all the people digging foxholes, and the dozers dragging supplies and equipment around on the sandy slopes, this once plant-covered area was now a big pile of shifting sand. All of the ground cover had been destroyed. The whole area would have been a dusty mess if it had not been raining.

I guess we should have been thankful that there was not enough of the fine black volcanic dust to make deep mud, but we were wallowing in enough of it that most of our green uniforms were smeared with black.

The beach was still being shelled, but not quite as badly as two days earlier.

Now there were several tank landing ships nosed into holes cut in the debris at the water's edge. These ships were moored to the beach with cables. Each ship had the bow doors open, and the ramps opened out on to the beach.

Unloading these ships was the job of our Division's Pioneer

detachment. The pioneers had their hands full trying to straighten out the confusion on the landing beaches, though, so to get some help they organized "labor gangs" from the replacement drafts that were coming ashore.

The labor gangs were assigned to finish unloading ships that had already been emptied of mechanized equipment and now had only boxed supplies. They moved the boxes from the ships to several storage dumps that had been set up a thousand yards or more up the beach, where units needing supplies could pick them up without getting in the pioneers' way.

All this unloading and delivery was done by hand. Stretching from the ramp of each ship up to the storage dumps were about four lines of men. The way the lines snaked their way through the confusion made each ship look like an octopus with tentacles. The lines were paired off facing each other, and staggered so that each man took a box of supplies from a man diagonally across from him on his left and passed it to a man diagonally across from him on his right. Then he took a new box from the man on his left and again passed it on. (In the facing line, each man took from his right and passed to his left.) This was real slave labor.

Of course the ships they were unloading, being "dead still" targets, were being shelled intermittently. But the pioneers and the replacement drafts helping them unload hardly even shied when a shell burst near them—they just kept doing their job, seeming to ignore all but the closest shell bursts. There was really no place to hide, even if they had wanted to. But I imagine that even if there had been some kind of shelter nearby each man would have stood firm there under the shell fire—scared shitless, but not wanting to be less a Marine than the man next to him.

When we visited the supply dump area we found another long line of men, infantrymen who like us were streaming through to get rations, ammo, water, and hand grenades to take back to their units at the front. Being on the beach again made me feel very exposed and uneasy, but—thank God—I had a place I could go. On each trip I nonchalantly shouldered a case of supplies and walked casually back up to our area, where the majority of people were only half crazy. Like every other Marine on that island, I was bound and determined that it would not be me who broke and ran from the incoming shells at the beach.

At this time, these chains of human "piss ants" were the only way supplies could be delivered to the front lines. There still were no workable trucks on the island; tracked vehicles were the only things moving, carrying mortar and artillery ammo up and bringing wounded back to the beaches for transportation out to the ships. We piss ants and many more like us met at this big pile and carried the boxes back up the hill to their units, through the shelling and small-arms fire, so others could keep on fighting.

We carried back cases of K-rations, hand grenades, 30-caliber rifle ammo, and five-gallon cans of drinking water that tasted as though the cans had not been rinsed when they were converted from serving as spare gasoline tanks for jeeps. These jeep cans were heavy (8.3 pounds per gallon) and awkward to carry—if they had to be moved very far it usually required two men.

Just before dusk all our help returned from the beach, bringing some more engineers they had found during the day. We now had almost thirty engineers in our little group, and a total of four light machine guns. No more H&S Company engineers landed until the fourth day, because infantrymen were needed on the island in the worst way.

Early that evening, even though I protested that I didn't feel well, I was one of the lucky ones that got to go back down on the west beach—again in the rain. Some of the people found some shadows to shoot at, but again I didn't see anything. (Maybe it was poor visibility in the rain or the fact that I was too miserable to care.) Now, with the advent of a temperature, I knew that it wasn't only lack of sleep that was bothering me—I was coming down with some kind of flu.

They sent out another patrol around midnight to reinforce us, but due to lack of any activity we finally returned to our area. It was almost 0130 before we were back in our foxholes.

Now I was really miserable, with a high temperature, a headache, and aching joints, either because of this flu bug or from fatigue and lack of sleep. Even though all my clothes were cold and clammy, soaked through by the continual rain, I was burning up with a fever. I felt so miserable when we finally got back to our holes that I just pulled my poncho over me and lay down in the wet sand.

That's all I remember until I woke up next morning, still under my poncho. I was warm, and all my clothes were dry. I felt a hundred percent better. I assume this was the result of the high temperature I had while lying under the poncho. The concentrated warmth had dried my clothes.

I guess nothing happened while I was asleep; the shelling sure hadn't bothered me. I was so tired that Benny had stayed awake all night to let me sleep.

D+3 (Thursday)

We moved again about mid-morning the next day, this time up to the southwest end of the main airfield. We were now in the 27th Marines area, and again in the center of the island.

The airfield was built on the extension of a shallow plateau. We were near the south end of one of the runways, which was built up about 25 feet above the surrounding terrain.

We were now about two thousand yards or a little better north of the 28th Marines lines around the foot of Mount Suribachi, and the front lines of the 27th Marines were maybe five hundred yards north of us. The Fourth Marine Division was on the other side (east) of the runway at this point.

It was still drizzling that morning. The shellfire seemed to be lessening, but that was only because the area the Marines held was slowly growing and the Jap gunners had lots more targets to divide their attention among. The shelling did not stop; there just were lulls in any one place when somebody else was getting yours.

Nobody seemed to know what to do with us. We still didn't have any engineer officers on the island, so we were still under control of Division Headquarters, and they found "make work" for us. The four of us who were mechanics were sent out to the equipment park. We were to look over our damaged equipment and to repair something, anything.

But we didn't have any of our tools or equipment to repair anything with yet, so we spent most of the day working down in the salvaged equipment area. We checked out the damaged and salvaged Engineer Battalion equipment, not really repairing anything, just tagging things that were salvageable and repairable. We wrote notes to ourselves on the hoods of the equipment in chalk.

The only productive thing I can remember that we did was to go back down and pick up some more rations and ammo from the landing beaches. This was also a day when several of us managed to wash our faces (there wasn't enough water for a shower) and get a shave and a good hot meal. We had souvenirs to trade, so we got first-class treatment on the LSTs. It drizzled off and on all of that day and night.

D+4 (Friday)

When we got up the following day the drizzle was still coming down. We were told to stand fast until some time later in the day, when the rest of H&S Company would be arriving. This was fine with us, who were following to the letter those old words of wisdom: "Never volunteer for anything."

In addition to having a much bigger Marine-held area to shoot at than on D-Day, the Jap gunners seemed to us "old timers" to be getting less accurate as more of their batteries were destroyed. The random shelling did not cease, though—there just were longer lulls in between shells in your sector. These lulls were dangerous, because they gave you a false sense of security. Then you could be caught out in the open when the next shell arrived.

In mid-morning, word spread that there were Marines up on the sides of Mount Suribachi. They were plainly visible to us down below—not many of them, so we decided that they must be just a patrol.

Everybody was passing field glasses back and forth, watching as the patrol neared the top of the mountain. We lost sight of some of them for a few minutes, then a yell went up that was heard all over the island. The patrol was putting up an American flag. It was small, but we could all see it, even without field glasses. (It was shortly replaced by a bigger flag, as shown in the famous photograph by Joe Rosenthal.)

There was cheering all around us—even the most cynical Marine who witnessed our flag being raised on Suribachi was touched deeply by the sight. It may be hard for people today to realize the pride we had in our country's flag. Later in the invasion, when the Marines controlled enough area for various units to set up headquarters locations (particularly support units that would mostly stay in one place), flags of all sizes began to appear. They were attached to sticks, poles, radio aerials, or any other thing that could provide visibility. It was very heartening to see all these flags flying when we visited the Rear. (I would guess that about half of them were U.S. flags. The rest, usually the biggest and best made, were Confederate battle flags. Today's "political correctness" would object to this display of the Confederate flag, but in that time and place nobody thought it was unacceptable.)

The Japs answered the appearance of the flag on the mountain with increased shelling down where we were—letting us know that they were still on the island and could still put up a good fight. For some reason, though, they never shelled our patrol on the mountain.

We figured that having our people up there was part of the reason the Jap shelling seemed to be getting less accurate.

Early in the afternoon, the rest of H&S Company started arriving on the island and joined us as we moved back to the west beach again. This time we settled in maybe a thousand yards north of our last location, and were responsible for protecting the left flank of the 27th Marines from possible enemy landings on the west beaches.

Arriving with the main part of the Company were a couple of 6x6 trucks to help us with the move. The only trouble was that they drew artillery or mortar fire any time the Japs could see them. Even with Mount Suribachi lost to the Japanese as an observation point, there were still high places on the north end of the island from which they could see us moving about, though maybe only 90 percent of the time. That 10 percent when they couldn't see you sure was the greatest.

These trucks had to be pulled up the slopes from the landing beaches behind dozers. Once they reached the more level areas, they were able to use six-wheel drive to move in the loose sand and transport our gear over to the west beach. I rode one of them, out on the right running board where I could exit fast if need be. The driver drove with his door open, with one foot on the accelerator and the other out on the left running board in case he had to exit.

True to our warning that any piece of moving equipment was a prime target for shelling, we drew incoming fire before we got very far. I didn't wait for the truck to come to a full stop—I faced out, jumped while it was still moving, and landed on my feet in the sand. Because I was facing out, though, the truck gave me momentum to my left, and my left ankle turned under me.

The shelling moved on after a few rounds. The truck must have rolled to a stop out of the Japs' vision. My ankle hurt real bad. It quickly started swelling up, and I couldn't walk on it at all. A Corpsman looked at it and assured me, after pulling and flexing it some, that it was only twisted. I was afraid to take my boondocker (a high-top shoe) off, because I knew that if I did, I wouldn't be able to get it back on any time soon.

Two of the guys helped me limp over to where our team was going to set up our machine gun. I started digging the foxhole while Benny carried over the rest of our gear.

We dug our line of machine guns in along the top edge of the bluff, setting up fields of fire down and across the wide beach below. Just below us were about ten amphibious tanks, each with its 75-mm cannon and 50-caliber machine gun. They were in place to repel an expected Jap landing on the beach tonight, and we were there as their only protection.

Several years later, after the war, I found out that one of the fellows who worked at the same office with me in San Francisco had also been in the Marines, and had served on Iwo Jima. I got together with him and it turned out that he had been in the 11th Amphibian Tractor Battalion, and had been in one of those tanks on the beach below me.

The Japs usually tried to disable tanks by blowing off a track with an explosive charge. Delivering the charge was a suicide mission carried out by a runner we would always call "Satchel Charlie" because he carried the explosives in a bag not unlike the demolition pouches I had carried off the landing craft on the first day. A Satchel Charlie would pop up and dash toward the tanks at top speed, activating the delay fuse on the charge as he ran. His mission was to throw the satchel under a tank before he was killed, immobilizing it and making it easy pickings for destruction by artillery fire. Our job was to shoot anybody who approached the tanks.

The hole Benny and I dug was at the right-hand end of a row of ten 30-caliber machine guns H&S Company had set up, about 25 feet apart along the edge of the terrace. We had no protection on our right except the steepness of the slope up from the beach. About a hundred feet behind us was a row of ten H&S Company 50-caliber machine guns.

In between these rows of machine guns, several rows of riflemen were digging in as protection for us. They were all new on the island this afternoon, and tonight would be their first night in a combat area. Hoping to prevent these new riflemen from firing at us by mistake, we had dug in during daylight, giving them a chance to see us below them and memorize our locations. They could not see the beach or the slopes below us, where the amtanks were. Only we in the machine-gun crews could see the amtanks. We told the riflemen we might fire downhill to protect the amtanks during the night, but that didn't mean the people uphill behind us were in danger. They were specifically instructed not to get "itchy trigger fingers" just because we fired; they were not to fire at all unless they were sure that the Japs had gotten around or through us.

Now that the whole Company had arrived, there were just two men left to man each machine gun. We no longer had a need for ammo carriers in adjacent foxholes.

Just at dusk we received an air raid alert for the island. About six twin-engine "Betty" bombers were on the way. It wasn't known whether they were coming to mount "Kamikaze" suicide attacks on the fleet offshore, or to bomb the troops on the island.

The possible kamikaze planes soon arrived, and ships all around the island fired at them in a true Fourth-of-July aerial display. One of the raiders flew southward along the beach right in front of us. He may have been hit already, but he was at almost the same height as we were, and all of us in the first row of machine guns fired at him as he went by. He crashed on the beach down near Mount Suribachi.

The whole air raid was over in just a few minutes.

Time to settle down.

"Hurry up and wait" is a very old saying in the service. It did often seem—during training, for example—that you would have to rush to be someplace at a certain time, only to get there and have to wait and wait.

Well, in combat the same thing happens. At times you are moving or are engaged in something that takes all of your time. You are busy, and time seems to fly. Then all of a sudden you must just stay put—you either aren't supposed to move, or can't. Time drags.

This staying quiet and not being able to move can make nights, in particular, terribly long. Sometimes at night there is no movement or noise along the front lines. As welcome as the chance to physically relax is, mentally it can be very tiring. There are times when the silence can cause more mental problems than all the noise of an artillery bombardment.

At times during the night you suddenly realize that all noise has ceased. The mind can play all kinds of tricks on you when there's no light from overhead flares and no noise. Suddenly you can hear movement and scraping sounds from every depression and rock pile around you.

Nights like that can take hundreds of hours to end.

On nights like that, some people fire their rifles and throw hand grenades for no real reason. This may partly be just for the comfort of hearing others nearby—the grenade explosions will spook someone in the vicinity, and they will make some noise too. Then several others join in, and before long at least you know that you are not out there all alone.

There were a series of passwords issued for use at night. Maybe this worked well in the rear areas, but they weren't used towards the front. Up there any movement or any sound such as talking would call attention to where you were, so everyone was very quiet after dark. There was no patrolling ahead of the lines, so there was no need for a password to allow patrols to return through the lines. The rule was that any movement could be eliminated in any way you felt appropriate.

No one left their foxhole or shell hole once darkness set in. There were no exceptions. Any movement or sound that could be detected around you was considered to be by infiltrating Japs. Of course, a lot of times the noise that drove you to the heights of anxiety was only a land crab out on a scavenging expedition, but you could never be sure. And if you had to give away your position in the dark all the time by calling for a password, you might as well turn on the front porch light.

Because of the number of Jap infiltrators that were killed within our lines nightly, someone had to be awake in each foxhole all night long. Since 90 percent or better of the foxholes at the front were two-man holes, that meant you only got to sleep half the night.

A few days of physical exhaustion and strain were enough to make you want to sleep for days. But being able to sleep only half the night at most (usually less) drugged your tired system with sleeplessness.

Any man who dozed or actually went to sleep while on watch in a foxhole significantly decreased his and his buddies' chance of survival. If he did survive, he was without a foxhole buddy from then on. He would have to stay by himself at night, or share his foxhole with another man who had slept on watch—which of course wasn't much better than being awake all night long.

So no matter how sleepy you got while on watch, you stayed awake. If you felt sleepy, you made sure that you kept your head moving all the time, never looking at one spot very long, as that would hypnotize you quite easily. If necessary, you did arithmetic tables in your head, you read books to yourself, you wrote imaginary letters—anything to keep your mind active, so you wouldn't doze off.

If you felt that you were losing it, you woke your buddy up. He would spell you for a while, but you had to make that time up to him before the night was over.

Chapter 9

FRIENDLY FIRE

D+4 (Friday) Night

It was dark now; a good time for infiltrators to try to get into our lines. Benny had the first watch. He was crouched at the front of the foxhole, keeping an eye on the beach below us. I was leaning against the back of the foxhole, sort of dozing.

Benny poked me and whispered, "The shit is about to hit the fan." Somebody was coming up the slope, and Benny raised himself up a little to look down that way. There was a shot, and he fell back on me, seemingly unconscious. There wasn't any way to get out from under him without standing up—a very poor thing to do right then.

I yelled to the hole on our left that Benny was hit, just as they fired a shot. I could tell from their muzzle blast that they had fired at something behind me and to my right.

I could feel the slimy wetness of Benny's blood all over me. I couldn't expect any help from a Corpsman, so I had to try to quickly dress his wound myself. Finding it in the dark was difficult, with no flares at all. But I managed to follow the trail of wetness to a wound in his forehead, about where the headband of his helmet would sit. The wound was about two inches long, with a small piece of bone protruding, and I started to put a field dressing on it. As I went to tie the tails of the field dressing around Benny's head, I slid my hand under the back of his head to raise it up. The little wet hole that my finger slipped into told me not to bother with the dressing: Benny was dead.

While this was happening I heard a lot of noise behind me (somebody was yelling that he wanted "that dirty Jap's samurai sword"), and I could tell that someone else had been wounded. I assumed that they and Benny had been shot by a Jap infiltrator, so I didn't dare call to anyone any more. I didn't want the Jap to know that Benny was dead and I was alone.

I worked around hastily and quietly until I could reach one of our ever-ready hand grenades. I pulled the arming pin and I was ready to throw it at any outside sound before some Jap could jump me.

Holding the safety spoon in place on the grenade with one hand and working only with the other, I finally extricated myself from under Benny's body. Now I got out a pistol and crouched in one corner of the foxhole, where I spent the rest of the night watching and waiting. I listened for any noise near me to throw the grenade at, and watched the faint light in the sky around the rim of the hole for any sign of movement to shoot at.

As soon as there was enough daylight for us to see to move about, Hank, from the machine-gun hole to my left, came over to see what had happened. He had a hell of a time getting the live grenade out of my hand, which had tightened up like a claw from holding the safety spoon in place all night.

We soon found out that a man in the hole right behind me had been shot in the darkness, at the same time as Benny. He was one of the new men, and realizing that he was wounded had caused him to panic. Disobeying his orders, he had left his foxhole and managed to run and crawl back through our company lines far enough to be helped. (He was lucky not to have been shot again by the other new people.) Once it was found that he had a head wound, he was helped out of the night lines and taken back to an aid station and a doctor.

A few hours later we learned that at first light he was back at the Engineer Battalion command post, at the very back of our unit, wearing a bloody bandage on his head. He told the people in the command post that he had shot a Jap inside our perimeter during the night and had immediately been wounded by another Jap. He said that the people at the aid station had tried to evacuate him to a hospital ship, but that he had refused.

The people he was talking to in the command post were also new to the island yesterday. To them he was a real hero, so some clown officer immediately wrote him up for a Silver Star, the third-highest medal for bravery. Another officer endorsed the recommendation, and the colonel commanding the Engineers sent it up to Division Headquarters within an hour.

These people never came down where we were to check the man's story. They were so far away from us that they didn't even know yet that one of our men had been killed. (This was back in the days before everybody had a radio.) They never did ask anybody out in the area what really happened. None of us were officers, so as far as the people in the command post were concerned, we were not knowledgeable enough to be worth consulting.

Meanwhile, to us "old-timers" on the island talking it over back at the beach line, the whole shooting incident just didn't seem right.

Benny's body had been removed from the foxhole. It was on a stretcher nearby, covered with his poncho. Finally, to settle the argument one of the fellows went over to look at Benny's wound in the daylight. He had to remove the field dressing I had started, to see for sure.

Benny's wound was from the back to the front. Only two shots had been fired, the second by Hank. He told us he had fired at the muzzle flash of the first shot.

The new "hero" arrived back amongst us, eager to see the Jap he had shot. When we ignored his boasting he became infuriated. He truly believed that we were jealously trying to deny him his glory.

The old-timers asked him where the Jap he shot had been. He told us that he had seen a head silhouetted in the light right there in front of his hole. He knew that it had to be a "dirty Jap" infiltrating our lines, so he took good aim and shot him. Almost as soon as he fired, he had been shot by another "dirty Jap."

Now he wanted us to give him the sword that the Jap undoubtedly must have been carrying. When some of the old-timers tried to explain to him what had happened, he wouldn't believe them. This man would never admit that he might have shot Benny by mistake.

The doctor of our unit came by later to see how the rest of us were taking Benny's death. When we told him what had really happened, he was flabbergasted. He told us that the "hero" had been scared shitless when he was brought in during the night, and had pleaded with the doctors at the aid station to send him out to the hospital ship. The field hospital had sent him back here to his unit instead, because his wound was only skin deep and certainly not serious.

No matter how much we old-timers protested, though, those stupid officers in the Engineers command post never asked Division to cancel the Silver Star recommendation. Nor, to my knowledge, did they ever ask the "hero" to return the medal. I guess they thought they would lose face if they admitted that they had been wrong, even this once.

When I watched the Operation Desert Storm coverage on television in 1990, I could only shake my head in disbelief at hearing the "experts" back here in the safety of their armchairs complain about some men being killed by "friendly fire." They seemed to think that combat is like a chess game, where you have plenty of time to plan what you will do. In actual combat, you move and react to situations from your subconscious, just trying to stay alive. A firefight is just too confusing for any kind of count of who killed who, and men can easily be killed by friendly fire without anyone ever realizing or knowing it. Of course it's a shame when any man dies, but it's a wonder that more people are not killed accidentally.

As an example of how easily accidents like the one that killed Benny can happen, here's a SNAFU that happened much later in the Iwo Jima fighting, up at the north end of the island.

The Japs had been driven backward to the north beach—a fairly wide, level stretch of land bordered on the south by half a dozen nearly vertical thirty- to fifty-foot bluffs. Units of one Marine battalion advancing from the south found themselves on top of the bluffs. To secure the area they had to make their way down the bluffs, clearing Japs out of caves along the way, and then attack the enemy on the level ground.

Getting down the bluffs was easier in some places than in others. The right-hand company reached the level area first, before dawn one morning, and began to sweep west across it. When they were part way across, Marines from a company on their left reached the top of the bluff, looked down, and saw shadows moving in the semi-darkness. They took them for Japs and opened fire with rifles and machine guns, killing a lot of the people in the first company.

Once this mistake was discovered, the battalion (or what was left of it) was removed from the island, and we never heard another thing about this.

Chapter 10

LEAVING "HOME" AND
GOING OUT INTO "THE WORLD"

D+5 (Saturday) and After

I am coming now to a period of time in which a structured account of events is impossible—all continuity disappears—and my reminiscences are no longer chronological. I have no guide posts, no references to tie remembered events to. Between running off one landing craft on D-Day and staggering aboard another one 36 days later, I am sure there are many days that I have no recollection of at all. I have a feeling that several of the things I have written about may have happened on the same day, early in my travels, and that the latter days are a complete blank, lost forever. After about day D+4, I don't have any concept of time. This may be just as well—it could be the only reason I didn't come out of Iwo any worse than I did. Several times in the first five days I had thought that "the shit was hitting the fan," but I was to be surprised at how easy it turned out for me. From here on out, it seemed like things always got worse, never better.

D+5 was the first full day the Engineer Battalion leadership was on the island. Starting early that morning they had their troops digging deep holes for them to live and work in safely. The sandy sides of the holes were reinforced with sandbags, and roofs were constructed by laying salvaged timber and steel rails on top of the sandbag walls, covered by layers of sandbags and more sand. Seeing their valuable officers so well protected from harm, all the enlisted men at headquarters naturally tried to do as well by themselves.

These H&S Company people lived in relative comfort, worked regular days, and stood regular watches at night against possible Jap infiltrators. They had hot meals, a medical dispensary, hot showers, and outhouses, all in duplicate—one for enlisted men and a much better and more private one for officers. Even out here, the officers had special privileges. They ate separately; and their head was surrounded by a canvas screen, while users of the enlisted men's head were visible to everybody for miles around.

It was often said by philosophers in the Corps that these and other "chickenshit" things were heaped on the enlisted men for a reason: to build up their frustration and hatred to the bursting point, so that when they were pushed off a landing craft onto an enemy beach they would take that hatred out on the Japs. All too often, the stupidity and pettiness of the orders we got from our own officers seemed to support that theory. We were always being prohibited from doing something quite trivial or inconsequential, and those prohibitions on us always seemed to result in additional pleasure or convenience for the officers. The orders imposed on us during our trip on the USS *Darke* certainly seemed to be an example of this.

But there were also many officers and senior NCOs who could arouse feelings of frustration and hatred in their troops just by being themselves. Some were born that way and never learned any better; for others, continual flaunting of the unchecked power their rank afforded them was a way of hiding their feelings of inadequacy and inferiority.

I vaguely remember that I spent the first couple of days after Benny was killed helping move H&S Company engineer equipment up from the east beaches to our designated area on the west side of the island. Dozers dug revetments in the sand to park trucks and jeeps and our machine-shop trailers. Once the big trailers were in place, we strung camouflage nets over them to hide as much as possible from the expected aerial attacks.

After that, about D+7, I became part of a team of engineers sent up to clear mines from a couple of big landing beaches (codenamed

"Orange" and "White") further north on the west side of the island. The plan was to try to open them for easier supply of the 26th and 27th Marines and the newly arrived Third Marine Division, as well as for quicker removal of their wounded.

These beaches were where the Japs had thought we would make our original assault landing, so they were very heavily mined. To clear them, sixty of us H&S Company engineers were sent up—three ten-man demolition squads and three tem-man mine disposal squads.

I was the assistant leader of first demolition squad. ("Nut-cracker 1" was our radio codename.) The leader was a fellow PFC engineer named Frank. Both of us were outranked by everybody else in the hastily assembled squad—one master technical sergeant, two sergeants, and three corporals. But the others had no demolition experience, so Frank and I were the "experts" and the others were to serve as riflemen.

The beach we were sent to first was big—about fifteen to twenty acres, I recall—and relatively flat, surrounded by higher ground. It was still under sniper fire from pillboxes up along the slopes. We were "guarded" by tanks, but their presence didn't stop the sniping.

There were many, many mines on that beach, all buried a few inches below the surface of the sand. To protect the beach from wind erosion, and incidentally to make mine clearance harder, the Japs had planted clumps of grass at eighteen-inch intervals. Each clump was about six inches in diameter and about eight to ten inches tall. The mines were mostly hidden in the clumps, but if you believed that was the only place they were, your buddies would never be able to find enough of you to bury.

Because of the continual sniping, you had to crawl along the rows on your belly, probing the ground ahead of you very carefully with your bayonet. You gently slid the blade in under each clump of grass or other suspicious spot at about a forty-five-degree angle. If the point of the bayonet met any kind of obstacle you stopped pushing immediately, because some kinds of mines could be set off by as little as five pounds of pressure. Then you carefully brushed away sand until you could see what your bayonet had touched. As you crawled you planted little white flags, which identified rows or parts of rows that were clear, and little red ones, which identified confirmed or suspected mines for later removal. Removing mines was especially dangerous, because some of them were booby-trapped.

There were several kinds of mines. Some were big, designed to destroy tanks and other vehicles, but the ones we hated most were small, deadly antipersonnel devices. One common antipersonnel type, about eight to ten inches in diameter and two inches thick, had a little detonator knob on top that about ten pounds of pressure would set off. Another type, about fourteen inches in diameter and six inches thick, required almost no pressure to detonate. Three eight-inch piano wires stuck out from the top of it like little springy feelers, and anything that caused any two of the three to touch would close an electrical circuit and set the mine off. The piano wires were easy to conceal among blades of grass, so we had to examine each grass clump extremely carefully.

It would have been nice to be able to search with mine detectors instead of bayonets, but each of these types of mines also appeared in non-magnetic versions that a mine detector couldn't find.

Among the biggest mines we found were 250-pound and 500-pound aerial bombs buried vertically, nose up, in deep holes. Connecting these bombs to the surface were "yardstick mines" (detonator cylinders about a yard long and two inches in diameter, with motion-sensitive feelers projecting through the sand).

We found so many mines that before long we were detonating them in groups instead of digging them out one by one. We used prime-a-cord, a highly explosive material that looked and worked like a length of cotton clothesline, to tie a line of small charges together. Next we'd place a charge on top of each mine, and then (from a safe distance) destroy the whole string at one time.

In addition to clearing areas of enemy mines, our demolition squads were also responsible for destroying confirmed and suspected booby traps. The only booby traps I ever saw were round and flat like a tuna can and probably contained about 8 ounces of explosives. In the center of the can was a small round plunger which when ejected by a spring would set off the explosive. A U-shaped safety clip held the spring in place until the trap was set. The trap setter would place a "bait" object—say, a pistol—on top and then pull out the U-clip with a string. This armed the trap: Anybody or anything that moved the object let the spring pop the plunger up and explode the device.

Theoretically, it was possible to attach a rope to any suspicious object and pull it from a safe distance, escaping the explosion if it was booby-trapped and getting yourself a souvenir if it wasn't. This worked great if you had the time to fool around like this and if you didn't move the object in trying to get the rope around it.

I mention pistols because they were the most frequently booby-trapped items. Usually they were near bodies we found when we moved forward first thing in the morning. But anything that the Japs thought some Marine would want for a souvenir was likely to be booby-trapped. It was much safer to set a small charge next to a suspected item and set it off than fool with trying to save the souvenir.

Whenever we detonated charges for any reason other than direct combat support right at the front, there was some risk that people nearby might mistake the explosion for incoming enemy artillery. To avoid spooking them, before igniting the fuse we always shouted out the traditional warning, "Fire in the hole!"

Those of us in the six squads of H&S Company engineers who were sent up to remove mines on the western beaches never returned to Engineer Battalion for duty. Division Headquarters took control of us for assignment to whatever unit was in the most need of engineers on any particular day.

The Division was generally headed north, but the units we were with went east or west if it got us north in the end. Most of the time we had no reference points to say where we were, or where we had been. There were paths, but no roads except the ones our dozers cut for us; and the area ahead had been shelled so heavily that maps were useless. The only terrain features they showed that were still intact were hills, each with a number (like Hill 215, or Hill 382) based on its height in feet. That sure wasn't much to orient yourself with. We went through two "towns" where nothing remained but a level stretch of ground with some pieces of wood and sheet metal scattered around.

The whole south end of the island, except for the area around the base of Suribachi, had been mostly loose sand. Somewhere around the first airfield, our northward push began running into harder and harder ground. As we got further north, the terrain we found was all hard rock, with a series of east-west gullies and ridges crossing our path and slowing us down. It was not unusual, as you attacked a ridge ahead, for the Marine beside you to be firing back toward the ridge you had just crossed, where Japs were emerging from their hiding places and shooting at you. That's being caught between a rock and a hard spot, I guess.

The jagged rocks were an obstacle even for tanks. The only way they could get up to help us was if we called in armored dozers from the Engineers to cut in roads. That meant more time for the troops to spend under Jap fire, which was more dangerous among the rocks than on the sands further south. Here the shrapnel and bullets could ricochet around, and there was no place to hide. True, you could form a little shelter by moving a few rocks around, but the rocks that would stop or deflect a bullet were too big to move.

I have read that the Army in Europe dug "foxholes" deep enough for a man to stand up in and roomy enough for two. The fancier ones even had grenade traps in the bottom, and log roofs for overhead protection.

Out where we were, there weren't any logs to get under; and shell holes, or any kind of depressions, were the preferred resting places. To us a foxhole was anything that you had to dig yourself—usually just deep enough to lie down in. If you wanted a hole to sit up in, you dug into the edge of a shell hole. On the south end of the island we always carried our entrenching tools to do that digging. But they were useless in the big rocks, so once we got halfway up the island, we threw them away.

The vegetation we found on the north end of the island also contrasted with the south. By our third or fourth day ashore, the manzanita-like scrub brush and green ground cover I had noticed in the sand the day I landed had been pretty much pulverized by shelling. I can't remember seeing any kind of living plant on the south end of the island after that. The north end of the island had lots of heavy brush or small multi-branched trees growing out of the rock outcroppings. Of course these trees were also completely "trashed" by the time we got up there. Their leafless, crooked, and twisted branches, some up to three or four inches in diameter, were scattered all over—just one more thing to impede our movement.

Our squad's first missions in support of the Division's northward march involved blowing up cave entrances, with the aim of preventing the caves from being used by enemy snipers and machine-gun crews. Before long, we found ourselves following on the heels of our infantry, sealing caves and destroying bunkers that they had bypassed (deliberately or inadvertently) in their mad rush forward. Many of these positions were still manned. Nobody wants to be buried alive, so there were lots of arguments from the Jap occupants over our right to seal them up in their caves.

The caves were fairly easy to seal, once we reached them. Most were no longer covered by supporting fire from other caves or machine-gun emplacements—the infantry had taken care of that for us—but some were still protected by snipers, hidden in well concealed spider holes.

Attrition among line company engineers and infantrymen trained in demolitions had by now stripped some rifle companies of their ability to clear hardened Jap positions blocking their advance. After some quick on-the-job training from real demolition people, we began to get requests for help. We were lucky to have had a chance to "practice" on mostly unoccupied caves for a few days before the requests got us up with the riflemen.

The farther north we got on the island, the more intact we found the elaborate Jap protective system for the caves and the occasional pillboxes we encountered. Up here, their positions all covered each other with interlocking fields of fire, and we needed help to attack and eliminate them. With our infantry "customers" and the riflemen in our squad covering us by shooting into the mouths of the caves and into the firing apertures of the pillboxes, Frank and I were able to work our way up and plant our explosives.

Caves were destroyed one at a time, following a kind of "blueprint" that we worked out over time. The riflemen in our squad, along with B.A.R. (Browning Automatic Rifle) men borrowed from the infantry unit we were supporting, would fire into the cave to keep any people inside from firing out. In the meantime Frank and I would work our way toward the cave, one on each side of the entrance. (He threw better left-handed, so he always took the right side, and I threw better right-handed, so I always took the left.)

Before starting, we removed our cartridge belts and anything else that would make noise or hinder us as we crawled. We wore cloth utility caps instead of helmets. We carried a couple of grenades in the side pockets of our engineer pants and tucked .45 pistols under our belts at the small of our backs. This left us free to crawl, dragging our explosives.

We would start forward, hopefully out of sight of anyone in the cave or bunker. In the case of caves, once we were in place and the moment was right, each of us would sling one of those 30-pound satchels of composition C into the opening. The two near-simultaneous explosions usually collapsed the roof in on those inside.

These charges had thirty-second delay fuses, so in order to deprive cave occupants of a chance to throw them back out before they went off, we had to ignite the fuse and count a while before we threw them in. Even so, the occupants sometimes managed to throw one back. By throwing in two charges at nearly the same time we caused enough confusion inside that we never got both thrown back at us. (I have seen combat films showing Marine demolition men with charges tied on long poles, which let them work in closer to a pillbox or bunker without exposing themselves to enemy fire. I guess all of the long sticks had been worn out before we got to the front, because I never saw this method used.)

After a cave was blown shut, often it would be silent only for a few hours. Then Japs would enter it from the tunnel complex that connected so many of the caves, poke a little hole through the dirt and rubble covering the entrance, and start firing at the Marines again. Some caves had to be "re-sealed" several times.

Before long we "graduated" to destroying the reinforced pillboxes or bunkers that were a permanent part of the Jap defenses. These naturally were harder to eliminate. Usually they had been surrounded by our infantry just recently and still had nearby Jap snipers or other light guns covering them.

In these cases the "blueprint" was modified. In addition to the rest of our squad shooting into the pillbox's firing aperture, the infantry unit we were supporting would fire at any other nearby Jap positions that might try to protect the pillbox.

Under this covering fire, which sometimes included help from tanks, Frank and I crawled forward from two sides, as in the regular blueprint. But instead of flingable satchel charges, we dragged special explosive devices called shaped charges. These were thirty-pound hollow steel cones, about twelve inches wide at the base and eighteen inches high, that would blow a twelve-inch-wide hole in a reinforced concrete pillbox. Our job was to make our way to the sides of the pillbox, set our charges on top, pull the igniter strips, duck, and wait thirty seconds for the charges to go off. It was important to stay down, because our buddies were firing into the aperture at the front. Sometimes they only stopped firing long enough for one of us to make that last sprint to the side of the box.

We were in little danger from the blast, because it was all focused downward through the roof of the box. In fact, it was not unusual for the explosive charge only to stun the occupants, so it was important for the Marines in front, as soon as the charge went off, to send their flamethrower man running up to kill any Japs still alive inside. He did this by sticking the nozzle of his weapon into the firing aperture.

Frank and I quickly learned to help by tossing hand grenades in from the sides of the aperture or through the newly blown hole in the roof. This was important, because most of the pillboxes, whether square or round, were built with a T-shaped concrete blast wall in the center to protect at least some of the occupants from incoming rifle fire. Our grenades kept the people inside stunned long enough for the flamethrower man and his buddies to get up to the firing aperture.

The farther north we went, the fewer reinforced concrete pillboxes and bunkers we ran into, but the terrain was very unfriendly. If you stood up on any ridge and looked ahead, the ground looked flat, but really it was cut every few yards by gullies and canyons running across the path of our advance. Cut into the steep sides of every canyon and gully that we entered were many more caves and machine-gun emplacements.

Any time the Japs spotted us in groups or saw us starting a morning advance from our lines, we could count on getting mortared but good. If the area you were entering was one they had already "zeroed in" (something you had no way of knowing until too late), they would really open up on you—and they were very good. You could expect hell.

As the artillery and mortar fire diminished from week to week, the accuracy and deadliness of the small-arms fire (from rifles and small "Nambu" light machine guns) seemed to increase. There was little apparent organized fighting, but the Japs were very well disciplined. They only fired if they had a target and could make the shots count.

Like everybody else, I use the word "snipers" loosely for all single soldiers firing rifles at us. There certainly were professional snipers out there—excellent shots, well trained and dangerous. A lot of the shooters, though, were not technically snipers by combat specialty. Any Jap who was separated from his unit continued to fight to the death. Whatever you called them, there sure were lots of them left to harass us every minute of the day and night.

The hard part was trying to find a single hidden man when there were maybe a dozen shooting at you. One guy would fire at you from distances beyond the rifle's accuracy limits, while another might not fire at you till you were within twenty feet of his hiding place. Some would allow themselves to be bypassed, playing possum for a day or two before coming back to life.

Advancing through the piles of rocks was a long, slow process. If these people kept hidden, it was impossible to spot them until they popped up to start firing. Later I wondered if our fatigue had made us miss telltale signs that they were there.

I had my share of close calls.

Once the unit I was with got pinned down, with shells from 61-mm mortars and the little 50-mm "knee" mortars falling around us like snowflakes. This was the first small-bore mortar barrage I was ever caught in, so it had to be early on, maybe in the area up around Nishi ridge. I was lying down between two small rock pillars, trying to make myself smaller. With the shrapnel ricocheting around me, I began frantically crawling forward looking for a more protected spot. I wiggled into a likely looking place, only to find it littered with bloody bandages (so it hadn't been safe enough for some Marine); the only other place nearby had a dead Marine in it. This was not a very reassuring location for any man to be in on his first encounter with intense mortar fire up among the rock piles. But eventually the mortaring let up, and we were able to get out of there.

Another time, also up near Nishi Ridge, we were crossing an open area that was being shelled. (This was while the Japs still had some large-caliber artillery left.) I was running almost upright for a change, because none of the shells were landing close enough to seem worth worrying about.

All of a sudden I was spun around and knocked down (possibly by a short round from our own artillery). I had been hit on my left side, right at the belt line, by a piece of burning hot shrapnel about two and a half inches in diameter. It had razor-sharp, extremely jagged edges and was still stuck into the cloth webbing of my cartridge belt next to my clip pouch. It had bent both clips in the pouch; if it had hit an inch away from there, I am sure it would have torn open my stomach.

The demolition squads did not have to stay on the front lines at night. In the evenings we were allowed to drop back, not all the way to the safety of the H&S Company area, but to a secondary line about fifty to a hundred yards back. That seemed like a long way to us, and we weren't as bothered by the infiltrators who seemed to continually harass the front lines. But the snipers and the mortar shelling were almost as bad, if not worse, back where we slept. It was nice to be able to sleep in shifts (sometimes), and be "fresh" for the next day's work, but you had to steel yourself every morning to get up and "advance" up to the front lines. Mentally, it was just as bad as if you had slept all the way back in the Rear.

There are a few exceptions to what I've said about there being no reference points we could use to tell one part of the north end of the island from another. One was the area of the third airfield. Usually you could see only about 25-50 yards from where you were, even standing; and the piles of rock, cliffs of rock, and gullies of rock you saw in one place were pretty much the same as the ones you would see around the next corner. So it was an amazing and memorable view when we came to the top of a bluff and saw below us a large, relatively level area where the Japs had begun rough grading for new runways. That area was also memorable as a sudden-death zone, where nobody could move without being shot at. It was bounded on the west by the ridgeline where we were and on the north by some hills, all still in Jap hands, that also had a good view of the unfinished surface. Anybody who tried to walk or run across it would draw fire from more than one spot.

Another unique terrain feature was a major obstacle to the Marine northward advance until we captured it some time around the third week.

Even after most of the Japs' big artillery pieces had been destroyed or driven into hiding, which as I remember took us ten days or so, their mortars continued to inflict extremely heavy casualties on us whenever we moved. Everybody had an idea of where the shells were coming from—you could see them at the tops of their trajectories, coming from somewhere in front of us. But the area ahead of the lines looked flat, with no ridges to hide mortars behind.

Then our infantry stumbled on an immense hole in the ground that hadn't been visible until they got up close. Some said it was the remains of an extinct volcano; to me it looked like an open pit mine, several hundred yards in diameter and mostly fifty to seventy-five feet deep. We called it "the blow hole." All around the sides, on several levels, were enough caves to conceal hundreds of mortars. The Japs could bring them out to the cave entrances when necessary, fire a few shells, and then pack up and retreat back inside to safety. Our counter-battery fire had been heavy but ineffective.

Discovering the blow hole enabled us to knock out these mortar positions at last. But it still took considerable work to destroy enough of these caves with fire from our bazookas (one-man rocket launchers) and tanks so that troops could get down in there and close off each and every cave. We did it, though; by the end of the third week, the volume of fire we were taking from the heavy (81-mm) mortars had lessened considerably.

But there were still plenty of other mortars, both 81-mm and 61-mm, firing at us from the mouths of caves all over the north end of the island. And until the very end there were plenty of the small 50-mm "knee" mortars left. Their range was relatively short, but it was much further than we could throw a hand grenade, and they made up in volume for anything they may have lacked in quality. I would swear that every Jap on that island had a knee mortar and was well versed in its use. Toward the end, they were firing them at us from cave entrances like rifle grenades. And of course shrapnel from a small mortar can kill you just as dead as shrapnel from a big one.

Chapter 11

LIFE "ON THE LINES"

As I sit here today in the safety and peace and quiet of our home, I stare into space, seeing these things I experienced and wondering if an accurate description of what happened is even possible. I know it's difficult as hell for me to try to express, let alone recreate on paper, the feelings of terror and helplessness that stick in my mind, or the feeling of resignation as the people around you are continually getting hit. It became a matter of whether you would be killed or just wounded—there was little doubt about your vulnerability. You would constantly say to yourself, really praying, "Please, God, make it just a wound when it comes."

I should be quick to point out that each man's memories are based on what he actually did there, not the overall military "big picture." Combat, to each man, really means just the area around you (maybe ten to twenty feet).

I have read that "if you talk about real infantry combat to people who have never experienced it, either you'll have trouble getting them to believe you or they just won't listen. But just about everything imaginable can happen in combat, and frequently does."

So I'll start this with two thoughts:

"A rifleman in combat is one of those things you are glad as hell to have been after it's over, but you sure aren't in a hurry to be one again."

and:

"Whatever the memories may be, they sure as hell will never leave us."

Night Combat

It is very hard to see at night.

The world is either pitch black or lit up with the greenish light of flares. As a flare goes off you have to adjust your eyes, just like when a camera flashbulb goes off in your face. On top of that, while the flares are falling they rock back and forth on their parachutes, making the shadows around the rocks and debris ahead of you constantly change shape and size. Is that the silhouette of a man you see along the side of that pile of rocks? You look away to the side for a second to clear your vision and now that "man" has moved.

Finally, once you've adjusted your eyesight and can almost can see what is out ahead of you again, the damned flare goes out. Now you can't see anything, and probably won't be able to for several minutes. Just as your eyes are almost re-accustomed to the darkness, there's a pop overhead as another flare is lit and begins floating to the ground. And so it goes, all night long.

But all bitching aside, there is an optimum method of seeing during the time the flare is in the air. You don't concentrate on a fixed spot, but you don't move your eyes around either—if you do, your imagination is likely to go wild and convince you that you're seeing Japs. Instead, you rely on your peripheral vision to detect any movement out there. You turn your whole head slowly from side to side, starting with the ground closest to you and working outward till the flare goes out. This is not a risk-free method—having your head up where you can see means that others can see you, especially if you make any sudden movement. Of course you can always pull your helmet down over your eyes and wait till some Jap slides into your hole with you ...

Offensive operations were also more complicated to carry out at night. For example, to synchronize actions it was imperative for someone in each foxhole to have a watch. All military watches and most civilian watches that people wore had luminous dials. It was hard to read the time from them in the darkness, but you would be surprised how far away the luminous face was visible. So all watches were kept buttoned up in a shirt pocket until a time check was needed.

Once the Third Division began a surprise attack at 0500, a couple of hours before daylight. (In a "normal" attack, naval gunfire would start at 0740 and the infantry would move out at 0810, allowing the officers to have their breakfast in the comfort of a dugout before coming up to the lines to watch the advance through their field glasses.)

On this night my squad happened to be staying up on the line to support a unit posted on the far right of the Fifth Division, with Third Division people on its immediate right. My squad was asked to help the unit we were with carry out its orders, which were to move forward with the Third and keep any gap from opening between the two divisions that the enemy could slip through.

The orders also specified that no flares were to be used until the Japs discovered the advance, and that if any of us fell down while moving on the unfamiliar ground through the darkness, we were not to make any noise. (Did you ever try to fall down quietly?) Actually, this attack turned out pretty well. The Third Division got quite a ways into the Jap lines while the Japs were still asleep.

Our fatigue added to the trickiness of seeing at night. Sometimes you were better off to close your eyes and concentrate all your energy on listening to the sounds around you. The eyes could be fooled, but your ability to hear at night could be surprisingly good.

Then again, the improvement in your hearing could be a mixed blessing. To detect infiltrating Japs in the darkness you had to strain your ears for any little sound that was out of the ordinary. Unfortunately, there was no way of distinguishing between the sound of a Jap crawling nearby and the sounds made by land crabs, little scavengers (much smaller than the ocean crabs you buy at the fish market) that were abundant on the island. Some areas were worse than others. On a quiet night, the sound of ten or twenty of these things crawling around was nerve-wracking to say the least.

To fire a rifle was to give away your position to every Jap within twenty miles, so as a sound slowly moved toward you, all you could do is wait till the intruder was close enough to stab at with your K-Bar knife. The tension was overwhelming. Finally, when you could not stand it any longer, you sprang out of your foxhole toward the sound.

Thank goodness all I ever encountered was a land crab out hunting for food. But there were enough Marines encountering infiltrating Japs every night that you didn't dare take a chance on what a crawling noise might be.

After we got back to rest camp in Hawaii, you had to be very careful of how you woke a person up, day or night. Most people (even some who never left the Rear area) slept with either a pistol or a knife in their hand, and would come up wild and swinging if they were startled in their sleep. We had had to surrender all pistols upon arrival at rest camp, to be stored till later. But most of the people from the lines slept with a knife in their hand all the time anyway, so you had to be very careful.

Up on the lines, a pistol was not your best defense if a Jap jumped you while you were asleep—he could easily deflect it so that you basically had no weapon. (A 45-caliber automatic pistol can also be rendered inoperative by grabbing the upper slide and pushing it back even a sixteenth of an inch.) A double-edged knife was faster and harder to deflect, besides which it was silent and didn't have to be reloaded.

When noise ahead of you on the lines at night signaled possible trouble, you normally did almost anything but fire your weapon, because its muzzle flash was a big homing beacon for infiltrating Japs. Knowing where a foxhole was, they didn't have to risk blindly stumbling into somebody who could stop them short of their goal of taking a Marine with them into death.

One of the best ways to keep your position relatively undetected was to toss a hand grenade at the approaching sound (if you knew that direction was clear of other Marines).

Our hand grenades were set off by a timing fuse that started its countdown when a spoon-shaped safety handle was popped free by an activating spring. The spoon was prevented from accidental release by a pin that held it and the spring in place. To use the grenade, you gripped it with your throwing hand, holding the spoon tightly to keep the fuse from igniting; then, with your non-throwing hand, you yanked out the pin by its attached pull ring; then you threw (releasing the spoon) and ducked.

Fresh out of the box, the safety pin was bent just enough to keep it from being pulled out accidentally, but not so bent that a good healthy tug on the ring couldn't pull the pin out through the holes in the spoon handle.

The safety pin was pulled out by hand—definitely not by the hero's teeth, as you see in some movies. If you used Hollywood's idea you wouldn't have any front teeth left after about the third or fourth grenade. Also you had to check the grenades on each new man who came into the lines to make sure that he had them attached to his suspenders by the spoon and not by the ring on the safety pin, which could accidentally set off the grenade if jostled.

At night, you laid out a row of grenades in a convenient spot alongside your foxhole, with their safety pins pulled halfway out of their spoons so that it took very little effort to get them out in a hurry. Once the pin was out and the spoon was sprung free, activating the fuse, there were five seconds till the grenade exploded.

Five seconds is a surprisingly long time. It was possible to throw a grenade at a Jap, have him pick it up and throw it back at you, and still have enough time for you to scoop the grenade up and get it away from you before the explosion.

After the spoon flew, if you had the nerve you could lessen the risk of having your own grenade thrown back at you by holding onto it for three seconds or so before throwing it. ("Mississippi one, Mississippi two, Mississippi three...") The only problem with that was that the sound of the spoon flying off would tell any nearby Jap where you where.

Jap hand grenades were somewhat similar, with a five-second timing fuse and a forked safety wire on top that was pulled out the way we pulled out the pin on ours. Instead of an activating spring like ours, though, their grenade had a detonator button that had to be tapped sharply on a hard object (a Jap soldier would generally use his helmet, or the stock of his rifle) in order to start the fuse.

When you heard that tap in the night you knew you had five seconds before a grenade would blow up—somewhere. You now had two options: You could fire your rifle at the sound of the tap (hoping that the tapper didn't know where you were) or you could silently wait till you heard the grenade hit the ground, and then try to jump away from it before it exploded. Each method had survivors who were positive that their way was best. We never heard much from the losers.

Under Fire

Incoming artillery is one of the most terrifying things there is. Mortar shells are bad enough, but artillery shells have ten times the explosive force and ten times the noise, and a shrapnel kill radius maybe three to four times greater.

Mortar shells fall slowly enough that in daylight you can see them coming. Standard practice during mortar barrages is for one man lie on his back and spot shells reaching the top of their trajectory, usually hundreds of feet in the air. He can easily judge where the rounds will fall and warn others to duck or run to another hole.

Artillery fire, in contrast, batters you with rapid multiple explosions, waves of intense concussion that can jar you so badly that you can't function, talk, or even think coherently. I can't begin to describe the terror and helplessness you feel, curled up in a fetal position, wishing you were invisible. Your mind is devastated. The flying shrapnel makes it suicidal even to raise your head up from your hole, let alone try to get up and run. The randomness of where the shells land is especially unnerving. Even in an area under intense shelling, there will be some spots that remain unscathed and others that are pulverized by multiple hits.

The artillery barrages we suffered during the first few days of the invasion were especially effective, because all the Jap guns were sighted in, or "registered," on preplanned target locations. When we walked into one of those locations, we'd be hit with extremely accurate fire. There was no advance warning; the first shells were on target.

As time went on, some of the Jap observation posts were destroyed, and our naval gunfire forced the Japs to move their artillery pieces to new sites. This required them to spend a little time zeroing in on targets, which sometimes gave us a chance to get the hell out of there.

The Jap observer would begin by firing a single white smoke shell as a marker in the general vicinity of the target. Next would come a second marker round, intended to hit on the opposite side of the target; then a multi-gun barrage of high explosive shells covering the area halfway between the two markers. If you were "bracketed" by marker rounds—or if a marker round landed anywhere near you, for that matter—you were in deep trouble and should get out of there as fast as possible, because the next rounds would usually be right on the money.

When you are under fire, your world is very small and very personal. Most of the time you are only barely cognizant of what is going on near you if it doesn't affect you.

The man running next to you is really not a part of your world unless he stumbles or falls, in which case he becomes at least partly your responsibility. (Exception: when coming out of the landing craft, you do not stop under any circumstances.) You have to find out whether he's been hit; if so, whether he's wounded; if so, whether what hit him was shrapnel (random product of a nearby explosion) or a bullet (aimed specifically at him by an enemy rifleman). If it was shrapnel, you can stop in your tracks to help him, but if it was a bullet you have to find a place to get yourself—and him, if possible—to cover.

Your thoughts continue: Am I alone now? Is the man on my other side still with me? Is anybody still moving? Is there a Corpsman near? Do I have any field dressings left? On and on it goes, as you try to find where the shot came from, or was there more than one shooter? I can hear several guns firing, but are they shooting at me or at people ten or fifteen yards down the line from me?

Your world is only maybe ten feet on either side of you; you are wearing blinders as far as things beyond that are concerned.

Filling Gaps in the Line

The Iwo Jima invasion plan called for the infantry divisions to replenish their combat losses from "Replacement Drafts" that were brought along with us on the ships. These were battalion-sized groups of enlisted men and officers, assembled in the States to provide instant replacements for men killed or badly wounded in the various Pacific island invasions.

On Iwo, as I've described, these people were brought ashore very early and used as stevedores on the beach by the pioneers until they were needed at the front. This was hard, dawn-to-dusk work, and very dangerous. There was no place to hide from the continuous shelling of the beach, and stopping work to look for a hiding place was not an option.

I had been a member of a couple of those units myself before coming to the Fifth Division. Just after finishing Combat Infantry

School at the end of January 1944, I was assigned to the 48th Replacement Draft. At the time it looked as though they might be sent to reinforce the First Marine Division (which had just landed at Cape Gloucester in the New Britains) or the Second Division (just back from Tarawa) or the Third Division (which was still fighting on Bougainville). Instead of going with the 48th Replacement Draft, though, I was sent to Combat Engineers School. When I graduated I was assigned to 54th Replacement Draft, which was probably headed for the Third Division (then just returning to the rear areas from Bougainville and Empress Augusta Bay) or maybe the First Division (possibly still needing replacements after its landing on Kwajalein).

I can remember how little training I had during my time in the Replacement Drafts. When I was in the 48th, we were only four weeks past boot camp and thought we were really hot stuff—in fact, we didn't even know the time of day.

I wasn't much better prepared when I was with the 54th. I believe that coming from it to the Fifth Division and getting six months of additional training before Iwo made the difference between confusion—or possible death—and a chance at survival.

Watching some of the Replacement Draft people up on the lines, I felt sorry for them. Most would have been helped with more training. Some, though, were downright uncomprehending of even the most basic things; either they hadn't had good instructors in the infantry schools (which I doubt), or they hadn't paid attention. These men's ignorance of weapons capabilities and use, and of the basics of field tactics, was very costly to them. There was no time to teach in the lines. You learned fast by watching and copying the actions of the quick, or you didn't survive. Some of the replacements were not on the line long enough for their names to be known to anybody in the units they were assigned to before they died.

Smells of Combat

There is another thing that should be mentioned here, but I am afraid there are no words to adequately describe it: that is the smell of death.

Some of us were lucky enough to get used to it gradually. When we first came off the landing craft onto the beach, all we could smell was the acrid smoke from bursting shells. (The Japs used a lot of picric acid in their explosives.) Before long the smell of scorched bodies in the burned-out bunkers began to mingle in. From then on the intensity grew, to the point that the sailors on the ships around the island told us that the smell carried clear out to them.

There is nothing I know of that smells worse than a rotting human corpse, bloated and split open in the hot sun. The bloating can last for several days, till it finally begins to dry out some. After you'd been on the line a few days, the smell would only bother you if you almost had your face buried in a rotting corpse.

Chances

It was almost impossible to be up with a rifle company and not get hit. The old-timers had words of wisdom for us "boots" on this topic (not soothing, but showing their deep understanding of combat): "Take it easy on your first cruise, son. If you're going to get it, that's all there is to it." This fitted in with what we'd been told time and time again by trainers and leaders who tried to keep us thinking clearly: "Fear is the relinquishment of reason," and "Doubt is more fatal than slowed reflexes." Good advice, but it was pretty hard to keep your cool when you were getting shot at, no matter what the old-timers and trainers and leaders told you.

The infantryman's basic trade, staying alive, is either learned or not learned in one day on the lines. He uses the instinct of preservation; he turns into a Mole, a Ferret, or a Cheetah, depending on the moment; and he will do anything to keep from drawing fire.

I quickly learned how to move through the worst of it. After all, anything can be learned—and learned quickly, when life is the motivation. Besides this, ludicrous as it may seem to anyone who hasn't been there, even in combat there are times when a premonition of danger sends a tingle racing up and down your back.

There were a couple of sayings that would float through my head at the damnedest times. One, which we had thought was half joking when we first heard it, was "Everything you do in combat, including nothing, draws fire." The other was the rifleman's conviction that "it only takes one to kill you." This was sometimes expanded to "It makes no difference whether you're killed by heavy artillery in a big battle, or by a lone sniper in a patrol action—you're just as dead."

Most people would say that an infantryman's outlook on life and death is very devil-may-care. I would classify it more as fatalistic. What else could it be, when every day you saw more and more of your friends killed or wounded? With every man that was killed, your unit just became smaller; there were no replacements. Because of the extreme length of time the Marines on Iwo had to stay on the lines, it looked to most of us as if we would continue to push forward until there were no people left. There was no letup in either the need to advance or the killing.

One common way of thinking about all this involved the law of probabilities—the idea that your chances of survival diminish in proportion to the number of times you are exposed to hazardous situations. This idea is undoubtedly true to a great extent, but most of the people I have ever run into who believed it were those who were safe in the rear areas. The man out on the lines isn't able to reduce his exposure to the probabilities, so he becomes a fatalist—realizing that he has no control over whether he lives or dies, and relying on some higher authority to determine when it's his time.

Many men expressed premonitions that they weren't going to make it. I'm not sure that this attitude, this feeling of helplessness, of being utterly abandoned, wasn't the downfall of some of those killed. After miraculously escaping harm from the mortar shell that exploded in my foxhole on the morning of D+1, I don't remember ever feeling that way, or having any doubt that I would get home. True, there were times when so many shells were coming in that if you were going to survive, you just had to be lucky—or under the protection of God. And I did worry a lot about the kind of wound I would receive, and I prayed that I wouldn't be bedridden for the rest of my life; but I was sure that I was going to live. I believed then and still believe that if you take reasonable precautions, then you will live as long a life as God intended you to live.

Because when the time comes, it is your time—whether you are in combat, or you slip and fall while chasing some naked blonde around the bedroom, or you maybe suffocating while sleeping under the silk sheets in your nice soft warm bed. There is nothing that you can do to escape the call when it's time. The only arguable point is whether you can take too many unnecessary chances and go to the head of the line.

The real worry was about wounds. Not all of them were bad— what we called "million dollar wounds" would take you out of combat without doing serious permanent damage to your body. You might be sent to the States as a hero, or at least to Hawaii, where you could sit out the remainder of the operation. (One example was the piece of shrapnel in the kid's ass as we came off of the landing craft. He told us when we got back to Hawaii that he was taken off the beach on another landing craft within five minutes of being hit.)

The wounds that everybody dreaded were the ones that leave you a cripple in a hospital bed for the rest of your life. (Our demolition officer, Captain Klotz, was shot through the top of the right shoulder while bending over. The bullet, which exited at his left buttocks, severed his spinal cord and he was paralyzed from the neck down for the rest of his life.)

Wounds disfiguring to the face were probably next down on the list of bad wounds. Then stomach wounds and, if it had to be, then the clean loss of an arm or leg was almost a relief as a way to get off the island.

But by far the worst thing that any man could think of happening to him was to be wounded and unable to prevent himself from being captured by the Japanese. The Marines went to great lengths to get their wounded off the battlefield. The Japs weren't above mutilating our wounded or our dead, so we were especially worried about their treatment of a wounded man. Men risked their lives and many died trying to rescue a wounded man to prevent his possible capture. You expected the others to do it for you, so you did it for them.

Resupply

One of the very unglamorous parts of being on the lines was that all supplies had to be carried up there on somebody's back. The terrain was generally too rugged for an amtrac, and even if the driver got up near the lines he would be such a target that he couldn't unload. So the tractors stopped back a ways, in a sheltered area, and each box of ammo, rations, or grenades had to be manhandled forward, along with those five-gallon water cans with contents that tasted like gasoline, and even medical supplies. (This work was usually done at the end of the day's fighting—just when you were feeling your best.) Sometimes two or three men from the demolition squad might have to spend a whole day crawling back and forth, bringing up more explosives.

Grenade boxes had easy-to-use rope handles on each end, but in spite of American ingenuity none of the other boxes had handles that might have made the chore of carrying them easier to accomplish in this dangerous place. About the only way to get the other boxes and cases up to the people was for each carrier to just hoist one up on his shoulder and take off running, at a crouch if possible. If a sniper started picking on you while you were carrying, all you could do was dump the box and look for a place to hide. (Some time try picking up a 50-60 pound box and running up a hill with it. Fun, isn't it? Then remember that nobody is shooting at you, and that when you get tired you can stop.)

What We Wore

In combat there is utter chaos mixed with total confusion.

There had been times in earlier Pacific combat operations when an officer had given orders to men not under his command and had not been obeyed, possibly because they hadn't realized he was an officer. (It was very dangerous to go into combat wearing any kind of insignia that might tell the enemy your rank, so nobody did. We knew the Japanese Army and Navy rank insignia and they knew ours.) An especially good leader can get his orders followed by men who don't know him, but that can't always be counted on.

In an attempt to solve this problem, a new insignia system was tried out in the Iwo invasion. Every man was to have a four-digit code number stenciled on the front and back of his jacket and the back of his backpack. The first digit, followed by a dash, identified your rank (1 for privates and PFCs, 2 for corporals and junior sergeants, 3 for senior sergeants, 4 for lieutenants, 5 for captains, and on up); the second identified your regiment, the third your battalion, and the fourth your company. The stenciling was color-coded to identify type of unit (blue for Infantry, red for Artillery/Tanks/Rockets/Mortars, yellow for Engineers/Pioneers/SeaBees, and green for Communications and other special units). Surrounding your four-digit number was a shape that identified which division you belonged to (a rectangle for the Fifth, a half-moon for the Fourth, and a triangle for the Third). For example, as a PFC engineer with H&S Company of the Fifth Division, my gear was stenciled in yellow, with the code number 1-411 enclosed in a rectangle.

This idea worked fine for the first few days, while the units were still made up of people who belonged in them. But the new people from the replacement drafts who were shoved into the units later didn't have these markings on their gear. Before long, so many of the original members of the line outfits were gone that nineteen out of twenty men fighting on the line either had no markings on their jackets, or wore markings for the rear-echelon unit they had belonged to before they were "combed out" and sent up to the front as infantry.

In fact, by the time my demolition squad was sent up to the front, it was getting harder and harder to find units at all. The attrition rate was very high, and there were no longer any replacements left on the ships. Every day more and more troops from the service units in the rear were sent up to become infantry, but there weren't enough of them to fill all the gaps. Most platoons no longer had officers in command. Some line companies that had started out with five full platoons had only two half-strength platoons left. Other companies had to combine remnants of their original troops in order to have even half-strength platoons. Still other companies no longer existed, except on paper—they had themselves been disbanded, with their remnants sent to bolster other units.

Under these circumstances we had more urgent things to worry about than uniforms, but that doesn't mean that what we got to wear wasn't important to us. In some situations it directly affected our survival.

Up at the front you were almost certain to draw sniper fire if you carried a carbine (which the Japs early on knew were carried by officers and senior NCOs instead of M-1 rifles) or a map case or a pistol. Before long, everyone carried an M-1 or a B.A.R. The more you blended in with the group, the better your chances of survival were. (Maybe one of the reasons the replacement troops fared so poorly during the campaign was that their clean uniforms set them apart from the masses.)

I remember from someplace that our combat uniform as Marines was a "two-piece herringbone twill fatigue suit, with high-top leather shoes." It also included the distinctive camouflaged helmet cover I've mentioned. These canvas covers for steel helmets were reversible to match varying environments, with a "desert" side in four shades of brown and a "jungle" side in four shades of green. On other island landings lots of the troops wore complete uniforms in one of these camouflage patterns. The Marines on Iwo had no such uniforms, for some reason, but to make sure that they were never mistaken for Army troops, they always wore the camouflaged helmet cover (brown side out).

Another thing that was being tried out for the first time in this operation, in addition to the new rank and unit insignia, was a re-designed utility uniform for the Engineers and Pioneers. Up to this time we had worn forest-green dungaree jackets and trousers that were fairly tight-fitting except for sailor-style bell bottoms. Our new jackets and trousers were baggier and more comfortable. The jacket had a big pocket on the back to carry your poncho in, and the trousers had cargo pockets on the sides that were especially conven-ient for retrieving needed items when you were under fire and hugging the ground. Also the pants were pegged, much easier to run in. These new uniforms worked so well that in later years the Army, as well as the rest of the Marine Corps, went to the same type.

Generally speaking, at the time we landed everybody wore pretty much the same uniform, but as the fighting progressed, what you wore became a matter of personal convenience.

The clothes of the troops up on the line were in terrible condition. All were filthy dirty, with ripped knees and elbows. We looked like hoboes, and were rightly referred to as "Raggedy Assed Marines." We looked even worse in comparison with the REMFs ("Rear-Echelon Mushroom Farmers," to say it politely). Not only were their dunga-rees in good condition, before very long they were even able to wash their clothes every day if they so desired. They were able to take hot showers (at a Division Headquarters "shower head" constructed by the engineers), to shave every day, and get six to eight hours of good sleep every night.

Chapter 12

WHAT WE CARRIED

All during the fighting it was odd to compare what gear the NCOs in different units had instructed their people to carry and what to discard.

Some people even had to wear their packs and bedrolls for most of the campaign. (It was dumb to burden a man that way.) Some carried lots of extra grenades and some carried extra bandoliers of ammo clips. Some wore their cartridge belts with suspenders and all of the canteens and first-aid pouches. Some people traveled very light, with just their weapon, a couple of grenades in their pockets, and a bandolier of ammo clips.

Especially when we got into all the rocks toward the north end of the island, just about everybody had to take all the gear off their cartridge belts and travel light. There was no way you could crawl amongst the rocks on your belly without getting something caught and having to make some kind of extra movement to unsnag it. You held your weapon in your right hand and carried extra ammo clips in a cloth bandolier slung over your shoulder. Your field dressing was carried in your jacket pocket.

My own personal gear was kind of a mixture. Because the difficulty of keeping a poncho on in the rains of the first several days, on one of my trips down to the beach I traded a sailor some souvenirs for a gray Navy rain jacket. I was able to wear that most of the time, except when I went on patrols. (On a later trip I traded more souvenirs for a heavy alpaca-lined foul-weather jacket that I later brought home and wore for many years.)

Like most other Marines, I used my helmet for protection against weather as well as against flying metal. Inside the steel pot was a dome-shaped molded fiberglass liner with a web suspension system that kept the liner about three quarters of an inch away from your skull in all directions. Inside the liner, between the cushion webbing and the top of the dome, there was almost a full inch of clearance. In this dry space I carried two small pictures of my girlfriend Helen (back to back and waterproofed), a package of cigarettes, and some toilet paper. Between the web and my head I always wore a utility cap (the USMC version of a baseball cap).

Over my long johns I wore a wool shirt with the sleeves cut off (like a vest). In one shirt pocket I carried igniter fuses; in the other, half a dozen blasting caps (wrapped in scraps of the shirtsleeves to protect against jarring). On top of all this I wore an old-type short field jacket, with a fragmentation grenade in each pocket and a bandolier of ammo clips over my left shoulder.

I wore the new special engineer pants, with a combat knife and a pair of fuse-crimping pliers on my belt on my right hip. In the front pants pockets I carried a Zippo lighter and a Boy Scout knife, and in the side pockets I carried a couple of field dressings and any assault rations (hard candies) I could steal along the way.

When we were moving from place to place, I carried an extra bandolier of ammo clips and wore a web belt with two more grenades, two canteens, two more field dressings and my poncho. These could be dropped anyplace and picked up later.

Explosives

The material we used most in our demolition work was composition C, a plastic explosive that came in foot-long blocks, each waterproofed with a thin layer of wax and about three inches high and three inches wide. These came sewed into light canvas pouches, each containing four blocks and weighing thirty pounds. A carrying strap three inches wide made the pouch easy to carry on your shoulder and convenient to throw when the time came.

Although composition C was about five times as powerful as

dynamite, pieces of it could be cut off the block and lit with a match to use for cooking purposes. Like TNT and just about all of the other explosive materials and devices we used (the very volatile prime-a-cord that I've mentioned was an exception), composition C wouldn't explode even if hit by rifle bullets. In order to set off the charge you needed some kind of detonator. Usually this consisted of a blasting cap (just an ordinary dynamite cap, to shock the composition C into exploding) plus an igniter or fuse to set off the blasting cap (after a delay for safety reasons).

Blasting caps (which were also the triggering device used to set off both U.S. and Jap hand grenades) explode very easily, and careless people over the years have lost fingers and eyesight from accidents with them. A cap dropped onto something, or squeezed too tightly in a vice or with your crimping pliers, will explode and set off any other explosive material nearby. Caps are never carried in the same pack as the explosives.

In battle conditions, a match or a burning cigarette was not a reliable way of lighting a fuse to set off a blasting cap. Instead you used a friction-type igniter. This was a pencil-sized tube that you attached firmly to the blasting cap, which you would then attach to the explosive. To activate the detonator you yanked on a little T-shaped handle at the unattached end of the igniter. Doing this was like pulling a big match out from between two pieces of spring-loaded sandpaper. The little handle came out of the igniter, along with a telltale puff of smoke telling you that the fuse inside the tube was lit. You had probably thirty seconds to the explosion.

The blasting caps Frank and I used were about two inches long, as wide as a 22-caliber shell, and hollow at one end. They came in little wooden boxes of fifty that we carried with us when we worked. To make a detonator you inserted the igniter in the hollow end and crimped the cap with special pliers to hold it firmly. Then you made a hole in the explosive (one of the handles of the crimping pliers was pointed to help you do this) and buried the cap, igniter end out. Finally you firmed the explosive as tightly as possible around the cap with your thumbs. If additional delay time was needed, you could crimp the igniter onto a piece of fuse cord, which you then crimped into the blasting cap planted in the explosive.

We also had some pre-assembled detonators, consisting of a pull igniter already attached to a blasting cap. They were designed to screw into ready-made sockets that some blocks of composition C and other explosive packages came with. These detonators came in little cardboard cylinders that looked like a cigar in your shirt pocket. They were a little safer to carry than ordinary detonating caps, but a rifle bullet or a piece of shrapnel would easily set them off.

TNT, another item in our demolitions kit, came in two-pound bricks, about three inches square and five inches long, each inside a waterproof cardboard box. Back in Hawaii, people did quite a bit of fishing using a handy-dandy TNT brick that had a hole punched in it, with a blasting cap inserted into the hole and an igniter crimped to the cap. The concussion when one of these went off would daze the fish and they would float to the surface; then you picked out the ones you wanted.

The biggest operational problem Frank and I had was getting any real power out of our charges. Any explosive, to be fully effective, must be confined in some way. This can be as simple as placing a solid object on top of the charge to direct some of the explosive force downward. The more weight is placed on the top of the charge, or the more tightly the charge is packed into a hole, the greater the explosive force transmitted in the direction away from the pressure.

When we had to throw bags of composition C into the mouths of the caves, there was no real destructive force applied to anything. Usually the charge merely stunned the people inside the cave long enough so that someone outside could either hose it down with napalm or throw in a couple of hand grenades. Once the cave's inhabitants were taken care of, a second charge would be set up over the entrance, with a few rocks on top; when that was exploded, usually enough of the roof fell in to close the mouth of the cave.

This is why we liked shaped charges. They had a metal casing, and the weight and the shape of the charge focused more of the explosive force downward so that we often didn't have to set off that second blast.

Our Weapons—a Quick Rundown

Rifle, caliber 30, model 1903 Springfield (or model 1903-A, with a pistol grip). This bolt-operated single-shot weapon was fed by a 5-round stripper clip that you had to remove when empty in order to close the bolt. The Springfield was a delight to handle and fire. The accuracy of its sight system made it a prized target rifle, and it was used extensively on the lines against snipers, but it was too slow in a combat situation. It later became a collectors' weapon.

Carbine, caliber 30, M-1. Ammunition for this gas-operated single-shot weapon came in 15-round box clips. It was light and easy to handle, but those were its only saving graces. Fairly accurate up to maybe 50 yards, it was okay for occasional use, but most people did not consider it good enough to stake your life on. Also, the Japs knew that carbines were issued to officers and weapons teams, so they made it a point to snipe at anybody carrying one.

Rifle, caliber 30, M-1 Garand. A gas-operated semiautomatic weapon fed by 8-round clips. This rifle, sturdy in action and reasonably accurate when fired from the hip, was the weapon of choice for most infantrymen on Iwo, and after the first couple of days there was plenty of ammo available for it. The M-1 wasn't perfect. It was somewhat heavier than the Springfield and (because it had more moving parts) a bit more time-consuming to clean. It jammed easily if the ammo clips were dented or dirty; and when you pressed a new clip into the breech, you had to be careful or lightning quick to avoid having your thumb smashed by the bolt slamming home. Also, its sights were sensitive; merely walking through brush could knock them awry, diminishing long-distance accuracy. All these flaws were minor, though, compared to the M-1's one serious drawback—the way it ejected empty clips. The firing of each round ejected the empty cartridge and fed a fresh round into the chamber, so you could fire eight rounds as fast as you could pull the trigger. When you fired round number eight, though, not only the empty cartridge but also the empty clip would be ejected, and the bolt would lock open to receive the next clip. This could catch you by surprise if you weren't keeping track of how many cartridges you'd fired and how many were left in the breech. Most of the time it was no big thing to run out of ammo and have to stop and reload. But that empty clip ejected with a very distinctive "ping" sound that told every Jap within a hundred yards you were out of bullets. This sometimes had very hair-raising consequences.

Pistol, caliber 45, M1911A. There were a lot of these around, but people up on the lines never carried them. The range was too short, and ammo for them was not always easy to come by up on the lines, although it used the same cartridge as the Thompson submachine gun. This was the weapon of choice of the REMFs.

Submachine gun, caliber 45, M1A1 Thompson. This had been a good weapon to have on other landings (which was why I had scrounged one for myself from a wrecked landing craft on the first day), but it was not a good choice on this island. It was heavy, reloading its ammo drums or clips took time, and it was a bitch to keep clean. I wound up leaving mine back on the truck.

Machine gun, caliber 30, M1919A4 Browning. This light machine gun could fire 400-500 rounds per minute, fed by 250-round belts. Its disadvantages were its bulk and general awkwardness. To move it required a minimum of three people, and the barrel got so hot that its rifling would degrade and one of the gunners would have to wear an asbestos mitten to change barrels. Otherwise it was generally a first-class weapon. It would work in lots of situations where others would have failed, absorbing all manner of abuse and punishment.

Automatic rifle, caliber 30, M1918A2 Browning. The B.A.R. delivered fire support to infantry units at high or low speed (500-600 or 300-450 rounds per minute). It could also be fired very accurately as a single-shot weapon, with a 20-shot magazine. It was heavier than regular infantry rifles, but considerably more mobile than the 30- and 50-caliber machine guns it substituted for (there were very few machine guns on the lines). All Marines on the lines prized the B.A.R. very highly.

Grenades and Ammunition

According to a book about weapons that I've consulted, the U.S. fragmentation grenades we used weighed about one and a quarter pounds, including an ounce or two of explosive inside a metal case that would break into some forty lethal pieces flying as far as thirty yards. That sounds about right, but the book also says that the average soldier can throw a grenade about 35 yards. (That's 105 feet! Hell, you'd have to be on the top of a mountain to throw one that far.) Incidentally, grenades were definitely not thrown like a baseball. The only way to keep from tearing all the muscles in your arm was to lob them—something like a basketball hook shot. You held the grenade in a stiff-arm pose and used the movement of your upper body to provide the throwing momentum.

All of the M-1 ammunition for the riflemen arrived on the lines in wooden boxes full of olive-drab cloth bandoliers, each containing ten eight-round clips. The clips could be pulled out of their individual pockets on the bandoleer fairly easily, and you were expected to reload your cartridge belt every time you removed a clip from it. But sometimes you used the clips up faster than you could replenish your belt, so you just carried the bandolier. (You generally had to keep the cartridge belt on in any case, because it had your canteens, first-aid pouches, and field dressings attached to it.

Ammunition for machine guns (both 50- and 30-caliber) also came up in wooden boxes. Every box contained six or eight waterproof metal canisters, each with an easy-open snap top and a collapsible handle for easy carrying. Each canister held 100 rounds of 50-caliber ammo or 250 rounds of 30-caliber ammo, already belted and ready to use.

Every fifth bullet on the belts we were sent was a tracer, thoughtfully provided so that the gunners could see where they were firing. One of the last things gunners did before dark was to strip each tracer from the belts they expected to use during the night. Tracers showed not only where the fire was hitting but where it was coming from, and the colors identified who was doing the shooting. (Jap tracers were green; ours were yellowish orange.) We in the infantry units did carry some of the loose tracers with us. They were good to use as markers when trying to show tanks or others where you had seen something.

Ammunition for the B.A.R.s was identical to M-1 ammo, but it came in special clips for automatic feeding. For some reason, new clips of B.A.R. ammo were in short supply, so bullets usually had to be stripped out of the M-1 clips and inserted in empty B.A.R clips. It was a good idea to save the empty B.A.R. clips, just in case. If you counted on getting new clips, you can bet your life that none would show up (and you can bet that the REMFs all had plenty of B.A.R. clips, too, even if the front lines didn't).

Ammunition for the 45-caliber pistols and the Thompsons had to be loaded in saved or salvaged clips. I believe carbine ammunition came in clips, but nobody on the lines carried carbines so I don't know for sure.

What the Enemy Carried

I don't remember all of the different kinds of small-caliber Jap weapons we found. The most popular among their troops seemed to be the Nambu light machine gun, which came in two sizes: 6.5-mm (25-caliber, more common) and 7.7-mm (31-caliber). The Nambu was fed by a thirty-round banana-shaped magazine that attached to the top. It had a built-in flash hider on the muzzle, a foldable bipod, and a carrying handle that looked like an old teakettle handle over the center of gravity on the top of the barrel. In the right hands it was an accurate rapid-fire weapon. (The Japs didn't have any "lefties" on the island; in fact, I think that every one of them had qualified as "expert marksman" on one before leaving Japan.)

The 50-millimeter Jap "knee" mortar was not what it sounds like. It was about knee-high in firing position (easily carried by one man), but its baseplate was designed to be set on the ground or a log for firing, definitely not on the user's knee.

These little mortars threw a shell the size of a hand grenade several times as far as a man could throw a grenade. They were very accurate in the hands of a trained user, and regardless of who was using them, they made up in volume for what they might have lacked in accuracy. According to a weapons manual the knee mortar shell weighed 1.2 pounds and had a range of 130 to 700 yards (further if special shells were used).

Some of the enemy gear we found was useful in helping us figure out who we were up against. Most of the Japs on the island belonged to the Imperial Army. Their uniform was olive green and their helmet had a star on the front. (I collected one of them one day to trade as a souvenir later). There were also some Jap Navy personnel who for one reason or another were assigned to fight on land with the Army. They were called Special Landing Forces; they wore Navy uniforms, which were black, but their helmets, weapons, and other gear were standard Army issue. Finally there was a small hard core of true Japanese Imperial Marines, who were also referred to as Special Landing Forces. They could wear either Army green uniforms or Navy black uniforms, but they could be identified by the distinctive Chrysanthemum and Anchor insignia on the front of their helmets. They were bigger than the usual Jap soldier, as well as being better trained and more fanatical.

Special Landing Forces wore heavy leather hightop shoes like our "boondockers;" other troops wore the split-toed canvas type shoes called "tabi."

Most Jap officers carried a sword, a map case, and a leather holster with a 9-mm Nambu pistol (which looked just like a German Mauser except for a round cocking lever). Some NCOs also carried swords into battle, though, so to identify a Jap officer for sure you looked for signs like a uniform made from a better grade of cloth.

Our Food

One of the things that were served all the time in military mess halls, both in the States and overseas, was a pressed cooked meat that came in cans. It was put on the civilian market after the war and can still be bought today—that's Spam.

Once we were overseas, the only time we ever had fresh eggs was the morning of D-Day. All other eggs we were served were reconstituted. The majority of meals were nothing but heated five-gallon cans of C-ration main courses, served with fairly fresh bread, which we always liberally covered with a mixture of peanut butter and orange or peach marmalade.

To make these dreary meals edible, every Marine carried his own bottle of catsup and applied it liberally to everything. I believe this is where the idea of putting catsup on french fries and eggs at fast food places came from.

Another favorite meal of the cooks in the service was chipped beef or ground hamburger, which they cooked in a white gravy and served to the troops on a piece of toast. This meal (it could be breakfast, lunch or supper) was known as SOS, short for "Shit on a Shingle."

In the Pacific theater we ate lots of meat and dairy products from Australia. We knew the butter was from sheep's milk, so when they told us the meat was beef, we suspected that it was actually mutton.

Bad as the meals in the base camps were, they were gourmet feasts in comparison to the field rations, which came in several varieties.

The Assault Rations we carried ashore when we landed were just small cellophane bags of hard candy, but they contained lots of sugar and tasted real good, so they were hard to find.

D-rations were solid chocolate slabs, a mixture of sweet and German types, that came in a waxed cardboard box about one inch thick by three by five. They looked like they had been packed in the early thirties, but you could use your K-Bar to shave slivers into a canteen of heating water, making a passable chocolate drink. The chocolate could also be eaten at night, or anywhere you couldn't light a fire. It was awfully hard to bite off, but it didn't taste too bad.

K-rations came in a waxed cardboard box, about an inch and a half thick by three by eight. Inside the box were two packages of hard biscuits and a small round metal container (about two and a half inches in diameter) that held one of three kinds of "spread": egg something for breakfast, cheese for lunch and minced meat for supper. There was also a packet of powdered coffee and a pack of four cigarettes.

C-rations came in cartons and boxes of various sizes. There were about eight or ten different canned main courses available, each of which was accompanied by crackers, condiments, cigarettes, matches, toilet paper, and suchlike. The only main courses I can remember were Beef Hash, Vegetable Stew, Kidney Beans, and Beans and Franks (officially labeled "Vienna Sausages with Pork and Beans") which was just about the best of them. After the war this product came out on the civilian market as Spam did; you can still buy it today as "Beanie Weenies."

Most of the people up on the lines had no way of cooking. If they wanted hot water in their canteen cup they had to build a little fire with scraps of cardboard from cut-up ration boxes. But we engineers, with our supplies of high explosives, lived the life of Riley. We cut off small cubes of composition C, which burned like a candle when lit, and used them to heat our chocolate or coffee.

Digging Equipment

Of course the most obvious items in this department were our entrenching tools, the little foldable shovels we all carried strapped to our combat packs when we went ashore. They included a hinged spade and a hinged pick, each of which could be folded against the short handle for travel or locked into an open position for excavating. They were nearly useless around the rocky northern end of the island, but they worked fine on the sandy south end, aside from being a little too small for efficient digging and a little too big for easy carrying. (When you were in a hurry you might leave one behind and have to resort to using the steel pot portion of your helmet as a scoop, or digging with your bare hands. This, too, worked okay around the south end of the island.)

Our other digging implement was that multi-use tool, the combat knife. True, it was no good as a shovel, but it made a good pick. It really was used for just about everything. You kept it sharpened for its intended purpose, but it got used so many other ways that I can't name even half of them.

At night when it was your watch, your knife was usually out, lying on a little cleared space at the front of your home for the night, along with a couple of easily available clips of ammo. When it was your turn to sleep, you settled back against the back of the hole with your rifle cradled in your arm, both to keep it clean and to have it handy for quick use; it was common practice to keep your unsheathed knife in your hand, even as you napped.

When you needed to get to a wound in a hurry, a sharp knife would cut through web packs, suspenders, jackets, dungarees, leather shoes and God only knows what else. The knife was the only tool we had for prying open all kinds of boxes and containers, as well as for preparing explosive charges. In the absence of eating utensils you used it as a ration can opener; as a knife to cut chocolate or dry biscuits, as a spoon to stir your coffee or soup, and as a fork to shovel food into you mouth when you got a chance to eat. The flat butt end of the knife handle made an excellent hammer, too. You could use it instead of the butt plate of your rifle to knock open those boxes that couldn't be pried open.

Identification

In the service everybody had to wear a pair of stainless-steel identification tags that listed his or her name, military serial number, blood type (only A, B, AB, and O were recognized then), and religious preference. Using these tags, medical personnel could arrange transfusions promptly if you needed blood; a chaplain could give you the last rites of the Church if you were a dying Catholic; and graves registration personnel could notify your unit if your body was found on the battlefield.

The tags were originally issued to be worn on a chain around your neck. Naturally the troops called them "dogtags," because they looked like tags you'd attach to a pet's collar.

Combat experience showed that clanking dogtags were a security hazard, so eventually leather cords replaced the chains and one of the two tags, instead of hanging around your neck, was threaded into the laces of your right boot. This way if your head was blown off, the people who retrieved body parts from the battlefield would still know that the bottom section was you.

If you were killed, one tag was buried with your body. The other, after being copied into your unit record books, was nailed to the back of the cross that was planted above your grave.

Chapter 13

NOT QUITE LIKE THE HOLLYWOOD MOVIES

Battle Lines

One of the things you should remember is that the lines on Iwo were not like the ones you see in the movies about World War I. The situation was fluid, and it was very easy to find yourself unexpectedly on Japanese real estate, with Japs on all sides of you. By the time our forward units had advanced past the second airfield, there were lots of Japs wandering around behind our lines, and there was continual sniping from any kind of hiding places they could find. Some of them infiltrated during the night, looking for food and water; others came to take at least one Marine with them to heaven; still others passed under us through tunnels. They reoccupied bunkers and caves behind us that we'd already cleared once, and started harassing us. We had to spend quite a bit of time going back to reseal cave entrances that had been closed at one time but now harbored snipers.

As shown in movies, wars involve continual firefights, with hundreds of people shooting at each other. This is not complete fiction—sometimes you do get a curtain of various kinds of metal thrown at you—but what happens ninety percent of the time is that you crawl along on your stomach from rock to rock, or maybe sprint from shell hole to shell hole, waiting to get shot at. The hard part is the waiting, knowing there's a good possibility that someone has picked you out and is drawing a bead on you; and that you could be dead without even hearing the sound of the shot that gets you.

A shot fired at someone near you is almost a relief—you are not the selected target at this moment. It is the waiting to get shot at, waiting for the artillery or mortar round to drop near you, waiting to get killed or wounded, that occupies all your waking hours. That is really what stress is all about.

What We Fought For

The Japs sure put up a hail of fire and shelling as the first B-29 made an emergency landing on the island. (The books say this was on D+12. If I had to swear to it I would have guessed that it happened almost a week earlier. Maybe D+12 was when the first B-29 was able to actually land, not just skid and scrape down the runway to a safe stop inside our lines.) The Japs were already sore that day, because for most of the morning transport planes from Saipan and Guam had been making emergency parachute drops of mortar shells directly to our mortar sections up near the front; they'd been experiencing ammo shortages.

The silk in these big cargo parachutes was very valuable, as it could be traded to troops in the rear areas for food. When the REMFs received the silk they cut it into rectangles, painted red "meatballs" on them, made a few marks to resemble Japanese writing, and then rubbed them in dirt to create "Jap battle flags." They then sold these to the ships at the beach, who in turn sold them to the transports they were offloading cargo from out at sea. Another source of silk for souvenir flags was the parachutes on the flares fired over the lines at night. The first thing each morning our troops on the lines collected as many parachutes as possible; somebody then took them back and traded them to whoever could offer the most or the best food in exchange. This may have been the beginning of a true cottage industry.

Actually, there weren't many genuine Jap souvenirs to be collected by anybody in their right mind. Most were buried in the caves as we closed them off. Some undoubtedly remained in the pillboxes we knocked out, but the explosives and napalm we used left a mess that we didn't have time to scavenge through. However, it was not unusual for me to look around to check on my eight-man squad and find four or five "extra" men—REMF engineers who were tagging along in hopes that we'd blow up a big pillbox that they could sift through looking for souvenirs to sell to the sailors at the landing beaches.

Whenever I got a chance to go to the Engineers rear area I would take a case of Jap hand grenades to trade with. These were true souvenirs that I had personally defused. The only other things I ran across up on the lines were Jap soldiers' personal items that mostly didn't seem suitable to collect.

It was frequently said by the old sages in the unit that "the Japanese fight for their Emperor and the British fight for glory; the Americans fight for souvenirs."

I cared little for souvenirs except as a trading commodity to get supplies, and it never ceased to surprise me how avid so many men were to get them, especially samurai swords, side-arms, and rising-sun flags. People looking for such things were sure taking their lives in their own hands. The closer we got to the north end of the island, the more time we demolition people spent destroying articles that we either knew or had good reason to suspect were booby-trapped. Particularly in the early mornings, as we moved up into territory given up by the Japs the night before, there was always a rash of calls about suspicious items. We found so many of them booby-trapped that it just became standard practice to blow up any obvious and tempting souvenir, no matter how inviting it looked. The fellows up in the line had learned long ago to leave that stuff alone.

Combat Crop Dusters

I remember being a little startled to see a pair of converted Navy torpedo bombers flying back and forth across the island, spraying DDT to keep the fly population in check. (This began on D+9, 28 February, I've since learned.) They looked like crop dusters, spraying fog from nozzles on each wing and leaving a big swirling cloud behind. It was really amazing, considering how low and slow they were flying, that the Japs didn't fire at them. (What if our planes had been spraying some kind of poison gas?)

Fighting Dirty

In the lines any kind of personal cleanliness was out of the question. Besides the dirt and sand that you were covered with from shelling, there were other even more nauseating things.

There was no man on the lines whose clothes weren't covered with dried blood from helping a wounded man at some time or other. You were also liberally covered with little bits and pieces of human flesh that had been thrown up by the continual churning of the shelling.

A shower was almost impossible to come by. If you did get lucky enough to take one, there were no clean clothes for you to wear when you went back up on the lines. New socks were worth their weight in gold.

The REMFs, who had started coming ashore on the fourth day of the invasion, were as different from the people on the line as a man in a white Palm Beach Suit would be from a filthy chimney sweep. One of the most disheartening feelings I had was to return to the rear and see how well these people were living, just a mile from where others were dying.

And they never shared any of the good things they had with the people from the lines. People from the lines were treated like lepers in the rear areas. Thinking about that, I wonder if it had to do with the people back there being shamed by their good luck, and hoping that if we went away there wouldn't be any war for them.

Lots of times at night there would be more firing in the rear areas than up along the lines. Those people back there were firing at every shadow that moved.

The first shower I was able to get was on a trip I made back down to the landing beaches around the fifth or sixth day. I traded some souvenirs to some sailors on one of the LSTs nosed in there and got a hot fresh-water shower and a hot meal. (I don't remember exactly what I brought, but they were authentic Jap gear of some kind.) It was sure nice to feel like a human being again, at least for a few minutes. I even got some clean "swabbie" (sailor) underwear and socks, but I had to put most of the same dirty outer clothes back on.

My only other shower in those five weeks was in a big outdoor shower that the engineers had set up right down at the south end of Orange Beach. It was open-air, accommodating maybe 250 men at a time, but no clean clothes or free meals. You take whatever you can get. The water was hot from under ground, and had to be mixed with salt water from the ocean to cool it down. I should mention that even here the officers could not mix with the enlisted men. Right alongside the big open-air shower, a small area had been surrounded with a canvas wall to protect the privacy of these most exalted ones as they bathed.

Another memory: The last evening on board ship we were all made to shave. The idea was that if you received a face wound you wouldn't get both dirt and whiskers forced into it. The wound would be easier to clean up and it would be much easier to reconstruct your face if need be. Coming on the eve of an assault expected to achieve victory in three days, this was a thoughtful policy. But as the fighting stretched from days to weeks, our leaders seemed less concerned with their troops' face wounds. In all my time on that island I believe I got to shave twice. And that may have been two more shaves than others on the front lines got.

Oh, well—don't do as I do, do as I say.

Whenever we went back to the rear areas, the REMFs were all shaved and in clean dungarees like today was a liberty day.

What We Left Behind

Thinking about personal cleanliness makes me think of sayings like, "It will scare the shit out of you," or "You will be scared shitless," meaning that fear causes something like diarrhea. I am sure that's true in some situations. But up on the lines on Iwo, it was usually only in darkness that you could be vertical, even in a squatting position, for long enough to defecate. During daylight hours you would be sniper bait if you stayed in one place without cover for even a couple of minutes.

What you needed was a place where it was possible to squat. Down on the sandy southern end of the island a nearby shell hole often came in handy, because you could scoop out a little hole and then cover your excrement. This little bit of sanitation worked wonders in keeping the smell and the fly population under control. But at the north end, amongst the rocks, you had no way to dig a hole or cover your excrement when you finished. The spraying of the island with DDT helped control the fly population, but there was no escaping the stench.

Of course when you moved into positions previously occupied by other troops, friend or foe, every shell hole was already a latrine. At the north end, I don't think the Japs ever gave up any pile of rocks to us without first leaving a smelly pile there for some advancing Marine to have to lie in. Even where they were all in caves and pillboxes, during the night they would come out and use all the available shell holes and rock piles—as you'd find when you advanced into the Jap lines in the morning. Sometimes in combat it was necessary to leap before you looked, and this could make your clothing even filthier.

When I've read novels about Vietnam, even ones written by people who were actually in combat there, I have been puzzled about the number of references to people urinating or defecating in their pants when they were scared. I never saw or heard of a single instance of that on Iwo. (I'm not talking about people killed or seriously wounded, who naturally lose control of the muscles that control these bodily functions.) I'm not trying to say that it didn't happen, just that as far as I can remember the effect was the opposite: People were just too scared to empty their bowels. I know I was—in fact it was well after dark the first day before I ever even felt I had to pee.

It was easy enough, once you got the hang of it, to take a leak day or night while lying on your side in a shell hole, but anybody who felt that they had to do more than that waited until after dark, and that was more like once every week or ten days than every night. When you needed to, if possible you scrounged an empty grenade or ammo box. Otherwise you used the steel outer shell of your helmet and tried to wipe it clean with some sand. For wiping yourself you used part of your skivvie (underwear) shirt, if you had any left.

Up at the north end there were not even any shell holes because it was so rocky. This made after-dark defecation an absolute necessity—otherwise a sniper was likely to get you before you even got your pants down.

The catchword as you moved out from a group, instead of, "We'll see you," or "Take it easy," was "Keep a tight asshole."

Brushing Every Day

Another thought about cleanliness: You never realize how much sand, dust and dirt is being thrown up in the air until you look down at your weapon. Having been trained from boot camp on to always keep your weapon clean and in good firing order, when you were in combat it got so dirty at times that you wondered how the damn thing kept working.

Even without all that "extra" dirt, after you had fired the M-1 rifle for a while you had to field-strip it and clean built-up carbon off the gas operating rod. While the rifle was apart you wiped everything clean with a piece of that old standby, your skivvie shirt. Then you lightly oiled the operating mechanism guts and reassembled the weapon.

Once ashore on Iwo, you were between a rock and a hard spot. You needed the breech mechanism well oiled, so that it would operate smoothly, but the oil attracted every bit of dust and dirt to it like a magnet.

Probably the most valuable thing that you carried with you was your toothbrush—not for your teeth but (whenever you got a break) for getting sand and other stuff off the bolt and chambering mechanism of your rifle. Sand on bullets being injected into the breech could keep the bolt from seating and locking the breech, and then the rifle wouldn't fire. You hoped that pulling back on the cocking lever would extract the bullet with the offending sand on it, and that when you released the lever the bolt would seat a new, clean bullet in the breech and the rifle could be fired.

Drilled into the stock of the rifle and protected by a hinged cover on the butt-plate was a compartment for carrying some cleaning gear: a small can of oil, a couple of cloth patches, and a piece of string to pull the patches through the barrel with. Cleaning the barrel with a string and a patch worked out fine at camp, but it had to be done sitting or standing up, which wasn't a good idea in combat. You could clean all of your rifle except the bore sitting up in a deep shell hole or even lying on your back; the bore you kept clean with bullets.

Nothing But the Best for Our Boys

Lots of the equipment that you see in the movies about World War II, particularly movies about the Army in Europe, was unheard of in the Pacific. For example, Army units as small as squads used "handy-talkies" to communicate. We Marines were lucky if we had radio contact from the company level back to the battalion level. The radios we had used in landings earlier in the war tended to become useless quickly because of salt water penetration. Also, all radios back then used filament tubes (rather than transistors) and could be damaged by the slightest jarring. On Iwo Jima we used radios only for communication between units that were ashore and the command units still on the ships. On shore, the Marines relied on runners for daytime communication between units up to battalion size. This system was reliable and provided confirmation to senders that their messages had been received. At night, most communication was by field telephone. Just before dusk, wiremen would arrive at each platoon's position, carrying a spool of wire that they would string from a hand crank phone there to the battalion switchboard.

Now if you were in MacArthur's Army I would imagine that you had lots of those neat things seen in movies, because "Dugout Doug" made sure that "his people" got all of these things in quantity, even to train with.

Even their Sherman tanks were a later model than ours. They probably had at least ten different versions of the Sherman by the time they invaded France in mid-1944. For the invasion of Iwo the next year, the only factory-made Sherman that the Marines had gotten was a "tank dozer"—anything else we had to cobble together in our field shops.

We did manage to acquire lots of the Army's good stuff through "midnight requisition," and we made it part of our extra gear as fast as we could find Army units that had it. This was true of weapons in particular. The Army had lots of fancy new weapons, even shotguns.

On a more official level, if by chance some Army gadget was replaced by a newer version, the older model might be given to the Marines. For example, we did get to use some up-to-date amtracs for this invasion. The old "Alligator" model that had been used to deliver troops and supplies at Tarawa and other previous invasions was made out of boilerplate and built like a bathtub. The sides were about five feet high, and anything inside had to be manhandled up and over the side to get it out. There were still lots of them around, especially for training.

The new "Buffalo" model could carry not only personnel and supplies but also small equipment, like jeeps and their trailers. Better still, it had armor plating and a rear ramp that could be lowered for easy loading and unloading. It was sure nice to be able to load wounded in through a Buffalo's back ramp and not have to manhandle them up and over the high sides.

There was also a small amphibian called a "Weasel," not quite big enough to carry a jeep. They were propelled by tracks with cup-shaped grousers. I have a feeling that these were only "lent" to us by the Army, because they didn't appear until late in the fighting. Toward the end of the Iwo operation they were used extensively for removing wounded from up on the lines.

All amtracs, old and new, were referred to as "tractors" (or occasionally as "phibs").

Teamwork

A couple of thousand yards west of Iwo Jima was a small island, maybe two hundred yards in diameter, that we were told was used by the Japs as a prison. With field glasses, you could see stone buildings out there built like an old fort.

At one point during the campaign our forces discovered that Japs were swimming in from there at night and infiltrating the western beaches. It was decided to send some Marines across the water to clean the island out. Before they could do that, though, somebody needed to soften up the island by dropping a few artillery rounds on it.

All the Marine artillery and the Navy ships were busy that day, so an Army 90-mm antiaircraft battery down at the south end of the island volunteered to help. I doubt if they fired more than 300 shells, but they fired them all in about two or three minutes. The shells were proximity-fused (a new type at the time); they were set to burst at a certain altitude—about 100 feet off the ground, I would guess. From where my buddies and I were, it looked like that little island was just obliterated by the shelling.

That was one place I was sure glad I was not.

Inter-service cooperation did not always work so well in the Iwo Jima invasion. At the start of the three days of pre-invasion shelling by the U.S. Navy, the command center's card index file listed 700 targets. The first day's bombardment destroyed less than two dozen of those targets. After two more days of bombardment the warships had still not expended all of their pre-D-day ammunition, and they had not destroyed significantly more of the known targets.

Any additional naval gunfire would have been immensely helpful to the Marines and in all probability would have shortened the fighting ashore, but the U.S. Navy was in a hurry to move its ships someplace where they could try to get more newspaper coverage than General MacArthur was getting in the Philippines.

The upshot was that no other island in the Pacific had been assaulted with so many of its defenses left unscathed.

This preference of naval officers for insuring the safety of their own asses, instead of the safety of the troops they were supposed to be supporting, was a very common thing, very prevalent in all ranks from the admirals in charge of the landing operations to the lowest ensign.

From time immemorial the Navy has felt that they were far superior to the Marines. This thinking continued even during the war, with these people behaving as if the Marines, not the Japs, were the real enemy.

During the war I was too far down the chain of command to fully appreciate the extent of this callousness. I thought that it was just over-exuberance, or "friendly rivalry" that sometimes got out of hand. But in later years I've read a lot about the pettiness of these admirals and how it led to the needless sacrifice of several thousand Marines. I can now see that I was way wrong, that lots of these Navy officers really felt that they were "God"—and due to their training at Annapolis they felt that the Marines were not worth the time to worry about.

If these people had not been in direct command of Marine forces, then I guess "inter-service rivalry" might have been an adequate description of their attitude. But by accepting direct command, they made promises to our country—promises that their actions indicated an unwillingness to fulfill. These officers told anybody they dealt with what that party wanted to hear, without any intention of ever doing what they said they would do. They were without honor, just cheap liars. It has sometimes seemed to me that by associating with these Annapolis types—supposedly America's best people—some of our Marine officers were led into their own dereliction of duty.

For God and Country

I would say that the old saw about there being no atheists in foxholes is pretty true. But even a young man whose belief in God is partly stimulated by fear can have a lot of sincere questions about religion that need to be explained.

While most Marines were southern boys, and belonged to the Baptists or some other fundamentalist denomination, the Corps also included lots of Catholics from the big cities up north. Interestingly, at the front you never saw ministers or pastors from Protestant churches. What you did see up there were many young Catholic priests, sent to give dying Catholic boys the Last Rites and absolution their faith told them they needed in order to go to heaven.

Going beyond ritual, these "salesmen" of the Catholic religion found many eager converts among battle-weary people lacking in confidence.

Here was a young man, not too different from yourself, who would sit in your foxhole with you and talk about anything you wanted to—home, school, football, politics, even your girl troubles. He'd eat the same food you did, or go without. He'd smoke, drink (if we could find any to steal), and swear as much as you did. He was a true friend in a time of need, a calming tie with a peaceful life in a world that we hoped to return to.

Many of us in that situation faced great temptations and confusing questions. How is it that these young men have enough faith in their religion to come to the front like us—but unarmed? Why is my minister not enough of a believer in his faith even to come near the front and offer me comfort and consolation occasionally?

More on Teamwork

About the time Iwo was declared secure, in mid-March, the Navy carriers we had been relying on for close air support were transferred to take part in the upcoming landing on Okinawa. Replacing them was a unit from the Army Air Force.

The Marine and Navy pilots from the carriers had been terrific. They flew practically down on the ground, strafing and bombing just a little ways ahead of us. We marked our lines with canvas panels, yellow on one side and fluorescent red on the other, so they (and also the little artillery spotter planes, which came in later in the operation) would know where they could fire without hitting us.

The first time we called for air support from the Army, we needed them to attack all along a ridge about 150 yards ahead of us, using napalm, rockets, or machine-gun fire.

Well, they sent us maybe a dozen planes, so high in the air that it was hard to tell what kind they were. I don't know if they could even see our front-line marker panels so far below them. From this great height they started dropping high-explosive bombs, which hit wildly, all over the place. Trying to escape them, we had to get up and run back towards where we had just come from. (Later I heard from people down from us that there were as many Japs as Marines up running, trying to get out of the way.)

So we lost ground because of Army Air Force "help." We never asked them for air support again. I imagine that was how they wanted it.

It always amazed me how little real help we got from other

branches of the service. In my view this was again the result of the pettiness of the officers in those branches. They were always complaining that the Marines were getting too many medals. Maybe we got more medals because more of us were getting killed.

The Chain of Command

At the front, nobody told another explicitly how something should be done.

By the time I got up to the lines, there were only two kinds of people up there—either you led or you followed. There were very few sergeants and corporals left, and even fewer officers. Some of the rated NCOs who were left were no longer capable of giving orders. But these people would follow a private who had the initiative to give orders and lead. Usually privates don't take "orders" from PFCs, but as far as I ever saw, those who chose to follow would without hesitation do as told by the ones who had chosen to lead.

In the case of my demolition squad, an order would come down telling us what the present objective was. We would talk it over and decide how to try to take it. Each man had a job to do to make the squad work, and each man did his assigned job without question.

If a special job (i.e., an especially difficult or dangerous one) had to be done, it was usually taken by volunteers—it's your life, you do it your way.

But if one man tried to move forward, anybody within a hundred yards of him would also move forward if possible, or provide cover fire to protect him. Each man was still responsible for the men around him.

That may sound like a contradiction of what I just said, but you will see that it isn't. We were all after the same thing—to get the job done as soon as possible and get out of there.

Chapter 14

POSSUM PATROLS
AND
THE "RIGHT KIND OF WAR"

One of the most discussed topics on the boat as we approached Iwo Jima had been the taking of prisoners.

Not one of the old-timers on board, the ones who had been in combat, had ever seen a Jap surrender. They swore that the Japs didn't believe in giving up, and that even when half dead, they would still be looking for a chance to take a Marine with them.

Practically every report we received confirmed the convictions of the old-timers. We had heard, for example, that of the 4,836 Japs on Tarawa, only 17 had surrendered. (Everybody was sure those seventeen were either Korean or Malayan slave laborers, like some who had surrendered on Guadalcanal earlier that year, or Japanese troops immobilized by severe wounds.) Japs in other places, such as New Britain, were suffering nearly as badly from starvation and disease as they were from Marine bullets, but they didn't surrender. Likewise, in the Marshalls and on Kwajalein and Eniwetok, they fought to the last man. In each battle, when the end approached, disillusioned and disgraced Jap generals and admirals committed "hari-kari." The last holdouts in the lower ranks shot off their heads with their own rifles or blew themselves apart with grenades, true to their Bushido tradition.

Given Jap practices like these, the old-timers said, it wasn't smart to try to talk any of them into giving up—or even to try to help their wounded by offering water or first aid. All any Marine with such humanitarian instincts was going to get for his trouble was a bayonet in his guts or a grenade blowing his balls off. If a Jap seemed to want to surrender, it had to be a trick—he was only playing possum, trying to get you close enough so he could kill you. The advice of the old-timers, which we followed whenever we overran a Jap position or otherwise encountered Jap bodies, was to send out a few guys on "possum patrol." They'd put an extra bullet or two into each of the sons-of-bitches to finish them off. This took some getting used to, but it was cheap insurance—a bullet only costs a dime—and you had to make sure before you checked the bodies for papers and maps that could help get this battle over with. Making sure that every apparent Jap corpse was really dead was not something that could be left till later; it was imperative that it be done right away.

The old-timers were positive that we would never have to worry that we might mistreat a Jap soldier who actually wanted to surrender. One of the old-timers, a corporal who had served with the old Fourth Raider Battalion, underlined this for us with a story about a night when his unit had been dug in a short distance inland on Vanguna in the Solomons.

Three Jap landing barges circled around and tried to land troops on the beach behind them during the darkness. The Raiders just turned around and fired at them as they tried to leave the barges. The result, said the corporal, was a slaughter. Only twenty or so Japs even made it off the barges onto the beach. All of them were dead the next morning except one badly wounded man who, true to form, was waiting for a Marine to come near enough to blow up. Someone shot him before he had a chance to arm his grenade. As for those Japs who didn't make it off the barges, about fifteen of them lay amid the carnage, all badly wounded and near death, but still conscious and waiting patiently with grenades and bayonets for a chance to get one last thrust in for the Emperor. The possum patrol eliminated these possums without hesitation or remorse.

The 23,000 Japs who were on Iwo at the time of the Marine landing proved to be as stubborn as those encountered in earlier Pacific campaigns. Years later I read that only 120 of them had surrendered to the Marines—less than one percent. I strongly doubt if that included any real Jap soldiers or Landing Forces personnel. The Army took over control of the island from us in late March, and I later read that in the first couple of months of their occupation 1,200 Japs had surrendered to them.

Among my souvenirs is a shrapnel-damaged 8½ by 11 sheet of paper with Japanese writing on one side and the following English message on the other side (printed over red, white, and blue diagonal stripes: "The bearer has ceased resistance. Treat him in accordance with international law. Take him to the nearest Commanding Officer. (Signed) C in C Allied Forces."

This paper is something I picked up out of some pillbox or bunker we had just blown up. It looks like it was fired in an artillery shell or dropped in a bomb from an Army plane. I didn't know we had used "surrender messages" like this in the Pacific Theater. I am sure that the Marines never distributed them, and I never heard of any Jap ever using one—well, not to surrender with, at least.

Most Jap soldiers and Marines, the old-timers told us, wore a cloth strip called a "belt of a thousand stitches" tied around their waist, next to the skin. This was a good-luck talisman made for each of them by his mother. She had traveled through the family's home town or province, getting one neighbor after another to sew one stitch onto the cloth until she had collected a thousand of them, each meant as a blessing or wish for the wearer's safe return. The Jap fighting men believed that wrapping this belt around the waist would divert enemy bullets away from their vital parts.

I saw quite a few of these belts, none fit to save as a souvenir, but amongst my war "stuff" is another kind of good-luck talisman. It's a leather pouch, about two inches long by an inch and a half wide and half an inch thick, worn on a leather thong around the neck. The pouch contains a little packet of soil from the soldier's home, along with several pieces of rice paper with writing on them that I'm told are prayers from the soldier's family.

Another souvenir-type item we often saw told more about Japanese attitudes toward surrender and death. This was a white headband, with Japanese writing on it, that all the Satchel Charlies wore. I found out later that these headbands were part of the Bushido code. The writing was a short, cryptic poem, a message to the wearer's gods that he was ready to die an honorable death—something like it would be for us to write a poem to St Peter. I also understand that the headband was supposed to be a protection against enemy bullets until the mission was completed.

Besides this inspiring way to announce your impending death, the code of Bushido also prescribed several rituals for taking your own life "honorably" rather than letting yourself be captured. The most honorable of these was what we called "hari-kari." That's where you disembowel yourself with a dagger. It was acceptable to have another man release you from pain by cutting your head off with a sword just after you had disemboweled yourself. For enlisted men it was acceptable to kill yourself with your own rifle or pistol. And if you didn't have the fortitude to do either of these, it was still considered honorable to step brazenly into the open, unarmed, and let the Marines shoot you.

So much for the value of life to the Jap soldier.

This kind of behavior was hard for us to understand. No Marine threw away his life. If you had to die, you wanted it to be for something. No matter how depressing the position you were in, you always had visions of coming out alive and returning to civilian life. The Jap soldiers were slaughtered unnecessarily because they so gladly threw away their lives, placing no value on their person. Recognizing this attitude may help us begin to comprehend what strikes us as their cruel and bizarre behavior on the battlefield.

I have seen it said that the American fighting man loathed his

Japanese adversaries because of their apparent fanaticism and indifference to death. I don't disagree with that observation, but it doesn't really tell the whole story. The Japanese seemed to get a grotesque pleasure from self-destruction, from planned death, whether by their own hand or by the hand of others. It was hard for us to get used to the idea that these people would so easily sacrifice their lives, seemingly for no real purpose. For somebody to sacrifice his life to kill another person, no matter how non-threatening that person's existence might be to him, was a puzzle to us every time we saw it happen. Why would you try to kill a Corpsman who was coming to your aid, for example? Or, pretend to surrender but then detonate a concealed grenade to kill both yourself and the people taking you prisoner? I guess you could expect a few true fanatics to go off the deep end in any war, but the wholesale Japanese dependence on this type of fighting was unfathomable. Other examples included "Satchel Charlie" sapper operations, missions by kamikaze pilots and the pilots of "baka" bombs, and "Banzai" charges by ground troops.

The banzai charge, in which an entire unit threw itself against our lines, usually at night, was one of the best known Japanese tactics on all the islands the Marines had fought on up to now. Once one of these charges was launched, there was no retreat—wave after wave of Japs kept coming either until they broke through or until every last man was killed by the Marines, sometimes well inside the Marine lines. At this rate several hundred Japs could be killed every night, resulting before long in their having no troops left to fight.

On our first night on Iwo, there was a small banzai charge against the 27th Marines up ahead of us, ("small" to everyone but the people who had to fight it). After that the Jap commanding general on the island forbade any more such attacks. Instead, each man was to make his death a victory for the Emperor by taking at least one Marine with him. The enemy continued that strategy for the rest of the battle. We eventually won, but it cost us more than repelling banzai attacks would have. (A few hours after I was taken off the island in mid-March there was a night attack against U.S. Army defensive lines around the airfield. Some people consider this a banzai charge; others, including me, don't think it was intensive enough to qualify.)

Instead of banzai charges each night, the Japs used what today would be called psychological warfare tactics against us. Many of them could speak pretty good English, and among other things they would hurl insults at us, hoping to get some Marine mad enough to fire his rifle. That could give away the location of his foxhole and allow Japs to kill him and infiltrate our lines.

That particular tactic failed, because the Marines didn't get over-wrought about the taunts. The Japs couldn't make us lose our temper by insulting President Roosevelt or his wife, for example, because we agreed with what they yelled; but we could get under their skin by yelling back "Tojo eats shit," or some such good thought. (With several Marines yelling back, it was harder for the Japs to locate and attack any one foxhole.)

A despicable, but more effective, Jap trick was to act like a wound-ed Marine pleading for help in the dark. This was a real hard one to ignore, and caused much trouble in our units. No man wants to be alone on the battlefield, especially when hurt. It has always been a given in the Corps that Marines will go to great lengths to rescue any man who is wounded, not just their friends; and a lot of Marines have been killed trying to live up to this unwritten oath. So these cries for help in the darkness were heart-wrenching to have to ignore. Al-though ninety-nine cases out of a hundred had turned out to be tricks, aimed at luring some Marine out of his foxhole and out in front of the lines, everybody always agonized over the thought that this time it might really be a Marine needing help.

On the lines there were continual demonstrations of the barbarity of even the individual Jap soldier. In addition to deception (the "wounded Marine" trick and fake surrenders), they tortured Marines who fell into their hands, and mutilated the bodies of our dead. They would deliberately wound one Marine—rather than killing him outright—in order to enable snipers to shoot others who tried to rescue him. They indiscriminately killed our stretcher bearers and Corpsmen, even when they were administering aid to wounded Japs. (For my money, the Corpsmen can never be thanked enough for their dedication to helping all wounded men.)

Not only were the Japs ready and eager to die for the Emperor, they also felt that being taken prisoner was the most degrading thing that could happen to them. To a Jap, anyone who surrendered was unworthy of being called a man, and this attitude was very evident in the ruthless way they worked captured soldiers and civilians to death—American and British troops especially—in the Philippines, the Dutch East Indies, Singapore, and Burma.

For all these reasons, the Marines took virtually no prisoners on Iwo. But there was another factor at work as well.

It may be hard to believe, but for probably the first twenty days I never saw more than a fleeting glimpse of a live Jap. We got shot at plenty as we tried to move forward, but much of what hit us was an impersonal hail of mortar and artillery shells. True, we also took deadly small-arms fire, and we shot back, but we never really had anybody to aim at in the darkness of the pillboxes and caves. We were only shooting at the muzzle flashes of an unseen enemy.

This situation didn't change much, but on occasion I did see running Japs, generally ones flushed out of pillboxes and bunkers by high explosives. When a live Jap appeared like this, the frustration of the people on the lines would boil over. They'd stand up, holler and shout like kids at a football game, with everybody firing at him as if he was a duck in the shooting gallery at a county fair. The hollering and cheering as he was hit and went down made the episode an exhilarating relief from our otherwise serious existence—a chance to pay the Japs back in some small way for our misery and the deaths of our friends.

But mostly the enemy was invisible. You knew he was there, because somebody was shooting at you, but you couldn't see him back in the darkness of the caves or through the small slits of the pillboxes or bunkers. It was sure not like in the movies.

Probably the most disheartening sight to us during the all the time we were on the island was the visible number of dead Marines, and the absence of any dead Japs. Those six dead Japs I saw by the pillbox on the first afternoon were an exception. Other than that I would say that until much later in the fighting you would be "lucky" on most days to see one or two dead Japs. If and when they were killed, they were in places like caves, pillboxes, and spider holes. You fired at muzzle flashes, but you very seldom saw the dead Jap. They were either buried in the caves, or burned beyond recognition in the pillboxes by the flamethrowers. An occasional man fleeing, or a Satchel Charlie, were about all we ever saw.

We, on the other hand, were out in the open, so when a man was killed, his body stayed in view. If possible, the body was quickly moved to a collection point, but for the first few days there were no collection points, so the bodies were just covered with ponchos and put together in rows. These little groups of poncho-covered bodies visible all over the place created the immediate impression that we were taking terrible losses and not hurting the Japs at all. We didn't begin to realize till much later that the Japs' losses were even greater than ours.

Our unexpectedly peaceful occupation of Japan after the war, and the generally friendly relations between the two countries in the decades that have followed, have made it hard for many people to remember or imagine how savagely we and the Japs fought against each other. It's easy to make fun of the bloodthirstiness of the REMFs, but in the heat of battle, the man up on the lines also felt a true and well founded hatred of the Japs. And in their belief that dying in combat for their Emperor would put them at the head of the line to get into heaven, there was nothing that Jap soldiers wouldn't do to kill Marines.

This was an entirely different kind of war from that fought in Europe, where the rules of the Geneva Convention were adhered to. What we fought in the Pacific was a simple war in which the Geneva Convention would have been a distraction, like pity. It was a war that did not require hatred, although hatred was neither forbidden nor condemned. In fact the whole psychology of the Pacific war allowed one to be perfectly objective while shooting down Japanese soldiers in a banzai charge or pouring high-octane gasoline into Jap tunnels and tossing in a lighted match.

Most of us Marines, most of the time, neither liked nor hated the Japanese. We killed them without anger or mercy, because it was our job. In this we were different from most Americans back home, who saw the Japs as yellow devils, slant-eyed and alien, forces of evil that had to be destroyed. Back home, they thought of the Pacific war as "dirty." They felt that the Americans fighting it were to be pitied and appreciated, even admired, more than those battling the Germans and Italians—who, except for Hitler and Mussolini and a few of their vicious followers, looked and acted and sounded like our neighbors next door or across the street.

In reality, the Japs were no worse than evil forces elsewhere, whether in Germany or Russia or at home, and the war we fought in the Pacific reflected that fact.

In Europe it was different. A German machine gunner kills ten of our men and then when things get too hot for him, he hangs up a white flag and comes out with his hands up. Even though the S.O.B. is a member of the Nazi party and has killed your brother and your best friend, you're supposed to pat him on the head, hand him a ration of Texas steak and give him a free ride to a stockade way back out of range of his own artillery. Next thing you know he's in a Prisoner Of War camp in Louisiana cutting cane, or in Illinois picking sweet corn. When the war's over, he'll apply for American citizenship, grab one of our girls, have a family, and then sit back, relax and enjoy the beer. All the time your friends are six feet under and missing all the fun.

Out in the Pacific, there was no favoritism. Everyone got what was coming to him. When the Marines hit the beach, that Jap machine gunner knows he's dead. He might last thirty days and kill twenty Marines, but when we land on his island he knows he's a dead man. We're going to get him sooner or later, and it ain't no use for him to come out with his hands up either. If he does, he gets five slugs in the guts; if he holds out, he gets fried with a flamethrower. There aren't any Japs cutting cane in Cajun country.

Most Americans found the Japanese way of war fantastically different and quite foreign at first, yet those of us who fought in the Pacific for any length of time quickly came to respect it. It was a war waged without mercy; a war in which those who surrendered were executed by their captors as spineless cowards and traitors to their own cause; a war that increasingly dictated the use of dumdum bullets and flamethrowers, napalm bombs and possum patrols. It was a war without privilege or favoritism, a war in which admirals and generals were killed as quickly and as objectively as Marine privates or sailors of the meanest rank.

It wasn't a good war…but it was "the right kind of war."

Some Closing Thoughts

The old-timers, the combat veterans who introduced the rest of us to the Japanese concepts of war, were sure that the only way that we could ever win the war was to kill every last Jap. Luckily, that never came to pass. It is hard to imagine what it would have been like if we had actually had to make combat landings on the mainland of Japan, but I guess that when the chips are down, if a woman or child is trying to kill you, you wouldn't hesitate to kill them first.

Although to some it might not make much sense, there is a great difference between killing armed people and killing non-combatant civilians. I have always been extremely glad that there were no non-combatant women or children on Iwo. At least as far as we were concerned, anything that moved on the island was an enemy soldier. There was no need to worry at night that there might be infiltrating civilians, as there had been on Guam and Saipan. (I've heard reports that our troops found women's bodies in some of the destroyed bunkers on Iwo. If this was true, they must have been some of the Japanese military's so-called "joy girls" who had been trapped on the island by the Marine landing.)

To encounter injured women and children, as I did later in both Japan and China, is very disconcerting. (And my opinion of the present-day women who are arguing that they should be allowed in combat is that they are out of their minds. But if they are that eager to go get maimed and degraded, then the services should allow men to stay home and be warm, clean, safe and able to sleep at night.)

Chapter 15

"A Funny Thing Happened on My Way to the Office"

As I sit here decades later writing some of these things down, one thing makes me think of another and it goes on from there.

I can't tell the whole story—many things I experienced were too terrible to put into words. I have no way of even beginning to convey what you feel as you see another human being torn apart, mangled, or maimed; no way to put down on paper what uncontrollable fear feels like, the screaming terror that lasts till you can't scream any more. That kind of terror numbs the conscious part of your brain and makes you just a living body, like one of Pavlov's dogs, responding to events in ways you were conditioned to by your training.

One thing that could help you stay sane amid all this horror was a sense of humor. The humor on Iwo was grim at best, but it was there. I have tried to write down here some of the oddities and the "lighter side" of existence in combat.

A Night at the Movies

There was so much confusion during the landing operations that lots of useless junk got to the beach, while things there was a crying need for got held up on the transport ships that were providing logistical support to the invasion.

Some of the transports offloaded all of their goods by timetables that had been established several months before we landed. The ships' officers paid no attention to what was happening on the beaches; they just tried to unload as quickly as possible so that their ships could leave the combat area and lessen the risk of kamikaze attacks. This haste and inadaptability would not necessarily have caused great difficulties if so many of the landing craft that were needed to deliver goods from ships to shore hadn't been destroyed during the troop landings.

An example: the timetables (based on the prediction that the operation would be wrapped up easily and quickly) called for a load of recreational gear for the troops to be landed on D+2. The load came in on schedule, but had to be dumped in a pile on the beach and left to rot, because heavy fighting was still going on there and no USO people would be allowed on the island for another twenty days.

Some enterprising Marines are said to have dug a movie projector and a small screen out of the pile, lugged them up the hill to a plane revetment on the other side of the airfield runway from us, borrowed a portable generator, and watched a movie that third night. (Were they REMFs? Well, they weren't up on the front lines, but then there wasn't really a Rear area on the island yet.)

I can easily believe it—that is a typical Marine thing to do.

Good Mixers

Once you were off your landing craft you quickly learned to tell the differences between various kinds of rifle and machine-gun fire, and you developed an instinctive ability to tell whether a shot fired in your general direction was ours or theirs.

As we moved north, there were times when this ability could be misleading. We began encountering and killing Japs behind our own lines who wore Marine uniforms and carried Marine weapons. A sniper armed with one of our rifles could kill several people before we realized that the M-1 sounds we were hearing were incoming rather than outgoing. The farther north we went, the commoner this got to be. Some Japs in Marine uniforms were very brazen and walked around during daylight hours. One of them even reportedly got into line for one of the hot meals that were at last beginning to be delivered to some front-line unit once every day. The story had it that he was the only guy in the line who wasn't questioning the ancestry of the cooks or complaining about the poor quality of the food, the easy life of the mess attendants, and the privileges of officers. People somehow ruled out his being a combat fatigue case, which left only one possibility—he was a Jap, and they shot him on the spot.

Passwords, Swear Words, and Catch Phrases

Because of all these infiltrators, the password system that was not used much up on the lines was taken more seriously back in the rear. If you had to move from place to place during hours of darkness, you were supposed to be challenged by guards who would require you to identify yourself with a password.

Our system was simpler than the countersign system used by the Army, where the guard challenges by saying one word and the person challenged has to respond with a different word. Instead, each night we were given a different category of words for use as challenge responses. Typical categories included names of states, automobiles, girls, college football teams, and baseball teams or players. The category for our first night on the island, for example, was "automobiles." When the guard asked you for the password, you replied with any automobile brand name containing the letter "L"—which was supposed to be hard for the Japs to pronounce. (I guess the idea was that anybody who answered "Lincoln" would pass and anybody who said "Rincoln" would be shot, but I have my doubts about how much security this would provide. Some of the Japs who yelled obscenities at the Marines at night, or insults about President Roosevelt, could speak English better than most of the Marines from Georgia and Alabama).

Even if you forgot what the password category was for that night, any answer relating to any of the typical categories would do for a start, and you could eventually convince the guard that you were one of the good guys. Anyhow, just about any Marine who got confused or forgot the password would start swearing; and there never was any

Jap who could think of all of the swear words that Marines used, let alone try to pronounce them.

While we were overseas, Eleanor Roosevelt was reputed to have said that all Marine Corps combat veterans, as they were rotated from the Pacific Theater back to the States, should be put in a special camp that would teach them how to re-associate with their fellow Americans.

She was sure that this (i.e., teaching us to be human beings again) could only be done in easy stages. The joke going around about this retraining was that you would be taught etiquette. For instance, you would be taught not to go home and yell down the table to, "Pass the fucking butter." When you graduated and went home you would be polite at the dinner table, and when you wanted the butter it was to be, "Please, pass the fucking butter."

A cartoon synonymous with the American forces everywhere and in every theater—any branch but the Marines—was a little drawing of a head looking over a fence so that only the eyes showed, with a long nose and eight fingertips hung over the edge. This famous drawing and the statement that went with it ("Kilroy was Here") appeared all over the world during the war, always inscribed by whoever got somewhere first. The Navy's Underwater Demolition Teams, which went in clandestinely ahead of amphibious landings to clear obstacles, left lots of these little signs on the beaches for the first wave of troops landing the next morning.

The Kilroy boast was a universal sign that some American had been there already. There were other sayings and phrases that you ran into everywhere as well.

One was a taunt that was always thrown at people headed into a new situation by the "veterans" who were leaving that situation. Whether you were going into boot camp, entering training camps, boarding ship, or boarding landing craft for the run to the beach, the old-timers would tell you, in a singsong voice, "You'll be sorree"— and you know, they were always right.

A Marine Corps maxim was "Ten percent never get the word." This was always true in every situation.

Another saying very prevalent in the Corps was to describe any situation that had gone wrong as "like a Chinese fire drill." I never thought very much about this comparison—I just accepted it as a traditional Marine Corps expression and let it go at that. But just as the dead Jap I saw outside a blasted pillbox on Iwo showed me that "hope you die with a hard on" was a curse grounded in fact, I learned after the war that "Chinese fire drills" were truly the height of disorganization. I was on occupation duty in Tientsin, China, and one night there was a fire at our barracks (formerly a Japanese girls' school). The local fire department was notified; by the time their men and equipment arrived, the troops who were on barracks guard duty had set up a bucket brigade and the fire was almost out. Now the comedy started. It was a true comedy, like the "Keystone Kops," to watch these people run up and down the stairs, yelling and blowing police whistles, bumping into each other, hooking up hoses that didn't have any water—large numbers of people who really had nothing to do but run around and look busy.

Having found out all these things, I'm just as glad not to have learned the truth of any other old sayings.

The Heat of Battle

There were parts of the island where the ground was so hot that it was easy to heat any canned rations we could find.

Some people got caught in shell holes in these areas. Pinned down by enemy fire and unable to move around much, they could suffer burns from being slowly cooked. In the worst cases, men got caught at dusk and had to stay put all night. By sitting on their haunches as much as possible they could avoid overheating their bodies, but by the next morning they were so badly burned on the bottoms of their feet that they had to be carried out on stretchers to the hospital ships.

The Rockets' Red Glare

I'm not sure what day this happened, but one evening the area behind us lit up like a Fourth of July fireworks display. All kinds of colored flares were fired into the air and there was wild firing of weapons, soon picked up by all the ships around the island.

We up on the lines we were bewildered. What was going on? Were they under some kind of attack back there?

After about fifteen minutes the noise and flares slowly stopped, and eventually we found out that some bored REMF radio operator had sent a message out over the air waves that the war in Europe was over. (That day was actually still some two months away.)

The Japs had a big rocket launcher that they fired toward the south end of the island from up on the north end.

When it was fired at night each rocket arrived with a long reddish-orange fire tail and was known amongst the Marines as "The Orange Blossom Special." (I told you all of these people were from the southern part of the east coast of the United States—that was the name of a fast east coast train, not unlike the famous "Wabash Cannonball.")

It took the Jap gunners a while to get their aiming down so that the rocket would hit on the island. While they were learning to control it they sure scared the hell out of all the ships around the island, but they never hit one.

They finally managed to hit around Suribachi quite a few times, but I never heard that they really hit anything valuable. The noise as it passed overhead was sure scary, but the long fiery tail was a sight to behold. In fact, it was downright pretty.

One of the Marine units my squad supported (probably a heavy-weapons platoon, but I don't know from which battalion) had small trucks with racks mounted in the back that held about fifty 4.5-inch rockets. When our infantry was about to launch an attack, these trucks would help them by moving up just behind our lines and blanketing the Jap positions with their rockets.

The Japs hated these trucks and would heavily mortar suspected launch areas as soon as the rockets were fired. One day I was taking my squad up to go with the infantry into an area that had just been rocketed. As I passed one of the launcher trucks behind the lines I stopped short—the driver was somebody I knew from training in Arizona, the only fellow I ever saw from school after I left boot camp in San Diego. We embraced like long-lost relatives, but not for very long, because the Jap mortar shells started to fall. We ran in different directions, and I never saw or heard of him again.

Babysitting

It is a statistically-established fact that for every man who fought in the Marine Corps during World War II there were nineteen men out of danger, backing him up.

The longer the fighting went on at the north end of the island, the more non-combatants crowded into the secured south end. Whether from boredom or from the desire to send home a "see—I was really there" item, many of them found their way into the area just behind the lines, where they were continually in the way.

This area was quite deceptive to the uninitiated non-combatants. They had a lackadaisical attitude toward cover that invited sniper fire and led to considerable unnecessary casualties. Many of these souvenir-hunters didn't even bring a weapon with them, and those who did bring one usually didn't have any ammunition for it.

The upshot was that souvenir-hunters got wounded and front-line troops had to drop back and rescue them, unnecessarily exposing themselves to sniper fire. Quite a few of these REMFs even managed to get out beyond our forward positions (there wasn't any boundary line painted on the ground) and our already harassed infantrymen had to extract them from the predicaments their unthinking souvenir quest had gotten them into. To advance into Jap territory for a military objective is risky but often unavoidable; to do it to save these dumb guys was to face unnecessary hazards.

But there was never a word of thanks, an offer of a clean jacket, or even a cup of hot coffee to show their appreciation for having their lives saved. I guess this service was something front line troops were expected to provide. (I don't remember that being taught in infantry school.)

I realize as I write this that for the first five days—probably for the first ten days—I was one of those REMFs. Although I may feel that this wasn't true for the couple of days at the very beginning, I'm sure the people up on the lines would have looked down their noses at my contribution.

The time from the tenth day to maybe the fifteenth day is hard to call. We engineers worked along our side of the front lines or were right behind the infantry, mopping up bypassed caves, tunnels, gun emplacements, and occasional pillboxes. There was plenty of sniping at us, and lots of shrapnel, but lots of times we were behind the lines, sometimes even a couple of hundred yards. Before long, though, that gap narrowed and we worked both sides of the front line. Whatever needed to be done, we did. So for at least the last twenty days of the campaign I can justifiably look down on the REMFs and consider myself an infantryman.

Cat and Mouse

We were up with some infantry one day, all trying to cross a fairly open space. We were faced by at least two snipers, possibly more.

There were plenty of big rocks to crouch behind in your dash. It could be made in about four short runs, from rock to rock.

When you have to move under sniper fire, the object is to keep moving. And if possible, doing something different each time you moved from cover.

We were always reminded that "doubt is more fatal than slowed reflexes." Here was a case where you didn't think, you did as you had trained to do in this situation. And again, "fear is the relinquishment of reason." Reason would tell you that what we had been taught was the best answer.

If you ducked out from behind a rock from the right one time, you might try the left the next time. Then maybe you'd pause before leaving the time after that, or sometimes not pause at all—anything to keep the sniper from getting a chance to draw a good bead on you. Several people moving at the same time can also throw the sniper's aim off.

This was a fairly routine situation, but out in the middle this time there was a new man caught behind a rock, who got scared when a bullet hit near him. He made several false starts, thinking each time that the snipers had him marked and would fire, then each time crouching back down behind the same rock. Instead of continuing to move, either sideways or even back, anything, he froze.

There is no way you can help somebody in that situation, except try to draw the sniper's attention away from the "sitting duck." We told our guy to stay put till some plan could be worked out, but after a few minutes, in sheer terror he finally made a break out into the open and was killed instantly by one shot.

Another afternoon worked out differently. My squad was out in front of our line, moving from right to left along it instead of straight forward from it as usual, because further forward there were a lot of gullies and ridges running parallel to the line. As we worked along—

scouting around, looking for caves to seal or bunkers to destroy—without realizing it we drifted further to the left than we had planned to.

We were taking turns moving from one rock outcrop to the next in an infantryman's crouch that was almost the same as walking upright, and dropping to one knee any time we stopped. We were not fired on at all during this time, and we never spotted anything unusual.

As evening approached, we decided to head back to the barn. We turned sharply left, dropped down off a little ridge, and walked casually and upright toward the rear, across a flat area about the size of a football field.

As we approached a gully on the south side of the field, we saw Marines hunched down in it, frantically yelling at us to get down under cover. We dropped down into the gully and they told us they had been pinned down there for several hours. The ridge over which we had just come was the Jap front lines, where all the fire against them was coming from.

To prove that they were pinned down, these Marines raised a helmet up on the end of a rifle. It was immediately fired at by at least one automatic weapon. They raised the decoy helmet several times in different places along the gully, and we got the same answer every time.

So we had walked over the tops of the Japs and then out across that clearing, with our backs to them, and they had never fired a shot at us; it was mind-numbing to be pinned down by them now, a few minutes later. We were not able to get out of that gully until after dark.

I saw things like this happen several times and they always puzzled me. One or two people would be up and moving in an area that was extremely dangerous, and inconceivably, not a single shot would be fired at them. Then someone else would try to move in the same area, and all hell would break loose. Since the war I've read several books that mention this phenomenon, so it wasn't just my imagination.

The explanation seems to be this: The men who didn't get shot at would typically be peons, doing some routine enlisted-man chore that didn't directly threaten the Japs and that was only dangerous because it had to be done out in the open, without cover or other protection. The Jap infantrymen watching them, so the theory goes, had been assigned similar mundane but dangerous work in the past. They would hold their fire until their American opposite numbers finished their task; then they'd resume normal sniping.

Living Off the Land

One day fairly late in the fighting, Frank and I went to a supply dump in the rear (way back, almost to the old landing beaches) to pick up more detonators for explosives. By that time, even though the north end of the island was still in the hands of the Japs, and the fighting up there was incessant, the south half of the island was full of rear-echelon troops whose only inconveniences were the noise and the dust. They weren't being shelled any more, and anyhow they all had nice deep dry holes to sleep in. They had showers and clean clothes, and above all they had food, good hot food.

At the front we had finally begun to get C-rations, small cans of food that came in maybe twenty different varieties and could be heated. At the front, they usually had to be eaten cold (sometimes, if you happened to be in one of the hot zones, it was possible to bury the cans in the sand and let the island's volcanic heat cook them).

We were also aware up there that the new Army "10-in-1" rations had arrived on the island (probably landed by some ship that wanted to avoid the possibility of kamikaze attacks). Some had made it as far as the area just behind the front, where they were available only for officers—captains or higher. But in the rear areas, we discovered, even lots of the enlisted men were eating them.

Our load of detonators and prime-a-cord from the supply dump was more than the two of us could easily carry, so we tried to thumb a ride back north along the main road. Not many REMF drivers wanted to pick up dirty, filthy Marines, especially when it was easy to see that we were carrying explosives, so we got a little more forceful. We stepped out in front of an Army DUKW (pronounced "duck," an amphibious utility truck moved by a propeller in the water and six big tires on land) and pointed our weapons at the driver.

Puzzled, he asked if something was wrong. No, we assured him, we just needed a ride. (We knew that the DUKWs were being used to transport supplies, and hoped this one might have pineapple juice or canned peaches on board.) We quickly loaded our boxes onto the vehicle and climbed aboard ourselves.

We told the driver that we needed help in getting the stuff we had up towards the front. He hesitated, as he shifted back into gear, but looking down the muzzles of two rifles, he said he would take us part way—as far as the food storage dump he was headed for.

While I talked to the driver, Frank checked under the tarp-covered load to see if there was anything good to eat that we could "requisition" without the driver noticing. He came and told me the whole load was 10-in-1 rations. This left us no choice: I leaned down and told the driver that my pal was having one of his shellshock "attacks" that made him dangerous and uncontrollable. He was delirious again and wanted to take this "tank" up through the front lines to kill Japs with.

I leaned in closer and told the driver that if he would take us up to our unit, I could get help to get Frank out of the vehicle and there wouldn't be any trouble. The driver was reluctant—he'd heard that it wasn't safe for moving vehicles up near the front. We politely told him he had no choice. Each of us told him that the other was unstable and dangerous, and that if necessary we would throw him out on the road and leave him. After some quick soul-searching, the driver agreed to drive us up as far towards the front as we could get.

We arrived at the unloading point up near the front, and had no trouble finding help to unload the DUKW. Within half an hour all the cases had been hidden in the area. We apologized to the driver for scaring him and turned him loose to return to the ship for another load of rations.

Neither I nor any of the units that got the rations ever got in trouble for this incident, or even heard of any complaint or investigation. It was just something that got lost in the war (and a few of those poor officers had to eat C-rations for a while).

I should explain that each 10-in-1 ration box contained three complete meals (breakfast, lunch, and supper) for ten men: cereal, coffee, hot chocolate, crackers and cheese, powdered milk, Kool-Aid, canned ham, chicken, and candy. The stuff tasted good, too. It was like a home-cooked meal. There was even toilet paper, in little waterproof packages, and a carton of cigarettes.

Nothing was too good for the "doggies."

My friend Kurt Holle had been a darkroom technician with the Photo Mapping Section before he went to the front with one of the mine removal squads. One day when he and I were back in the rear area, we visited that unit and were told that they were spending all their time taking pictures of officers for them to send to their hometown newspapers. We thought it was only right that we should have our pictures taken to send home to our parents and girls, so we did, and I still have copies. (Note: the photographic record of the fighting on Iwo is surprisingly sparse, considering how important and tough and long the Iwo campaign was, and how many resources were devoted to documenting it. The Navy had a forty-man motion picture team out in the Pacific and the Marines had fifty men out there from the Fleet Motion Picture Office. In later years I've learned some things that may help explain why. One is that of the sixteen Marine cameramen killed in combat during the war, six died on Iwo, as many as on Tarawa, Guam, and Saipan combined. Also, MacArthur was landing in the Philippines at about the same time, and took up all the news space.)

A Visitor

One day up on the front I was crouched in the protection of some rocks, resting, and was intently watching some other people in a firefight against a Jap-held cave near us. As I tried to decide what was the best way to get alongside the cave safely, two men suddenly slid into the shelter with me.

I immediately knew they were "new guys," because their dungarees were not all dirty or ripped. One was older, maybe even in his forties, so he had to be an officer. He looked around at what was going on in the area, then rolled on his side and took out a pack of cigarettes, which he offered to me and his runner before lighting one himself. When he rolled over I saw on the pocket of his uniform his stenciled rank and unit insignia: 9-111. He was a general from Division staff.

He spent some time with me, asking all kinds of questions about how the fighting was going. He was not after the "bullshit" kind of answers. He wanted to know just how it was with my squad, how tired we were, how hungry, were we getting explosives? What was happening amongst the men because of the shortage of officers? How long could we last without replacements? And so forth. I answered his questions as well as I could. (To his "shortage of officers" question I replied, after a pause, that it was really a big relief not to be ordered around by people who had little or no experience in the lines.) He thanked me and took off down the line to talk to somebody else.

Fire Drill

I heard after leaving Iwo about a marvel of engineering that we used against the Japs on the island.

A very effective alternative to high explosives for destroying pillboxes and caves was napalm, but getting it up to where it was needed was a challenge. The usual way was on the back of an infantryman, in two separate tanks with a combined weight of about eighty pounds. One tank held enough napalm to squirt flame for about seven seconds and the other had enough propellant to shoot that flame as far as 100 feet. Also available on Iwo were some flame tanks. They carried more fuel and propellant than one-man flamethrowers, extending the duration and range of the flame while offering some protection to the operators inside the tank.

Neither method was ideal, because of the large amounts of napalm required to close some of the caves. In an effort to do better, a 10,000-gallon fuel truck was modified to fire a napalm mix from two tanks using high-pressure pumps and 1½-inch fire hoses. The hoses and the nozzles were connected together so that one operator (who wore an asbestos fire suit obtained from one of the aircraft carrier crash crews) could open and close both nozzle valves simultaneously. After the truck had sprayed enough napalm into a target cave, a Marine near the cave would throw in a thermite grenade to ignite the mixture. Scratch one cave, and on to the next.

(Gosh! Those dumb infantrymen and line company engineers—we'll show them how it's done. We'd better give the officer who thought this up a Navy Cross just for being out of his dugout.)

A typical Jap-held cave was selected for a trial of the new concept. The first thing the project leaders discovered was that the fire hoses were not long enough to shoot flame all the way to the cave entrance from where the truck was initially going to park. The road would have to be extended to get the truck closer. So the leaders called for an armored dozer to clear a road up to the front door.

But the Japs in the cave didn't play fair—they shot at the dozer, and the leaders had to call in some infantry to help protect this valuable piece of machinery.

Also, because of the inhumanity of using napalm, the leaders decided that we should get somebody up here to ask the Japs inside to give up and come out before we set the place on fire. This message was shouted to the Japs by some captured Korean laborers who were brought back up to the front under guard; but for some reason the Japs, instead of giving up, shot back at the Marines and their prisoners. (We found out after the surrender of Japan that the Japs considered Koreans to be "sub-humans" who were definitely not trustworthy.) I understand that the REMF officers who had come up with this Bright Idea were very put out by the Japs' refusal to cooperate. (But no Japs on Iwo had surrendered willingly yet—why should we expect them to start now?)

Finally the dozer got the road cut in. The driver backed the tanker up to within range of the entrance and started the pumps. The hose operator fired a few test squirts, then a big squirt into the cave, after which he shut off the nozzles, and the thermite grenade was thrown in.

Nothing happened. The leaders decided that more napalm was needed, so the operator turned the nozzles on full for a bigger shot.

Just then, the Japs in the cave threw the burning thermite grenade back out. It rolled towards the hose operator's feet and exploded, igniting the mixture from the nozzles. The resulting fireball knocked the operator down and caused him to drop the hoses with the nozzles still open wide and under pressure. The hoses whipped around uncontrollably, covering everything and everybody in sight with flaming napalm. The tank truck was destroyed and several Marines were badly burned, some fatally.

In the confusion, the two Korean prisoners ran into the fire and pulled the hose operator out of the burning mess (he was pronounced dead on the scene), and a Marine saved the tanker driver from the vehicle. The Marine was later awarded a Silver Star; I don't know if the prisoners were ever even thanked.

So we went back to the old method: a couple of infantrymen, a flamethrower, and a couple of engineers to seal off the caves as we got the time. Pillboxes still had first priority.

Chapter 16

HEROES, WOUNDS, AND RIBBONS

Act Like a Man

There is a big difference between being afraid and being a coward.

Men who are afraid are tense, they're nervous, they sweat a lot when it's time to move up, and they can be almost paralyzed when the shells start falling. I haven't talked as much as I could about the noise, the dirt, the smoke, the whining shrapnel, and the absolute terror that you feel as you try to cross the beach or some other open area under intense fire.

We were definitely afraid at times like those, but the old-timers told us that we should never let it worry us—that only a moron wouldn't be afraid when he was in danger of losing his life. Everybody is afraid, they told us, but most people's fear was visible only in a negative way, by their silence. Being scared, they summed up, doesn't keep you from doing your job

I don't think that in combat you have any real control over what you do, or how you act. It seems at times almost as if you are watching yourself from outside, that you are not in your body. Your movements and actions are on "autopilot"; you've been trained to behave in a certain manner, and that training takes over. Probably more present in the back of your mind than your fear of personal injury is the thought that you do not want to let the others down in any way, least of all by being less of a man than they are. You don't ever want to feel that through some action of yours, or some failure to act, another man was wounded or killed. I think that would be too much to have to live with. But I'm sure there were others who had different motivations for being able to keep going.

No matter where you go in the Marine Corps, only time actually spent in combat makes you a "real" Marine. The more combat time you have, the more worthy you are in the eyes of the Corps, and the more willing people are to respect your judgment. I guess you could say that combat time confers status, which in many cases is worth more than stripes or even bars.

Before Iwo I accepted this attitude as part of life in the Corps, but didn't really understand it. Back from combat now, I realize that this attitude was fostered by the senior NCOs to take care of those who, like most of them, had served in combat and made the Marines what they were.

War Stories

Although those of us who were sent northward with the infantry as members of demolition squads never returned to our home battalion for duty, that doesn't mean that we never visited there. Anybody who was sent to the rear for supplies would try to stop by H&S Company to see if we had gotten any mail, and maybe to pick up some personal items for himself or other squad members before returning to the front. For us, though, the H&S people were definitely part of the rear echelon now. Even people we had been close friends with before we left the ships became strangers to us.

This alienation from our former buddies was not deliberate on our part. The only way I can think of to describe the changed relationship is to say that we were now senior-year college students, while they were still boys in high school. There was no longer a common bond.

Even when we and they got back together in Hawaii later, we hardly knew each other. In our conversations it seemed like we and they were not even talking about the same things. Our outlook and understanding of life were no longer the same as theirs. Their interests seemed so juvenile that they were boring to be around. What they wanted to hear from us was war stories like John Wayne movies, full of heroics and glory. To us their innocence was disturbing; we knew real combat wasn't like what they imagined, but we were unable to articulate for them the things we had witnessed, because of the horrors they recalled for us. The scenes were still vivid in our minds, but we had pulled into protective shells and become quiet. They felt we were just being aloof, and they gradually stopped asking us to drink or play cards with them. If they could have shunned us like plague victims they probably would have (I guess we were "infected" in a way); as it was, we were tolerated but ignored.

I understand now that the stories they wanted to hear were the only tie they had with the real war. Having been two or three miles behind the front lines was almost like having been back in Hawaii. They had lived in a relatively safe area with very few inconveniences, working regular hours every day and enjoying clean clothes, hot meals, showers, and the ability to get regular sleep; for them the war had been almost a lark. Now they wanted to hear stories of heroics and people who were winning medals, so that they could bring them home to dazzle their folks and in later years tell their children what they did in the big war. They also needed war stories to pass on as they drank beers at their local VFW. (At a VFW meeting, you could tell who had been in combat and who hadn't very easily by what they talked about. Combat people, of any branch, only talked combat to others who had been there.)

The rear-echelon guys wanted us to entertain them with exciting tales of life on the front lines; what we wanted was a chance to forget war and think of pleasant things—like home and GIRLS. But even if we did try to explain to them something memorable done by one of our own engineers, it meant nothing to them because they had no gauge or guide to apply it to. Without knowing how impossible it was even to move from point A to point B at the front, there was no way for them to understand what tremendous feats some of our "little" stories were describing. We were unable to impress on them the fact that in combat, doing ordinary or normal things was in itself heroic. They were uncomprehending. Our descriptions meant nothing to them. We were talking about two different things. It was like we were talking two different languages.

Maybe this failure to communicate was because in combat, unlike in the movies, there is no music soundtrack, no dimmed lights, no cuts from the opening shots to the moment when the hero prevails over all. Real combat is a dull thing to talk about. It sometimes took hours to move just a few yards. Our former buddies had no more idea of what combat was like than most of you, reading these words now.

The best that I can do to explain it to you is to say that every man on the front lines is a hero. If one of them is lucky, an officer will see him perform a dangerous thing and he'll get a medal.

The medals do not always reward those who should really receive them. They do pump up the spirits of the troops behind the lines, though. For them, medals are the only criterion for being a real man. The man on the line who receives a medal is likely to be bewildered. Chances are that his act of "heroism" was a common occurrence. He doesn't feel he did anything that every other man hadn't done a hundred times, and whatever he did hadn't been to win a medal, anyway—he probably did it to save the life of another Marine.

Up on the line, life and dignity survive because of caring. The best explanation I can think of is the Golden Rule: "Do unto others as you would have them do unto you." You have to help each other if anyone is to survive. It's as simple as that. Nobody took blind chances; everything that was done was a calculated risk. Sometimes the cards didn't turn up right, and you paid with your life, but you always tried. A man pinned down or in trouble could always count on help. A wounded man knew that he would be gotten back to medical aid by somebody, as quickly as possible.

And the Marines never left their dead.

Officers and Gentlemen

I am sure you will be able to tell from my stories that in the eyes of some of my officers, I was not a "good" Marine. I always had a loathing for people who issued chickenshit orders, just to prove that they had the power to make you obey them. Having experienced the leadership of good officers earlier in my brief military career, I have always felt that I had something to base my judgment on. I was one of about a hundred members of my boot camp graduating class who volunteered for training in the Marine Raiders. My rifle range score qualified me only as a Marksman (the lowest passing grade), but I had still graduated as a PFC for other reasons, and the Raiders accepted me (probably because they were short of people).

At that time, the Raiders were the elite of the Fleet Marine Force. They were being modeled after the British Commandos, the most highly trained assault fighting force in the free world.

This Raider training was cut short, very short. Within a couple of weeks or so after we arrived at Tent Camp 3 in California, the Raiders were disbanded by order of the Joint Chiefs of Staff in Washington DC. (The word we got was that the Army wanted to be in charge of all elite fighting units, and their political influence greatly outweighed that of the Marines.)

Even this short stint with the Raiders dramatically changed my preconceived view of how officers should act. In the Raiders, about the only difference between officers, NCOs, and enlisted men was that officers were better at everything, so they got paid more. Everybody worked, ate, and slept in the same place—there was no special area or quarters for Officers and NCOs. Company officers were referred to by their surnames and never addressed as "sir." But by the same token, if you were given an order by someone who was willing to lead, you did what they told you. There was time during the post-training critique that was held late every night to talk about who had the right to boss you.

The people who were dug in so deep and safely in the rear areas on Iwo were completely different. They would not have known what leadership was if it stepped up and bit them on the parade ground. They may have been good pencil pushers or paperclip counters—they may have truly believed that counting those paperclips, in their shellproof dugouts, was the way to win the war—but they had no leadership qualities at all. Still, they were "officers and gentlemen by an act of Congress," and had to be treated as such.

On the assumption that the officers of my unit were representative of the officers I was likely to encounter in peacetime, I decided that I could never last very long in the Corps after the war. I just didn't have the temperament to be a good stateside or rear-echelon Marine.

Being detached from the Engineer Battalion and sent to the front relieved me of the rear-echelon idiocy. Amongst Marines, real Marines, I enjoyed a freedom that was refreshing. I was not harassed with petty nonsense, just told to get my job done to the best of my ability. And I believe that whatever I had to do, I did without shirking. I never had to be ashamed to face another man for letting him down. I believe that I upheld the "best" traditions of the Marine Corps.

Bad as the pettiness of our leaders was, I think our situation was made even worse by our monstrous chain of command. According to the textbooks, any time a unit—say, a regiment—was sent into combat, one of its three battalions and all of its the special troops (like Engineers, Artillery, Medics, Signals, Motor Transport, and Headquarters staff) were held back in reserve. So two battalions went forward into combat, but each kept one of its three companies in reserve. And of the two companies from each battalion that went into combat, each kept back one of its three platoons in reserve. And from each platoon only two of three squads went forward and one was kept in reserve. After subtracting all these reserve forces, a regiment that started out with a full strength of a thousand men could wind up sending well under half that number into combat.

Of course, units in reserve don't stay subtracted indefinitely—the reason they exist is so that they can be committed as needed to fill gaps. After a few days on Iwo, though, the infantry squads (the people doing the actual fighting), were being shrunk by casualties and not seeing any relief. At the same time, the colonels looked around their bunkers and saw no reduction in the size of their staffs, so they must have thought the front lines were at full strength too.

Before long, the advances called for every morning were being made by very few men, and then when they didn't gain the objective that the colonel had picked out on his map, he called them shirkers.

You can say what you want about bravery, but dead men, and badly wounded ones, can't advance. The failure of some of our senior officers to recognize this doesn't say much for their intelligence and other qualities.

Officers were very rarely able—or willing—to see the cowardice of the "shirkers" among their fellow officers. Most of these shirkers were smart and ingenious, and used these qualities to ensure themselves safe duty in the safer places. They were easy for the enlisted men to spot, though: they were the ones who talked the loudest about bravery, but who seemed to find so many important things to do just as the unit was moving out. They were the ones who always had to stop and straighten out some piece of gear or check a "situation" on the map long enough to be behind and not in front of their men. And if they were with the men, they were the ones who had to stop and talk to somebody in the rear on the radio whenever the going got tough.

It is hard to say, never having been in a position where I had a choice, but I guess that if I had the chance that the officers back in the headquarters command posts had, I would have been dug in as deep as they were. But I'm not sure I would have been able to kid myself that I was really doing my part for the war effort.

I think that what rankled us more than anything was the officers' superior attitude towards enlisted men. Some displayed plain overt contempt; others just disregarded your existence. These misguided souls honestly believed it was only right that they, being officers, should be protected. After all, they had college degrees to prove how smart they were, and Congress had told them that they were gentlemen. They would talk loudly, amongst themselves and to the troops, so everyone would know that they were not ordinary riffraff like the enlisted men who were being sent up to the lines.

They were sure, I now believe, that without the great decisions they made in the depths of their bunkers the war could never have been won. (I'm not so sure what those decisions were, or what difference they could have made.) So to boost each other's egos, and prove their worth, they awarded each other medals for "planning," "display of spirit," and "leadership."

They also needed these medals—as many as they could get—in order to impress people after the war, when they again "heeded the call" and ran for public office. The medals enabled them to cite their leadership ability and war record as proof of their qualifications. The war is long past now, but I have a tendency to question the integrity of any man who runs for an elected office, particularly if he says he was an officer and boasts of his wartime achievements and all his medals. To me, he is immediately suspect.

My dislike of officers in general, because of the cowardly ways of the headquarters types I knew (unlike how even the lowest private behaved in combat), was reinforced at every turn in the "gray area" behind the lines of the combat zone. I must say, though, that not all officers were shirkers. I know from personal experience that the few officers I came in contact with in combat, real shooting-type combat, were good people.

Perhaps because they were thrown to the wolves, so to speak, as we were, the officers who were in infantry units and line companies were what I would expect officers to be. I imagine that they were as scared as we were, but they never deserted their men, nor failed to lead by example. Maybe they had no choice in being where they were, same as the enlisted men, but they acted like men. They took the same chances, at times even more than necessary, trying to keep things moving.

Chapter 17

UP IN THE FIELDS
WHERE THE MEDALS GROW

There was a fairly small number of awards that could be made to individual Marines for acts described as "above and beyond the call of duty." ("Duty" would be things you were required to do—I never found out what kinds of things you were not required to do, particularly in combat.)

The lowest award was the Letter of Commendation, just a formal entry in your record book to the effect that you were a little above the average Marine. These entries were supposed to be the basis of all promotions. The individual was supposed to be called before a battalion formation at which the letter would be read to all the troops. (When we returned to Hawaii, so many LOCs were awarded that they didn't even bother to call out the names of those who had received them, let alone read them to the troops.) Recipients of some LOCs also received a ribbon to wear.

One level higher in prestige was the Bronze Star, a medal awarded for "conspicuous bravery." This added an extra five dollars a month to your pay. Next above that was the Silver Star medal, which added ten dollars to your pay. Above that came the Navy Cross and then the highest of all, the Congressional Medal of Honor (CMH). I don't know how much extra pay came with these medals. In addition to these awards for achievement and valor (things you accomplished) there was the Purple Heart medal, awarded for things that happened to you (being wounded).

One sign of the hellishness of the Iwo Jima campaign is that 27 CMHs were awarded for actions during those five weeks—almost exactly a third of the total number awarded to Marines for all World War II actions (82).

The distribution of CMHs and other awards within the Fifth Marine Division tells a lot about what the Marine Corps was like in those days. Counting replacements, 23,141 men served with the Division on Iwo. About 896 of them (3.9 percent) were officers and 22,245 (96.1 percent) were enlisted men. Division members were awarded 1,184 valor medals for service there (14 CMHs, 95 Navy Crosses, 331 Silver Stars, and 744 Bronze Stars). Of those medals, officers got 283 (23.9 percent), enlisted men 901 (76.1 percent). Another way of looking at this is to say that one in three officers got medals, and one enlisted man in 25.

The Marine Corps expression summing this all up is "Semper Fidelis," which can be translated several ways. The most genteel, perhaps, is "I've got mine, to hell with you."

The distribution of Purple Hearts was similar to that of valor medals, for reasons that are worth some study. The rules said that to be eligible for a Purple Heart you had to be treated by a doctor. But up in the front lines there were no doctors. When a man was hit, his first medical aid came from a Navy Corpsman, who stopped the bleeding, administered morphine, and prepared him to be moved to one of the aid stations in the rear. The only places doctors were to be found was in those aid stations, where the wounded could be protected while they received field surgery or other treatment before being removed to hospital ships.

The rule requiring each Purple Heart to be authorized by a doctor may have been based on the assumption that all seriously wounded men would be treated at the aid stations. That may have been the case in the first hours of the fighting, but the combat units all quickly ran short of men because of the high casualties. So no one who was not seriously incapacitated ever left the lines. To leave the lines was to place your friends and buddies in even more jeopardy, because they would have to continue with one less Marine to help them.

Each man's constant thought was something like "if we can only get to the next little rise, or past this bunker, all the shooting will end;

then we can all rest, not just me." Without this little scrap of hope, there would never have been any incentive or reason to move forward. So at the front, wounds that were not life-threatening or disabling were treated by a Corpsman, and the man continued on with his unit.

All these true wounds, inflicted by the enemy, were never recorded, much less the other injuries and medical problems suffered by troops in combat. I don't think there was any man who had been at the front very long whose hands didn't look like he had been in a fight with a lion. Scrambling amongst the rocks it was awfully easy to get your hands, elbows, and knees all scratched up. Then between the dirty surroundings and the oil you got on your hands trying to keep your weapon clean, these sores never healed. And even in the chilly weather most of us came down with a form of the "creeping crud" under our arms, under the belt and especially between our legs, from not being able to keep clean. Redness and rawness in these areas would quickly develop into infections that could be as bad as athlete's foot. It took some time under very painful treatment with lots of "Jensen violet" fungicide to complete the scabbing and healing process. Another troublesome type of sores was regular athlete's foot, which came from not being able to clean your feet or change your socks; it caused the skin between your toes to peel off in big strips.

In the meantime, our heroes in the rear areas were treated by a doctor any time they went to an aid station. Any officer who wanted a Purple Heart could get one (the doctor was right there, eating at the same officers' mess and sleeping in the same bunker). And even among the enlisted men in the rear areas anybody cut himself opening a C-ration can—or got a splinter from the rough lumber used to build a new latrine, or suffered any other kind of scratch or bump—rated a Purple Heart. Not a single Purple Heart went to any of us sixty men on the mine and demolition teams.

In my wanderings I was told that my name was being put in for three decorations: two Letters of Commendation and a Bronze Star.

A Letter of Commendation

I learned about the first LOC from an officer in the Division's Tank Battalion, which my squad was working with early in the northward push (near what must have been the second Jap airfield).

The Japs up in this area had developed the tactic of throwing what we believed were chlorine gas hand grenades into the air intakes of our tanks. The tank crews, like just about everybody else, had early on discarded the bulky and seemingly useless gas masks we had been ordered to come ashore with. Now they were in a tough spot. If they opened the hatches for fresh air and tried to run for cover, they were fair game to be gunned down by surrounding Jap troops. The only alternative was to get gas masks and wear them inside the tank, which was cumbersome and uncomfortable.

Our tanks always worked in groups of four—one up front to do the dirty work, a second up front to cover it, and two more in back to cover the two up front; every so often they would exchange positions.

On the day I was to be commended for, I was back with the third tank, one of the two covering from the rear. I was talking to the crew inside through the phone that all tanks carried attached to the back of the engine housing. (Visibility from inside tanks was notoriously poor when the hatches were closed, so whenever possible we tried to have a man outside serving the crew as an extra pair of eyes. Keeping the crew informed as to what was actually happening outside, what to shoot at and what not to shoot at, was an important function. More than once I was shot at by a tank crew that didn't have an outside observer and mistook me for an enemy.)

As I was talking with the crew in tank #3, tank #1 in front came under machine-gun fire from its left. Everybody looked in that direction, and tank #1 turned its turret leftward to fire back. At that moment, a Satchel Charlie appeared from out of the rocks to the right and ran at top speed toward tank #2. Several of us fired and he went down short of the tank.

He didn't seem to be carrying a regular demolition satchel, and I speculated on the phone to the crew of tank #3 that maybe he had been coming to plant some kind of gas grenade in tank #2's air intake. Tank #3 relayed that thought to the other tanks by radio, and they and our infantry units agreed not to shoot at me while I went up and searched the Jap.

All the tanks and infantry nearby fired at any caves and holes they could see as I ran out in the open, made sure the Jap was dead, took the canvas bag off his shoulder, and ran back for cover behind tank #3.

On opening the canvas bag, I found I had hit the jackpot. Inside were four or five round glass bottles, about three inches in diameter, each filled with a liquid, sealed with wax, and covered with something like a fish net.

An officer sent the bottles by runner back to Division right away for analysis. I found out from the tankers next day that the liquid turned out to be only hydrochloric acid. When one of these bottles was broken in a tank's air intake it would release some chlorine gas— just enough to irritate the crews' eyes and noses and cause panic, but not enough to do any real damage. This meant that there was no need for the tank crews to wear gas masks after all.

That officer was wounded and evacuated from the island a couple of days later, leaving behind no paperwork related to a commendation for me.

My Second Letter of Commendation

A different officer praised me for another service I did Tank Battalion a week or two later, up near the south end of he third airfield. Division Headquarters sent my demolition squad ("Nutcracker 1") up there to destroy a tank that had broken down, supposedly damaged beyond repair, and keep the Japs from using its guns or posting snipers in it.

We found the tank sitting out in a relatively level area. The crew were still inside, where they had been all night, protected by the three backup tanks. I went with Frank, the squad leader, to ask the officer in charge of these tanks why we should destroy the disabled one if it was good enough to stay with all night.

His answer was that a Satchel Charlie had badly damaged the track at the left front where it made contact with the bogey wheels; the track would come off if they tried to drive the tank. We told him that the rest of the tank, including the other track, seemed intact—why not repair the damaged track? He said that his men were scared to be outside of the tank, and besides they were only crew, not mechanics.

I offered to fix the track if the tankers had the necessary tools and parts and would provide protection while I sat out in the open doing the work. They did, so I did. A spare idler wheel was carried up by infantrymen, and extra infantry appeared in the area to keep things "quiet." Three of us worked for probably three or four hours, getting the damaged pieces off and new parts on. Then I had the tank drive forward a little at a time as the individual track plates were replaced and rejoined into a new track. It was really no different from repairing a tractor.

Division was notified that the tank had been destroyed. At the end of the fighting, the salvaged tank was shipped out with the equipment belonging to the Engineer Battalion. Back in Hawaii, the Tank Battalion got a brand-new tank to replace the "destroyed" one.

The second Tank Battalion officer was killed two days after this incident, leaving behind no paperwork related to a commendation for me.

My Bronze Star

The recommendation to award me a Bronze Star came from an officer in one of the infantry units—probably the 26th Marines, which I worked with in the "Gorge" area at the north end of the island—but I'm not sure. As the Fifth Division fought its way up the island, my demolition squad's work had gone from clearing mines on the beaches to destroying cave entrances behind our lines to attacking enemy-held pillboxes and caves hand-in-hand with infantry units that surrounded them. (The infantry had their own demolition men, but there was too much of this kind of work for them to do it all, and before long my squad had fully taken over the responsibility.)

The job the officer told me he wanted to see me decorated for was for me just another bunker, but it was one that hadn't been surrounded yet. The Japs inside the bunker had been causing trouble for several days, firing out of the concrete machine-gun emplacement and keeping a Marine infantry unit in the vicinity pinned down.

I was able to work my way out around the side of the bunker, come up to it from behind, and set off a shaped charge on the top of it. The explosion stunned the Japs inside just long enough for me to drop two hand grenades in through the hole I had blown in the roof. In the resulting confusion an infantry flamethrower operator was able to advance and hose down the firing aperture, destroying most of the people inside. I did have an argument with one Jap who tried to exit out the back. I won.

By destroying the bunker, I enabled the infantry unit, which had taken several casualties in the couple of days they had been stalled there, to resume its advance.

The battalion Sergeant-Major told me later that our battalion leadership back in the rear had disallowed my Bronze Star recommendation. According the rules, in order for you to get a medal, whatever it was that you did had to be seen by two commissioned officers—one who would write up the citation and a second who would countersign it. In my case, the only witnesses were one officer and one sergeant. (After the first few days on Iwo it was extremely rare to see two officers in the same place on the front lines.) Not only that, the officer I'd worked for was killed the morning after the incident, and the sergeant two days later.

I didn't make a fuss, because I didn't think that I had done anything out of the ordinary. I assumed that the officer who praised me was new on the line and didn't realize that what I did was nothing more than others did. (Thinking back now, I'm sure that any officer alive up there at that time had to be new.) What I did was what had to be done, something I'd done a hundred times by then, so I never contested the "official" decision.

"My" medal was one of fifteen Bronze Stars and Silver Stars that the line companies recommended be awarded to members of the demolition and mine disposal squads for our service at the front. All fifteen medals were disallowed by Battalion headquarters for similar "technical" reasons. Instead they "saved" the medals and awarded them to members of the Battalion staff. (Mine went to one of the REMF officers for "keeping the lines of vital supplies to the front areas flowing smoothly during this difficult time." This meant that he was on the island, dug down in some hole so deep that he never bothered the troops, leaving some sergeant alone so the work could get done.)

At an awards formation after it was all over we were told that "some" award recommendations had been disallowed because it didn't look good to the people in the line companies for so many to be given to people in H&S Company. The announcement did not mention that actually every single recommendation had been disallowed, and that disallowing them left the officers with almost twice as many medals to pass out amongst themselves.

That's pure Semper Fi.

Part of my reason for not pursuing the awards I was recommended for was a kind of mental block I developed as I saw so many REMF people I knew getting undeserved valor medals and Purple Hearts. To fight the REMFs for the medals that were due me would be to lower myself to their level. Instead, I accepted the lame excuses for not awarding me anything. (I'm not bitter about this. The Bronze Star and the Purple Heart, if I'd received them, would have gotten me home from overseas six months earlier than I actually made it; but maybe that was God looking after me. I have always felt that the time I spent in Japan and China after the war was a pleasant and rewarding experience I would never have gotten any other way.)

But there was more to my restraint than my scorn for the REMFs. I was also held back by a sense of guilt and unworthiness. All the people I was with, the people I cared about, told me I had earned these ribbons and medals and should fight for them. But I didn't feel right about doing that. If I had won the fight and accepted the awards, I would have felt that I was riding on the coattails of others, so to speak—profiting off of their heroism. That, to me, was the lowest thing a man could do. I honestly felt then, and still do now, that many others did far more than I did. If they didn't get medals, then I certainly wasn't worthy of them either.

I know this may sound strange to you, but I felt that I hadn't really done my share in the fighting. I saw people around me getting wounded and killed, and thought they were the ones who should have the medals. Through all of the fighting I was in, I was never wounded seriously enough to require any hospitalization. This seemed to me to prove that I had not tried hard enough, and my shame at not having done enough to be wounded has bothered me for all these years.

Many years after the war, at a Marine Corps get-together, a VA hospital psychiatrist told me that this guilt I felt for the suffering of others is a well-known combat neurosis. He told me that men felt this guilt because they accused themselves, for the most far-fetched reasons, of being accessory to the processes that had wounded or killed their friends. By rational standards, he told me, coming through the fighting with a whole skin didn't disqualify those men—or me—from being a hero.

But rational standards were not those of someone who passed through Iwo. To me, true to my line company "breeding," the heroes were always my betters, those who were not coming back at all.

Other Awards

In addition to individual decorations, there were special ribbons that could be awarded to entire units that performed outstanding feats in the face of enemy fire.

The whole Engineer Battalion, for example, received a Presidential Unit Citation (PUC) for demolition and mine removal during the first three days of the fighting. Everybody involved in the fighting that the award was for was entitled to wear a special ribbon with a star in the center of it. Unit members who were ashore during the citation period but didn't have an opportunity to blow anything up were also entitled to the ribbon with the star. People who were members of the unit during the citation period but not ashore got to wear the ribbon but not the star. As usual in our outfit, though, this distinction was soon lost. Even the troops who were still out on the ships during the citation period got to wear their ribbon with the star on it. Oh, well, Semper Fi.

Later in the fighting the Engineer Battalion was also awarded a Navy Unit Commendation (NUC), one step lower in prestige than the PUC. Again everybody got to wear the ribbon with a star on it, no matter how deep they were dug in their "command post." So even the stars pinned on award ribbons to identify the people who had actually been in combat had their true meaning adulterated; more proof of the superiority of the officers.

Other PUCs and NUCs were awarded to various infantry outfits that fought their way up the island. Those of us in the three demolition squads and the three mine disposal squads were with them during the tougher fighting and we were included in their citations, which meant that all of us received both the PUC and the NUC several times.

The trouble was that when it came time to count up all of our awards (more awards meant more "points" and an earlier return to the States), none of the citations we'd received for service with other units showed on our record books. We were told that the Engineer Battalion had no record of what we had done or where we were while we were on the island, and that there was no way they could obtain such information. So naturally these awards of ours couldn't be counted.

Semper Fi…again.

Heroism Revisited

I have yet to figure out the rationale for giving commanding officers Silver Stars and Navy Crosses for battles that their men were in. On Iwo the officers were always way back from the lines. Lots of times they couldn't even see the fighting, and had no contact with the men doing the fighting. And true to form, if these officers, safe in their dugout, found out that an attack had stalled under withering enemy fire and high casualities had been suffered and the men had returned to the relative safety of their own lines, the commander would send a runner forward and tell them to attack again. It sure was no skin off of his ass if the troops had to try several times before some other idea was tried. The loss of half of his men meant nothing to him.

Too many decisions were made from too far back, and too deep in the ground. Many objectives could have been reached with less loss of life if approached in a different manner, a thinking manner, but ignorance and vanity prevailed.

Also, there was far too much value placed on mechanized equipment. (After all, it had a dollars-and-cents value, and was hard to replace out in the Pacific battle area when damaged—unless you were in MacArthur's Army.) Too many men's lives were wasted in trying to overcome enemy positions that should have been destroyed by tanks or armored half-tracks. Too many officers, in a hurry to get their medals and get back to the dugout, rushed troops into advancing, when by waiting a few minutes we could have gotten mechanized help and suffered far fewer causalities.

For the troops there comes a disheartening moment when it fully dawns on you that you are truly expendable—that you have been thrown to the wolves. You are basically written off the books, and nobody outside of the few people you are with cares if you come back alive or not.

To a certain degree it's understood, just from your having joined the Marines, that you are putting yourself at risk for an important cause. But when you are in big units, it's a lot easier to feel that you are doing something for your country and the folks back home. When you're at the very end of the road; when you've been sent to do something which, win or lose, will mean absolutely nothing toward the final outcome; when you nevertheless must put your very life on the line, gambling that you will live through whatever ordeal is ahead, just so some officer can say what a hero he was (and you can bet your bottom dollar that he doesn't go with you)—at times like these there's no way not to feel depressed. You feel reduced to the level of the Japs you are fighting.

None of these observations are unique or new. In his book *Semper Fi, Mac: Living Memories of the U.S. Marines in World War II*, Henry Berry tells the story of an interview with one of his ex-officers.

> I hate to tell you guys this, but after the battle of Okinawa all the officers got together and we decided who should get the medals. Believe me, the officers got first consideration. I mean, that's the name of the game. You know, Semper Fi.

At a division reunion Berry met another man, much decorated, who told him:

> You know, the secret is to be near a colonel when you do anything special. It ain't what you do—Christ, half the guys in combat deserve medals—it's who sees you do it.

Come to think of it, I guess that was how our colonel's driver got a Bronze Star. Not that the colonel ever strayed out of his reinforced bunker, or that the driver ever got near the front. My guess is that he got his medal for driving down to the beach to pick up the colonel's 10-in-1 rations.

Hell, Frank and I could have brought him some 10-in-1s if we had only known.

Another author, Daniel da Cruz, in *Boot: The Inside Story of How a Few Good Men Became Today's Marines*, has some wise things to say about how award recommendations are written:

> The Medal of Honor has been earned by, and awarded to, Marines from private to general, but cynics can detect a pattern in which the act of valor that wins the private a Bronze Star, and the captain a Silver Star, and a colonel a Navy Cross, will earn the general a Medal of Honor. Dozens of privates have died to protect their shipmates by smothering with their bodies the blast of enemy hand grenades, posthumously winning the [CMH]; to date no general has fallen on a hand grenade. The citation of a general, who probably didn't fire a shot, is likely to read: "his tenacity, courage and resourcefulness prevailed against a strong, experienced and determined enemy, and the gallant fighting spirit of his men under his inspiring leadership enabled them to surmount all obstacles."

"No such vaporous generalities embroider an enlisted man's citation," Da Cruz says, and quotes an example:

"During the assault on Iwo Jima, assailed by a tremendous volume of small-arms fire ... [Sergeant] Cole boldly led his men [through a barrage] of flying shrapnel and personally destroyed with hand grenades two hostile emplacements. ... [When halted by three Japanese pillboxes] he delivered a shattering fusillade and succeeded in silencing the nearest ... before his weapon jammed. Sgt. Cole, armed solely with a pistol and one grenade, coolly advanced alone. Hurling his one grenade ... he quickly withdrew, [returned to his own lines for grenades], again advanced, attacked and withdrew. He ran the gantlet of slashing fire a third time to complete the total destruction of the Japanese strong point. Although instantly killed by an enemy grenade as he returned to his squad, Sgt. Cole had eliminated a formidable Japanese position, enabling his company to continue the advance and seize the objective. ... He gallantly gave his life for his country."

I remember that when I first enlisted I was afraid I would never get to fight in the war. That may have been one of the reasons for the shortness of my stay in the Navy's V-12 College Training Program—all the program meant to me at the time was that I wouldn't get into combat in time to win a lot of medals.

I think every boot Marine wants to get all the medals he can—they sure look pretty on your uniform. But when the chips were down, it turned out that the medals meant nothing, except to the REMFs. Up where the real fighting took place, the sarcastic rallying cry was always "Okay, saddle up. Let's move out, there's no medals left here." On the lines it was the respect and trust of those around you that really meant something. "Valor" was so common at the front that it was hard to understand how any one man could be singled out as being braver than another.

I guess that maybe that's why they found it easier back in the rear to write each other up for medals than to award them to real fighting men. The REMF officers had college educations, and a command of English, and lots of time, and their imagination had not been blown to hell. They could easily turn out a little fancy prose for a citation that would make anybody or anything (even a REMF or a jeep) sound like a hero just for being on the island. After all, as the saying went, "They don't give medals for what was done—they give them for what somebody says was done."

People on the line didn't have time to write up each other for medals; they were trying to stay alive.

After returning to Hawaii, lots of the fellows got their chests tattooed (on the right side, where any medals the officers had let them have would be pinned if they wore a uniform blouse) with the following message to be displayed at the gate of heaven:

> St Peter, Sir:
> Another U.S. Marine reporting for duty.
> I've already served my time in Hell.

Chapter 18

THE GORGE

Iwo Jima was declared "secured" on the 15th of March, but fierce fighting continued for ten more days as we moved slowly northward and began to enter and take the last pocket of resistance, a rocky ravine we called "The Gorge." (This area was known as "Death Valley" in many books. I think every newspaperman and writer gets his jollies by using that name. It seems to appear in every battle and in every war.)

According to the history books, our assault on the Gorge was put off on purpose until after that victory announcement. Americans had already raised a hue and cry about the massive Marine casualties on Iwo, and it was clear that this final battle was going to be especially deadly. Postponing it allowed the numbers of men wounded and killed fighting at the Gorge to be conveniently added to the total Iwo Jima losses at some later date, unnoticed by most people at home.

We knew the Gorge would be deadly because of intelligence from captured laborers and discovered documents indicating that the Jap commanding general had his headquarters there, guarded by the real diehards of his command. These included most of the Imperial Marines on the island, along with other Special Landing Forces units that were not quite as good as the Marines but much better disciplined and fiercer fighters than any of the regular Army units we encountered. According to official U.S. histories, there were at least 1,500 Japanese troops in this ravine (that means there were more). They had all taken a special vow to die for their emperor. Copies of this "Courageous Battle Vow" were found later. It reads as follows:

> Each man will make it his duty
> to kill ten of the enemy before dying.

Until we are destroyed to the last man,
we shall harass the enemy by guerrilla tactics.

Anticipating the savageness of the Japanese defense, our commanders decided to mass all American troops possible for the final push. The front-line troops were moved up to the near rim of the Gorge, where they waited until everybody else caught up and closed in around the edges. (The commanders didn't bring in any fresh troops; they just massed the tired, worn-out people who had spent weeks fighting their way up the island. Their thought seems to have been that, tired though we were, we knew how to fight the Japs and would likely suffer lighter casualties than new troops would.)

The ravine we found in front of us was shaped like a funnel, about five hundred yards wide at the inland (south) end and less than two hundred yards wide at the deeper north end, where it met the sea. The seven hundred yards from end to end were strewn with rock and riddled with caves and little side gullies.

The Gorge was deceptive to the superficial observer. It was entirely possible to stand at its edge or its mouth and study its steep slopes and cliffs at leisure. There was absolutely no sign of the Japs, no movement and a lot of the time no shooting—generally only silence.

It was even possible for small patrols to move around on parts of the ravine floor. But any time they came too close to a Jap-held cave, or any time the Japs decided they were a profitable target, there would be a flurry of small-arms fire from several well hidden locations.

This was the worst of the bad terrain we had started meeting down near the first airfield. The ground had gotten harder and harder as we moved north, and more and more we found holes, caves, or what-have-you that had been dug into the near-vertical faces of the canyon and gully walls. The digging must have been hard work, but the resulting chambers gave the Japs better protection against our attacks than anything they could dig in the sands further south. There were probably more caves per acre in the Gorge than anywhere else on the island. Although no Marine who'd survived this far was adventurous enough to crawl in and find out for sure, it appeared that most of these caves were connected in groups by tunnels. I guess the only good thing for us was that up here where the Japs could dig caves and tunnels, we ran into fewer reinforced concrete pillboxes and bunkers.

When we did find pillboxes, there was always an elaborate defense system dug in around them. Besides being strewn with lots of boulders and big rocks, the Gorge was heavily fortified, with the few pillboxes backed up by lots of caves (natural and man-made), machine-gun emplacements, spider traps, and trenches. The pillboxes and machine-gun emplacements were dug into the walls of the ravine, so that the ones on each side could cover the fronts of those facing them, and there was no back to defend.

All of these positions were well camouflaged. A machine-gun emplacement dug into the face of a cliff typically had room for two or three men to stand and fire their weapon, but the firing aperture might be no more than two or three feet wide and a foot high, covered outside with brush and plants.

Once a cave was discovered, it was sometimes possible for our troops to stand on the rim of the Gorge and hit its opening with anti-tank rockets. But all the cave openings were so cleverly concealed that they were almost never discovered until they opened fire on a patrol or group. Even then, they were hard to spot. The Japs used smokeless powder, so the only way to see where the fire was coming from was to see the muzzle flashes of the weapons, which they tried to hide by firing from well back inside the caves.

There was really only one way into the Gorge—right down the middle of the hard rock floor. Our armored dozers put in a major effort to cut a road for us there. Every so often they would back out and tanks would enter to neutralize the caves as far in as they could reach. Then the tanks would back out and the dozers would return to work on another fifty feet of road.

We started at the wide end and worked our way toward the narrow end where the Gorge met the sea. Someplace in there the Jap commanding general and most of his staff were holed up in caves. The Jap troops protecting this command area were sure acting like true Imperial Marines.

Because of the terrain, there usually wasn't enough maneuvering room to allow us to bypass any of the fortified positions. They covered fields of fire that held everybody up until each position was eliminated in turn. Tanks firing from the floor of the Gorge and rockets launched from up on the rim could sometimes help, but mostly the only way to clear out these Jap positions was with explosives and flamethrowers.

The Japs had no artillery left by this time, and no full-sized mortars. The troops in the caves did lob their small "knee" mortar shells our way, but we lost few or no Marines to Jap shrapnel wounds. Instead, whenever they got a chance, the Japs swiftly and surely picked us off with single sniper bullets—generally in the head.

We weren't hurt by Jap shrapnel, but shrapnel casualties caused by our own side were a different story.

Artillery fire into the Gorge was useless, so we never requested it. The pillboxes and machine-gun emplacements were cut into the face of the cliffs, so only a direct hit could do any good, and the spider holes and snipers didn't seem very vulnerable either. The Japs in them would just move back in the tunnels until the barrage was over and then crawl forward, ready to shoot at us again.

In spite of our not requesting it, artillery fire poured in. (According to one book I've read, as many as eleven U.S. artillery batteries—that's 44 big guns—were firing into the Gorge to "help" us in this battle.) And why? Because REMF officers who needed some combat time to fatten up their personnel files and get themselves recommended for awards found this a safe and easy method: They would come up to the front, call in a few artillery rounds, "win" their medals without exposing themselves to enemy fire, and then go back to the south end of the island and crawl into their safe dugouts.

This grandstand quarterbacking wasn't harmless, either. Although the rounds our noble officers fired could keep the Japs hunkered down, they could also keep us from getting close enough to blow the cave mouths shut with explosives. That left the cave occupants free to return and snipe at us later in the day. For our own safety, we who were down on the floor of the Gorge had to move back out of the way of this folly. (While we were being "helped" there was no way we could do anything. We had no communication with these artillery batteries.) Some of us didn't get out of the way fast enough, and became "friendly fire" casualties.

The artillery barrages impeded our work and caused us needless casualties, but we had no officers to complain to and get them stopped. The REMF officers came up to the front, caused trouble, and then left. Nobody ever tried to find out if their efforts were needed, or whether they helped or hindered the people on the ground.

I read later that by the time we entered the Gorge, the combat efficiency of the Fifth Marine Division was rated at thirty percent. My first thought was that this must have included the REMFs, because it often looked more like two percent up where I was.

One platoon our demolition squad was sent to help always stands out in my mind. When we finally found it, it had only three men left, two PFCs and one private, out of an original 36 to 38. The private had been on the island longer, so he was the Marine in charge. For units in such bad shape, it was a real boost when our demolition squad (eight men, often with some souvenir-hunting riflemen tagging along) showed up to help clear enemy positions in their area.

Most of the companies were now around fifty to sixty men, down from 240, and were commanded either by a brand-new lieutenant from a service unit in the rear or by an old Sergeant. Most platoons were run by corporals. Battalions that had landed with 36 officers and 885 men were down to about fifteen officers (mostly headquarters staff) and maybe 300 men, mostly wounded, and so tired that they couldn't think straight or move faster than a shuffle.

Those of us who survived long enough to take part in the fighting around the Gorge were not the same men we had been when we poured out of the landing craft a month earlier. We even looked different. Very few of us wore our steel helmets, for example, because they did not stop rifle bullets, which were about all the Japs had left to kill us with. I wore my utility cap instead—it was less trouble when you had to run.

There was not much running up here, though. Most of us had been on the lines for at least fifteen to twenty days with no relief and no replacements. There didn't seem to be any end to the number of caves that still faced us. It looked more hopeless every day. Few of us remained, and we were so tired that we moved like zombies if we moved at all. We had no strength left. By this time, you just accepted that the odds were against you, and were merely waiting for the shock of the bullet that you'd feel only if it wasn't instantly fatal.

It seemed that even if the Japs didn't get you, the physical exhaustion and emotional stress would do you in.

This was a bad state of mind, because it dulled your senses. You were no longer as observant as you had been, and I'm sure this added to the number of needless causalities we suffered. Nerves were frayed from artillery and demolition explosions, and there was not a man up there who wasn't wounded or bandaged in some manner. We were all walking wounded.

It was about this time that I came closest to being seriously hurt while I was on Iwo. On the day the island was officially declared secured, I was working with an infantry unit at the entrance to the Gorge. We were on a flat area facing a long, low ridge honeycombed with caves. The caves and the spider holes supporting them had halted this unit's advance. Four tanks had moved up to support us. I was standing with two infantrymen at the rear corner of one of the tanks. They were about alongside what would be the right rear wheel if this were a panel truck, and I was around the corner from them, about where the rear license plate would be. I was using the tank's external phone to tell the crew inside what the infantry was going to do, how and when, so they would tell the other three tanks by radio not to shoot at us.

The next thing I remember is awaking on my back, tightly bound to a stretcher and unable to move. My eyes were completely bandaged, and shells were exploding around me. From the hissing sounds just before the explosions, I knew we were taking fire from little Jap "knee" mortars. It was terrifying to be unable either to see the falling shells or to try to get out of their way.

My only contact with the world was a radioman in the next shell hole over who was trying to get help: "B.A.S. (Battalion Aid Station), this is Blue Cannon George." For what seemed like hours he called frantically, without ever getting an answer.

Finally a Corpsman reached me. In response to my many questions he told me I was at a collecting point, back several hundred yards from the fighting. Someone had strapped me down so that I could be moved. The firefight had heated up and there were now two of us wounded awaiting transfer back to the Battalion Aid Station. The two infantrymen who had been with me beside the tank were dead. Because I had been unconscious for some time it was possible that I might have a head wound, so he couldn't give me a morphine shot. He didn't know about my eyes; he was not the one who had put the bandages on.

There were more mortar rounds falling; somebody called for a Corpsman, so he left me.

Lying there thinking about being blind for the rest of my life, I felt sorry enough for myself that I started to cry. I must have cried a lot: the tears diluted the blood sealing my eyes shut and allowed light in under the bandages.

When the Corpsman came back I told him I could see light, so he agreed to at least change the eye bandage. When it was removed, I could see. It turned out that my eyes had been bandaged as a precaution, because I was unconscious and my face was bloody. (I was covered with the remains of the two infantrymen.) The Corpsman unstrapped me and checked me over. Aside from a bad headache and a ringing in my ears, I was deemed to be okay and could return to my squad.

When I got back to the lines, Frank, the squad leader, told me that the Navy had sent their apologies for firing a "short round." It had exploded almost on top of the two men who had been with me beside the tank. They had been killed instantly, but the corner of the tank had shielded me from the shrapnel.

Chapter 19

BACK TO THE LAND OF SHOWERS, HOT MEALS, AND TRUE SLEEP

At about ten o'clock one morning my squad was relieved, taken out of the lines, and sent back to the rear area.

I remember almost nothing of that day. I found out later that the date was March 25th, and that our commanders had decided that the Gorge, where we had been fighting for the last ten days, was cleaned out enough to let the Third Division finish the cleanup. Trucks picked us up at the front and took us back to the west landing beaches (White and Orange), where we were to wait for small landing craft (LCVPs) that would shuttle us out to the transports that afternoon.

Back in Hawaii later, friends told me that I had been waiting at the beach with them when a couple of Corpsmen stepped up, took my M-1 and handed it to the man behind me in line, then pulled me out of line and led me to a bigger landing craft (probably an LCM). This was great—there was no line to stand in, and there was even enough room that I could sit down against the side of the boat and go to sleep. And sleep I did.

It turned out that this boat was only for the wounded. We were taken out to a hospital ship where those most badly hurt, still on their stretchers, were placed on pallets and lifted from the LCM up to the deck of the ship by cranes.

The rest of us were "walking wounded." We saw a landing net hanging from the deck of the hospital ship and assumed that we would have to climb it to get aboard. A Corpsman told us that we could if we wanted to, but that we could ride up on the pallets after the more seriously wounded were all removed.

Several of us thought we were okay, so we started climbing. Part way up the side of the ship I panicked. I couldn't climb up any farther—my hands and arms were so weak that it felt like I was going to lose my grip on the ropes and fall. I locked my arms through the net and hung on for dear life. To be so close and yet so far—I thought for sure I would fall back into the LCM and crack my skull, or into the ocean and drown.

Two sailors quickly came down the net and helped me up to the deck. (I wasn't the only one that made a fool of myself and had to be rescued like that.) This was the only time I ever boarded a U.S. Navy ship without saluting the Officer of the Deck and requesting permission to come aboard.

I'm sure we were the cruddiest-looking bunch of people you have ever seen. No two of us had on the same "uniform." We were filthy dirty and I'm sure we all stank so bad that people shied away from us, but we were too tired to care. (I can remember that the nice clean rear-echelon types who sorted us out—taking names, serial numbers, and units in an effort to find out who was still left alive—were in clean uniforms, with bright clean stateside rating marks.)

Once safely on deck, I and the others (there were only maybe twenty of us that were able to walk) were told to strip down bare-assed naked and set aside any personal items we wanted to save. Everything else—clothes, cartridge belts, canteens, first aid pouches, helmets, and shoes—went into a pile on deck to be buried at sea. You could keep your combat knife and—after a sailor checked the magazine for live rounds and returned it to you—your pistol.

I used my utility cap to hold my K-Bar combat knife, my Boy Scout pocket knife, my Zippo lighter, my crimping pliers for explosives, and my waterproofed picture of Helen.

Naked, I carried my .45 and my cap with all my belongings along a passageway to a spot where I was directed to pile them while we were each given a quick boot-camp style haircut. That done, we were pointed to a fresh hot water shower and told, "You may stay as long as you like. There is shaving gear on the wash basins. There will be clean clothes and hot chow when you are ready."

After a long shower, time out to shave, and then more soaking under the hot shower, we were given all new clothes—standard Navy issue work shoes, blue dungarees, and white skivvies. We were also given oversize Army dungaree jackets for the cold weather.

After we were dressed, we were taken to the crew's galley. I don't remember what we had to eat, but it was hot, it was good and there were several main dishes, all served to us sit-down style. The cooks looked on appreciatively as we devoured the food, all we wanted to eat. I do remember that at the end we had all the ice cream we wanted. We were told that any time, day or night, for the next several days we could have all the food we wanted to eat. This big meal was too much for several of the men, and they got sick.

We were also told that we could sleep as much as we wanted until we got back to Hawaii, and that we would be checked over more thoroughly by a doctor in the next couple of days.

The ship I had come out on carried 2,000-plus Marines, about 400 men in each troop compartment. Each man had an area about 6 feet by 2 feet by 18 inches for himself and all his gear, including his rifle and backpack. The ship I was on now could carry 6,000 troops easily, but there were only about 300 of us on board, less than thirty in the compartment where I was. The aisles were wide and the racks were only two high instead of half a dozen.

One rack was about chest height, so that a Corpsman could tend the more seriously wounded. The other rack was below that, about four inches off the floor, and when not in use was chained up out of the Corpsman's way.

These racks were wider than those on the troop ship, maybe three and a half feet wide, and had a pipe railing around them about six inches high so you couldn't roll out in rough seas. The rack was covered with a mattress maybe three or four inches thick that had a white fitted sheet on it. I can't remember whether there was a top sheet or not, but the blankets were heavy white Navy hospital blankets.

I can remember that you didn't have to leave your rack for compartment inspection every morning, but the Corpsmen asked you, if you didn't get up, to stay in it until after the inspection was over. The Corpsmen made the racks most days, so the sheets and blankets were always clean. The whole compartment, besides having so much room, was amazingly clean. The floors were battleship gray, and I'm pretty sure they were linoleum, because they were swabbed every day before inspection. It was very impressive to lie there in my bunk at almost floor height and look across the sparkling clean floor. I still recollect the compartment as being not only sparkling clean, but light, airy, and very quiet.

Four of us in my compartment were considered walking wounded; the rest were semi-ambulatory. We four got up every day and went to chow; we also helped the Corpsmen keep the compartment policed. The others were waited on and fed by Corpsmen. Some of them could get around, when necessary, with help from a Corpsman. Never in all my time overseas did I ever see a Navy nurse, except for some on the streets of Honolulu.

After a couple of days of eating and sleeping, I was examined by a team of doctors. When they finally got through with their examination, plus several surprise night-time checks, they decided that all I had was "combat fatigue". (Amongst the troops this was called "the thousand-yard stare"; in World War I, it had been known as "shell shock".) I would live.

I told the doctors that I was experiencing poor eyesight and hearing on my left side; they seemed to think that these problems would go away with rest. Well, they didn't. Six decades later I still have headaches all the time, sometimes worse than others, and I have trouble with vertigo. I get sick very easily if I turn or move fast in certain ways, but that's a small price for still being alive.

The doctors explained to me that "combat fatigue" was just being bone-tired and completely disoriented. Your reflexes slowed considerably, and you no longer made conscious decisions. You could still do anything you had previously learned to do, but you didn't know how you did it or why. (I believe that.) Apparently it was caused by extreme fatigue, nervous exhaustion, and lack of proper food. Spending day after day physically worn out just allowed your mind to sink into utter stupefaction. They told me that this was a way the brain tried to keep you from going crazy. Thank God for that.

I have thought much over the years about the mental and physical beating that we took under fire. Even if it had only been the constant noise of our own heavy guns, I don't know how any of us could have lasted as long as we did. But when you add to that the strain of being shot at all day long, it seems to me that we must have had nerves of steel to last more than one day.

Now that we were under way, all of the "walking wounded" who had been released by the doctors were asked to help the crew run the ship. Once I was certified as well enough to perform light duty, I was asked (asked, mind you, not ordered) to work in the crew's mess. When I got there, the old Chief Petty Officer in charge took one look at me and assigned me to run the bread slicer in the galley.

This meant that just before every meal I had to put the fresh baked loaves of bread through the slicer to supply any of the seven galleys on the ship that wanted some. Sometimes this work took ten or fifteen minutes. Other messmen came and got the sliced bread; I didn't even have to deliver it.

The rest of the time was mine, and because I now worked for the bakery, I got my meals with the cooks. (The second day there was a big birthday cake for one of them.) I was the only Marine in the galley and they all treated me like a little kid.

All I did was eat and sleep, just what the doctor had ordered.

The way the sailors on this ship acted towards the Marines was a welcome change from my previous experience. On our way out on the USS *Darke* there had been nothing but trouble between us and the sailors, who were on their first month out of the States. They acted like the Marines were worse enemies than the Japs. Most of the sailors on this hospital ship had been out of the States for over two years and had been at several landings. In fact, they had just carried Army troops to the invasion of the Philippines, where they took a kamikaze hit. They were on their way back to Hawaii for repairs (two flooded compartments in the aft part of the ship were sealed off), but they were detoured to Iwo to bring back wounded. Even the officers treated the wounded like human beings and not like we all had the plague.

During our trip back to Hawaii it was announced over the ship's P.A. system that President Roosevelt had died. I don't think his passing meant that much to us, who had seen so much death, except that he had been the only president most of us had ever known.

We spent our time after returning to Hawaii preparing for the big landing in Japan itself, but instead the atom bombs were dropped and the war ended. We were sure glad for those bombs. They meant that we wouldn't have to make a combat landing on the mainland of Japan, which would have meant almost certain death for too many of us.

I did go to Japan and then into China as part of the U.S. Occupation forces, but that's a story for another book.

Chapter 20

AFTER IWO

When we got back to our home base, Camp Tarawa on the big island of Hawaii, the Fifth Division was already beginning to receive replacements, both men and equipment. Everybody had to work hard, because we were now getting ready for an even bigger invasion than Iwo and there wasn't much time.

It was no secret that this time we would be invading the home islands of Japan. Exactly where we would be ordered to make our landings was the topic of much discussion, but it was also no secret that we were going to face a bloody fight no matter where we attacked. According to "Tokyo Rose," we would be met not only by the Japanese armed forces but by women, children and old people brandishing pointed sticks and willing to sacrifice their lives to keep us from their homeland She broadcast that we would suffer far greater losses than we had on Iwo—that we were in fact on the verge of total annihilation.

We were already staging equipment for this landing, and the order of battle for each unit was pretty well established, when the first atomic bomb was dropped on the Japanese city of Hiroshima. We generally got little information about what was going on outside our camp, but soon we were told that a second bomb had been dropped, this time on the city of Nagasaki. A few days later, on a normal work morning, we were told over the loudspeakers in the training area that Japan had surrendered and the war was over. Dumbfounded, we returned to our tents and talked this surprise over amongst ourselves and then with the people in the tents around us.

The news, welcome as it was, was hard to comprehend. We would be able to return to our homes in the United States alive, not in coffins. However, we were soon told that we must physically occupy

Japan before we could go home. We quickly set sail and made our initial landing on Kyushu, the southern most of Japan's four main islands, on September 22, 1945.

To our great surprise and relief, our landing and the subsequent occupation by US Forces of all the islands of the Japanese Empire met no opposition. In fact, the local military helped us from the very first hour of our landing. After a couple of days we began to be inundated with kids, who came looking for food once they saw that we were not mistreating or punishing people in any way. Next, seeing that the kids were fed and treated well, the rest of the civilian population began to appear. They treated us first with tolerance, but soon with guarded displays of welcome.

An early order of business on Kyushu was to clear the quays of the Naval Shipyard at Sasebo of debris from the U.S. bombings so that the harbor could be opened to U.S. ships bringing in supplies. In support of this project I was sent to help in the construction an all-weather road up the middle of the island. On the farms in that area we met the people—the real people of Japan, not the military—and we were impressed by them. They responded well to us, too, and soon we were treating each other as we would neighbors at home.

Around the first of December I was hurriedly transferred to take part in the U.S. occupation of Tientsin, in China. At that time Tientsin was an "international" city. This meant that before the war and the Japanese takeover, at least seven foreign countries had held territory within its boundaries and exercised authority there instead of the Chinese. The U.S. Marines had now taken over the governing of those seven cities-within-the-city until the foreign powers returned to reclaim ownership.

My new job would be to maintain seven new diesel electric generators, one in each of the little colonies. My duties required that I travel freely through the city each day. But given the quickly rising power of the Chinese Communist party and their unconcealed animosity towards anything representing the U.S., it was dangerous for a single U.S. Marine to be out of our compounds by himself. Therefore I was assigned a bodyguard (consisting of four armed Japanese soldiers from the Japanese Army compound a couple of blocks down the street from where we were billeted) and a command truck to transport us. The same four soldiers were detailed to me every day, and of all the surprises I got during these postwar months, this became the biggest: These soldiers and I soon became good friends. They had been conscripted and were as glad as I was that the war was over, but they were still willing to protect me.

On the first of May, 1946, I was allowed to return home to the United States, where I was quickly discharged. Among the first things I did was to call Helen Ulrey in Flagstaff, Arizona. I followed that call with a visit, and we were soon married.

We set up our first home in Berkeley, California. I was told that I could not get into school for another year and a half, so I went to work for the California Division of Highways. Three years later, with some night schooling plus daily on-the-job training and lots of help from some of our neighbors (all returned veterans with experience in the same fields), I qualified for and passed the examination to become a Civil Engineer.

As an engineer I worked on freeway construction in the San Jose, California area for forty years before retiring. During that time Helen and I raised two boys. I gave my off-work time first to the Boy Scouts, then Little League; later I served as a fire commissioner, and as a home owner I became involved in the incorporation of the city of Cupertino, California.

Shortly before I retired from the Highway Division we moved into a rural area south of San Jose, where we built and operated a whole-sale fuchsia nursery. During the years I ran that business I hybridized and patented twenty-five new varieties of fuchsias.

Then we retired again and this time moved to Fortuna, in northern California. I soon became a uniformed volunteer helping in the local police department. In that role I served as an advisor to young people, male and female, interested in Law Enforcement careers.

Fifteen years later I retired again, this time because Helen became ill. She died sixty years and six months after our marriage. In addition to our two sons, we by this time had five grandchildren and eight great-grandchildren. (This narrative was originally written in 1989/ 1990 as a history lesson for my family; it has not seen the light of day until now.)

As you have been able to tell, there are many things that I still clearly remember. Some of these scenes are burned so vividly into my mind that I still see every graphic detail in them after many decades, whether I want to remember them or not. And after all these years I have not found what type of trigger causes these scenes to surface in my mind.

It's not as bad at night now as it was when I first came home. It was especially bad on Helen when we were first married. She would be the innocent victim of nightmares in which I was trying to get out of the way of a fired sniper round, or to reach some kind of cover as the mortar shells started dropping.

In these—to me—very real happenings, my actions were brought on by reflexes learned in combat. In real time if you were lying down, you were always a sort of a crouch, with one foot pulled up for leverage. Then when an emergency arose you were able to instantly jump or throw yourself up and over into another nearby hole for cover.

Now, in the middle of the night, I would react to this dreamed threat in the same manner. If Helen was lucky, I went out of bed on my side, onto the floor. But sometimes I tried to jump towards her side of the bed. When this happened, I usually became entangled in the covers and fell on her. At other times I would wildly throw an arm back for some reason and hit her in the face or chest.

After all these years sometimes I still have these flashbacks, just as vivid to me as ever. They eventually stopped causing physical damage to Helen, but in some ways they're worse for me these days. Now they seem to run in a pattern in which I'm unable to do something either to help someone else or to save myself from some impending catastrophe. There is still terror in these dreams, but now much frustration also.

My heavenly protector from that first night on Iwo has stayed with me over all these years. I'm sure there is no way that I can ever thank Him for His protection. But I do hope that over the years in little ways I have done things and said things that will pass on to others my appreciation for His guidance and assistance. This is too great a gift to ever forget.

Howard

IWO JIMA, OR THIRTY-FIVE DAYS IN HELL

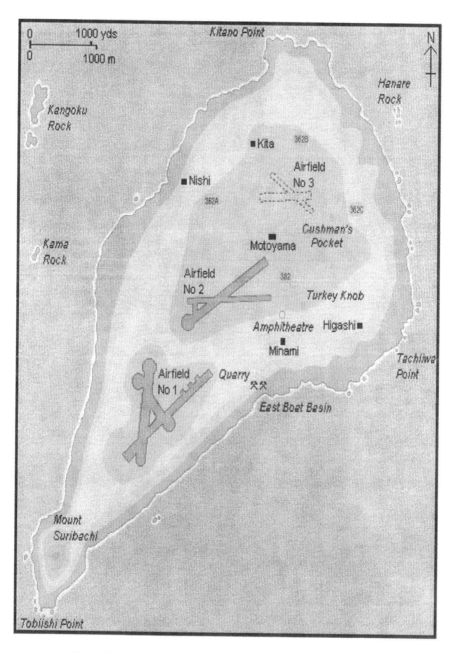

Iwo Jima Map A: Overall Geographical Layout

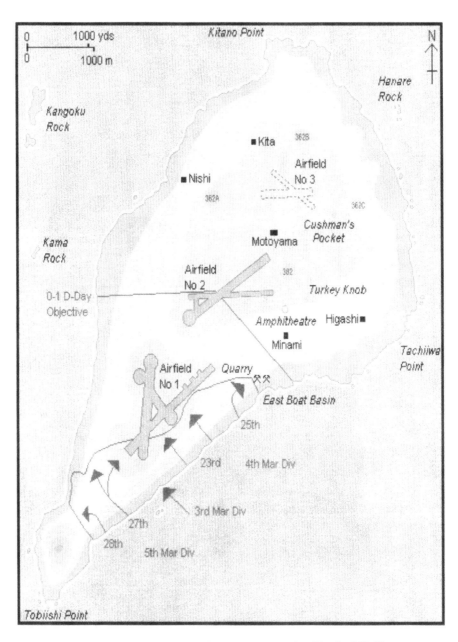

Iwo Jima Map B: Line of Advance at the End of D-Day

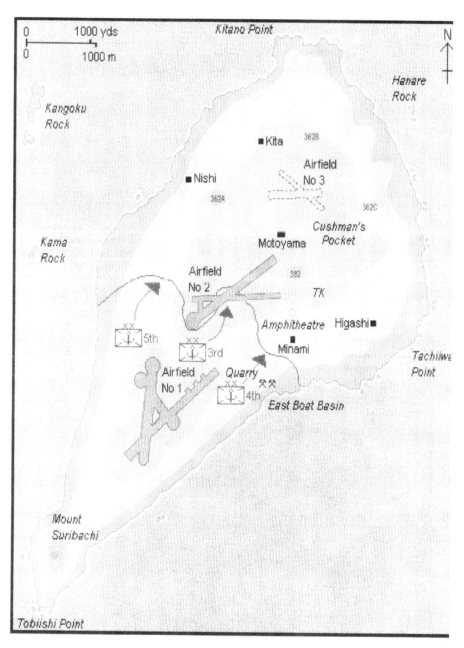

Iwo Jima Map C: Line of Advance at the End of D+5

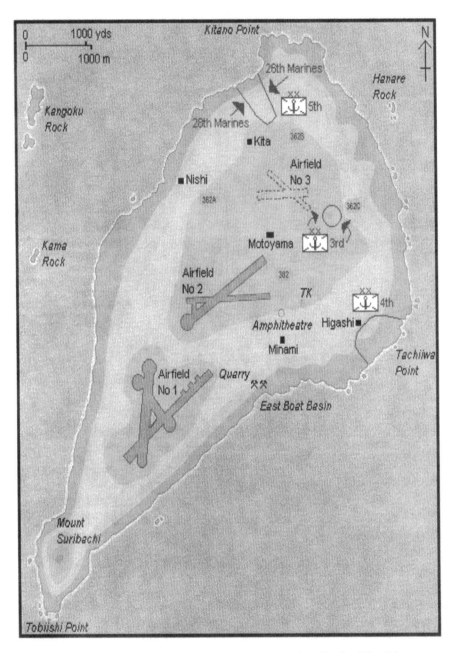

Iwo Jima Map D: Line of Advance at the End of D+26

SCENES OF IWO JIMA

Life and Death on Sulphur Island

As experienced by
Raymond C. Miller
Sgt USMC

THERE IT WAS, where for days there had been only endless ocean. An island, almost beautiful, once calm upon the sea, now smoke and dust and noise and everything a-boiling.

THERE IT WAS. I'd never see it like that again; a fearsome beginning of the day but not the start of the story.

My name is Ray Miller. During World War II, I served with H Company, 3rd Battalion, 28th Marine Regiment, in the Fifth Marine Division. This division, reinforced, numbered some 20,596 men.

I'll tell you some of the things I saw in that war. This is not a history of a military operation. It is personal feelings of how it struck me, the emotions and the stories of what I have to tell.

We were all just ordinary guys called upon to do extraordinary things we would never have done "back home." How we lived and thought differently while in battle is an interesting and thought-provoking study in the contrasts between who we were and who we became—those of us who survived.

Chapter 1

HOW I GOT THERE—JOINING UP

The regular peacetime Marine boot camp was many weeks long. However, the United States had just entered the war and the Corps was hungry for bodies. So the San Diego Marine Corps Recruit Depot (MCRD) was put on "fast"—just five weeks long. My class got an intensified abbreviated program. Life changed in a hurry. The method was simple: boil 'em all down to basic "man stuff," then re-build 'em into Marines.

With so many new recruits coming through, the camp needed extra coaches at the rifle range. I had done well during my unit's one-week stint at the range, so I was selected to help train men who were only about four weeks newer than I was. To be honest, I'm not sure I had ever fired a rifle before, but the coaches who trained me got the credit for my getting good scores. I enjoyed being a coach. I smile when I think that these "boots" that I was coaching looked upon me as an experienced veteran Marine. All the coaches wore campaign hats that looked great and much more "official," if that's the word, than the regular headgear issue—overseas caps, I think they were called.

Alas, the fun of being an "old salt" to the boots I was training was short-lived. The Camp Commandant's daughter, Rose Arnett, would come to the range and come over to visit with me. Out here in this almost woman-less world I thought this was great because she was very pretty, I liked her, and she had a little Ford convertible. But just as things seemed to be getting good, I found myself transferred to Camp Elliott, another Marine base nearby. I've always thought that this happened because one of the lieutenants at MCRD also wanted her attention and I was in his way. The duties at Camp Elliott were awesomely boring and I really wanted to get out of there.

Most of the time none of us had much say about what happened to us; we just kept quiet and did what we were told. I was fortunate to have one little "connection" back home to use if I really needed it. And I needed it then. I had always (Always? I was only 18 years old!) wanted to go to Alaska. I knew we had Marines there so I wrote to my father, who had the connection, asking to be sent there.

A few days after the letter back home, I was called into the first sergeant's office where he asked, "Miller, who do you know? I got this order here with pink ribbons all over it. Get your sea bag packed; you'll be going to San Diego tomorrow to join a bunch of boots on the train to Puget Sound Naval Base. Then you'll be on the next ship to Alaska."

And so I was.

The Trip to Alaska

Fifteen months at the naval operating base in Kodiak was an interesting experience. It was far from "ordinary life." We all got a little nuts up there after a while, an experience not too different from those of millions of military men all over the world for centuries. We were not with old friends and family and girls and wives and children—the life in which we were brought up. So we did things a bit differently in Kodiak.

I mention this as it has a bearing on the story I have to tell; how I felt and fared with the unusual things that happened in the service and especially in combat.

Life was different. It was different because there was now a new set of rules to follow to "get along" and to do my job.

I had enjoyed my years in high school, because I was curious about everything and enjoyed learning. I was in drama and in singing, in some sports and did some writing. I drank beer and really had a hell of a good time.

Life was different in Kodiak—likely different from what any of us were used to. In Kodiak, I had some friends and had some good times. I played some ping pong, went to some movies, went for walks, shot some craps, did some reading, and played cribbage. I got a perfect 29 hand playing with Jack DeNoble. I would go on walks with "Coco" Whittemore where we talked and talked of many things. I remember the better things, and though doing guard duty is far from exciting, I was there because I had asked for Alaska (and got it).

The weather was unusual—lots of wind and not as much snow as you might think. We were in the flow of the (warm) Japanese current, but the winds came down out of Siberia and the differences in temperature produced incessant meteorological turmoil.

The winds—"Williwaws" they were called—rarely stopped and never came from just one direction. And rain? We had rain! The weather was not dull. The duty could be called dull, but we were doing an important job there. Who else was going to watch the north Pacific?

It was highly expected that the enemy would jump across the Aleutian Islands to attack the United States' west coast.

As if to substantiate this expectation, the Japanese did occupy the outer islands of Adak and Amchitka. Who knows where else we'd be fighting them? Our commanders didn't let us privates in on planning the war, but we did learn that there were high-level thoughts of our going over through Siberian Russia to attack the Japanese homeland. The military had arranged for some classes in Russian to be taught at Kodiak and I was one of the willing students. Remember; I liked to learn. Nazdrovya!

It wasn't all dreary in Kodiak. Two of my fellow Marines, who were making money on the side tailoring uniforms in the attic of our two-story barracks, received transfer orders and put their business up for sale. A buddy, Dale Riggle, heard about this and told me (or maybe it was *me* who heard about it and told *him*—that was a long time ago!) In any case, Dale and I bought this little business. The sellers gave us a few minutes' instruction in tailoring and sold us their equipment (a sewing machine and some sewing supplies) as well as a record player and lots of records. We worked our little enterprise at night or at other odd hours and could listen to great popular music while we made money. Along with the business, we acquired an official price list blessedly approved by the Colonel, our commanding officer.

While we swept away boredom and listened to tunes, we made a tidy sum. You see, there was an official Navy Tailor Shop on the base, but their service was not known for its speed. You could get your new stripes sewn on there if you were willing to wait three months—or you could come to us, maybe pay a little more, but get it done right away. That way you could get a photo taken really quickly to send to the folks back home, so Mom would be even more proud and so your (ex-) girl friend would feel tons of guilt for just letting some 4F guy kiss her.

We also got in some interesting field experiences in Kodiak. Once the High Command arranged for us to carry out maneuvers with the Army. About five miles from our barracks and Fort Greely, the nearby Army base, there was a broad area called "Bell's Flats," just a few feet above high tide. The official plan for the exercise was that we Marines would march out to the flats and set up a line of defense to protect our bases against an "invading force" played by the Army. We would spend the whole night there in foxholes, or whatever we had prepared. The invaders would approach—by sea if necessary—to breach our "sturdy" defenses if they could; we would repel their attack if we could. At the conclusion of the exercise in the morning, we'd march the few miles back to camp.

So we Marines set up our defense perimeter and waited for the "invaders." As I recall, not a shot was fired, but I'm sure there were umpires out there in the dark to evaluate the performance of both sides.

In addition to the Army and the Marines, though, there was a third "contender"—weather. It was a dark, blowy, rainy night at Bell's Flats—the very stuff of Shakespeare. The official plan, a great way to train fighting men to do their job, turned out not so great from the standpoint of personal comfort. As the darkness wore on, we were doing our job right, defending our turf, but the third contender was winning. Few times can I recall being so physically miserable. We were thoroughly soaked and frozen. Regardless of whether we won or lost this engagement, an unhappier group of souls you would find nowhere.

Here in nature's miserable feast, man's imagination pictured the dilemma of choices—a chance with his favorite movie starlet or a good hot shower. Shakespeare couldn't have set the scene better. As each man pondered his options, with little to look forward to but a long, unhappy night—it must have been 11:00 p.m. and we were only beginning to feel the sting of this trial-of-men—word came from the colonel that our defending forces had proven equal to the task of protecting the island. The exercise had proven most worthy and was now "complete." Trucks would soon appear to take the weary defenders home to their barracks (complete with hot showers). Hundreds of cute starlets would go unsatisfied, and all the participating Marines suddenly fell in love with their colonel.

After I had been in Kodiak several months, the time came for the station armorer to return to the states and they needed a man to fill that job. That sounded interesting to me, so I applied for the position (called "Armorer and Artificer"—really) and got it. I enjoyed caring for the weapons and learning more about them. There was lots of scuttlebutt (rumors) about when and on what ship we would leave Kodiak. Every new ship that came in was a possible candidate in the rumor mill. Even an old Russian ship came in with a woman doctor on board—also spicy grist for the mill. Someone came up with the wild idea that we would be stateside bound on a destroyer! How about that for a good one? As it so happened, we finally left there on an old WWI four-stacker destroyer converted to a small cargo troopship, the USS *Fox*. We had a very interesting rough ride across the Gulf of Alaska in December. One day we steamed all day at 20 knots or so (probably the ship's limit), but got not one inch closer to Seattle!

Chapter 2

BACK IN THE STATES

Returning to the States was like going to heaven. I got to meet girls again. We were at Puget Sound Navy Yard (PSNY). Liberty in Seattle was great. I had left for Alaska before they had invented WACs and WAVEs and Lady Marines (sometimes called "BAMs"). These new species were happily in abundance in Seattle. The first or second night there I heard of a dance at the WAVEs barracks and arrived with my considerable interest showing. I was in Bremerton for several weeks, having many a wonderful time in Seattle. On the Black Ball Ferry Line over to Seattle, one could pick up a date if one didn't have one already. You'll recall, I had some money from Alaska (where could you spend it?), and found places ashore to buy good meals and good times.

A few days after arriving in Bremerton I was granted furlough (first in two years) to go home to Wisconsin to visit my family. I got to ride on an old train with poorly heated wooden coaches for five days across all of the dozen or so long western states. I had left no wife or girlfriend back home, but it was very nice to see my folks again. I was a hero to them even though I had not done a hell of a lot to win the war—yet.

Home to See My Grandmother

I have a favorite grandmother. My dad's mother, Ida Miller, had four children but only one grandchild: me. If I became a favorite grandchild, it's just a matter of statistics. She lived in Chicago, 185 miles south of where I was raised in Wisconsin. I would see her at least twice a year, and in the summer for a few weeks. She would take me to movies, on trolley rides, and rides all around Chicago on the elevated trains. This was the grandmother every kid should have. She was so very good to me. I loved her dearly.

When I went away to the war, she was concerned. She loved me very much and let me know it. We had so much fun together. We didn't need to talk too much about our closeness; we just enjoyed it. She would give me little gifts my parents wouldn't ever think of.

Although I didn't write to her, my father would send my letters home to her. In time, her health failed and my father moved her from Chicago to our home in Wisconsin. He figured that I had enough to worry about, so I never knew that she was ill and with my folks, where they could care for her in her declining health. I never knew about all this until later. As best she could, she followed the news and worried about her little grandson in the war. My father would show her my letters and keep her up to date with what information he had.

She was in steady decline while I was away. Of course, as I said, I knew nothing of this. My folks took the best of care they and medical science could render and she savored each little bit of information about me.

When I returned from Asia after the War, safe again, I phoned home to tell my folks I was back in the United States. My father told his mother this. She smiled...and then died.

Chapter 3

JOINING THE FIFTH MARINE DIVISION

I returned to the Pugent Sound Navy Yard, in Bremerton, looking forward to interesting new assignments. I didn't wait long. The word came to pack up the old seabag again (I was getting good at this) and jump on the train for California. I was going to join a "line company" (about 150 Marines, the guys who do the fighting) with the Fifth Marine Division, then forming at Camp Pendleton—a big place in southern California.

In Alaska, we did our jobs as assigned and on days off from the guard detail we had "school" to learn more of what we needed to know about military matters. But, at least speaking for myself, we didn't get a lot of physical exercise. That really wasn't an important consideration—until now!

Our new division was being assembled with a few men from Alaska, some paratroopers and Solomon Islands veterans, and probably some "boots," too. And we had some sergeants with lots of experience in the Corps. This was certainly a blessing as these were the guys in the know who really ran things. They had the valuable experience most of us didn't have.

Thinking back now of all those guys at that time, I get sentimental. This would be my "family" for quite a while. At the time, I doubt if many of us knew how close we would get.

We were about to get the training of our lives. It began with our company commander, Captain "Whoozis" (sorry, I've forgotten his name), and lots of running up and down those dusty roads out there in the hills, and running up and down the hills as well. Our captain, who ran with us, of course, had been an Olympic runner. (Weren't we the lucky ones?) While we poor suckers, who were far from being in shape, struggled to get enough wind carrying rifles and packs while our legs were falling off, old Cap'n Whoozis flowed along like the breeze. For him it was a walk in the park; for us it was murder.

There was much more than physical fitness going on here. While I can only speak knowledgeably for myself, I dare to speak for others in saying we were all slowly becoming well-oiled cogs in a big organized machine. This would pay off later in staying alive.

In this book, I am more interested in telling you of feelings and impressions than about bald facts of war. The sensation of camaraderie becomes more intense as time goes by working daily with these men. The sense of "peer approval" looms large as why we do what we do to "get the job done." There's a great deal of that: "Get the job done, good, right and fast."

Again, speaking for myself, but now with a degree, graduate work and experience in psychology, I can attest to the weight this great motivator has on one to do "more than one can do." None of us wished to be seen as slacking, in any way, from the duties that had now become inborn religion to us. I guess this is the stuff that makes Marines Marines.

Captain Whoozis told us that when we ran the roads and hills with him, we would *not* fall out of the formation unless we passed out or our legs broke. I never saw a single man fall out, even though I know just about all of them were in as much pain as I.

It would be extremely humiliating to faint or trip or in any other way step beneath one's own pride as a man and a Marine. This is important shit! This is what glues it all together. You will hear me talk more about this same attitude later when things get even more serious.

Another one of the "rules" that seems to make it all work is that every Marine is first a rifleman. All those going through boot camp must "qualify" on the rifle range—do it until they get a good score. I don't really know how the system makes it happen, but all Marines get the necessary training in basic riflemanship—even if you're going to be a cook or truck driver or clerk or whatever, you are first a rifleman.

The company's Table of Organization (the "T.O.") included one job for an armorer. I had learned that trade in Kodiak and had been promoted to the rank of corporal with Ordnance as my occupational specialty, so I got the job. My duties as the company armorer were to provide a suitable storage place for the company weapons and replacement parts as well as a place to effect needed repairs. This didn't mean that I wasn't also a rifleman. The rules called for each man to re-qualify on the rifle range at intervals to keep his skills up to snuff.

I was assigned to the company headquarters platoon, which consisted of the company commander, the executive officer, first sergeant, cooks, quartermasters, clerks, and so forth. In battle, my usual duties would be suspended, as would those of some others. We would become "spare parts," to be used wherever needed—as messengers, litter bearers, or riflemen on the line as necessary.

In addition to my armored duties, my possible future as a "spare part" got me selected to go to a variety of "schools" to learn about such duties as transport quartermaster (how to load and unload a ship for combat and other purposes) and demolition trainer (how to teach others in the company some details of the various demolition devices and equipment). I admit that I felt honored to be chosen to receive and later pass on to others this important knowledge, as well as to serve as librarian of some of the manuals and other official information.

But I was still a rifleman. I trained in the field to acquire and improve many of the skills I had been taught at one stage of the training or another, I learned to "snoop and poop" (our favorite colorful expression for working one's way through the brush unnoticed) and to worm along on my belly—with rifle—to be as one with the earth and minimize exposure to the bullets that flew just above the head and body both in practice and in combat. I also learned how to be a part of a team that would direct fire into the aperture of a gun emplacement (to keep the gunners inside too busy defending themselves to spot a trained Marine creeping up around to the side, starting a fuse, and flinging into that opening a satchel charge or some other noisy explosive to obliterate them. (A satchel charge is similar to a schoolboy's book bag containing several pounds of TNT instead of books. There's a strap on the bag useful for carrying and flinging.)

These were pertinent realities at which we needed to be good. I needed this practice at these skills to help get the job done when this was for real in the future. So being a "spare part" was an interesting challenge I accepted—as if I had a choice.

Another interesting and challenging part of our training was learning how to board a ship, with all our necessary gear; and how to load into landing craft and assault a real island out there in the water. We did this many times, and if we didn't get expert at it, we at least had the experience and were not too surprised when the day came that we had to do it for real.

And that was truly the plan.

To Hawaii for More Serious Training

After several months at Camp Pendleton, the Fifth Division went down to the docks in company formations, ready to get loaded onto ships bound for Camp Tarawa in the highlands of the big island Hawaii. Well, you know how it is in company formations, all the platoons together and awaiting the word to pick up the seabags, load on the trucks and get over on to the ship. This all takes a little time.

Hal Wolfe and Tom Dahldorf were both in the first platoon, and to pass the time they did some singing together. They had begun getting together and singing back at the tent camp at Pendleton, but I didn't learn that until later. Having done some singing myself, both in a quartet in grade school and in my high-school chorus, when I heard them singing during the wait at the docks I went over and joined in.

Hal would start singing the melody of some old song and Tom would add some tenor harmony. And they sounded pretty darn good to me. I wandered over and threw in some baritone notes and a bit of bass now and then when needed. Finally the trucks came and we got busy with the business of getting aboard and getting organized on the ship.

With little to do while going to Hawaii, we got together and did some more singing. We knew we needed a bass singer and somehow soon found Ted Pyle. Or, maybe he found us. We were really singing reasonably well, we thought, and were sure having fun. For a while, at least, the war seemed far away as our greatest problems were to make good harmony and enjoy it when it came out right.

One of the ship's crew who handled recreational and other activities passed the word that there would be a talent show on board in a couple of days and anyone who wanted to perform was welcome. So, in addition to several other acts, we sang two songs.

The ship was blacked out at night, part of wartime precautions. In the dark, we'd be out on the deck singing. We had no music to follow, we just sang what sounded good—ear music. Occasionally someone would stop by to listen. On one particular evening, after we had finished a song, a high squeaky voice in the dark commented, "That was some fine barbershop singing, fellas." He came closer and introduced himself.

"I'm Tim Webber. There's an organization of men who sing this kind of music. It's called the Society for the Preservation and Encouragement of Barber Shop Quartet Singing in America— SPEBSQSA—and there's even a chapter in the Fifth Division. You can sign up and be a member for fifty cents a year."

He got our money, signed us up, and we were "barbershoppers." Just like that. None of us had ever heard the term "barbershop music" before, and now we were members!

We docked at Hilo, on the big island of Hawaii, and boarded trucks for the trip to the broad plateau near the volcanic lava fields. Located there was Camp Tarawa on a very large cattle ranch with plenty of room for both us and the cattle to do our respective "things." We continued training as we had done in the States, but after "recall," the bugle call that marked the close of the business day, we'd go to chow and then amuse ourselves as we wished.

Often in the evenings and on weekends with little else to do, we'd get together and sing. We got pretty good at this, and we even had a name: "The Tune Timers." Occasionally we were asked to sing at some event or function and even got to sing at some distant village church functions. There wasn't a lot of entertainment available up in them hills, you know.

We went to chapter meetings of SPEBSQSA right there in camp Tarawa. Our quartet sang and we listened to others sing and had lots of fun. The chapter president was Bob Crosby, who in civilian life was bandleader of "The Bobcats" and brother to Bing. There were a couple of dozen guys in the chapter, including the secretary, Tim Webber, as well as General Keller E. Rockey, the Division Commander, who turned out to be a barbershop lover.

Near our camp up there on that broad plateau was a "steakhouse" (and one other house) at a lonesome intersection of two roads that maybe didn't really go anywhere. At the steakhouse, you could get something a bit different from what sold well in the chow hall. And one could get a beer. (Beer was readily available at the camp.) It was a nice place to socialize and sing. On one of our occasional trips over there, in came Tim Webber with a communication from headquarters SPEBSQSA and a musical arrangement of a barbershop song! Up to this time, we had never seen a barbershop arrangement, with notes for each of the four voice parts. We just sang "by ear" whatever sounded good to us.

At one of the chapter meetings we heard of a quartet contest that we could enter. SPEBSQSA was organized into about fifteen large districts of several states and provinces each, and each year the Society held district contests as well as an international convention that included contests. Because several quartets (and even chapters) had recently formed in the Pacific region, the Society had now designated a new Pacific District, which would soon be holding a contest in

Honolulu. We were excited. We knew nothing about this stuff, but it was sure more fun than our "day jobs." The Marine Corps, always with an eye to good publicity, sent our quartet to the contest in Honolulu. It was held in a hall at the naval base, with about a half dozen quartets competing before a panel of judges that included the mayor of Honolulu, the base commandant, and maybe a couple of musicians. By dint of good fortune, and lots of practice, the Tune Timers were pronounced winners in the contest. We thought we sang well, but what did we know? We had a lot of fun. By today's judging standards, we'd be well down on the list.

SPEBSQSA's next international convention was scheduled for July 1945 in Detroit, and the Marine Corps was planning to send our quartet, the Pacific District champions, to take part. But by the time of the convention, the events I'll discuss in coming chapters had left one of our members dead and another we knew not where, and there was more war ahead; we didn't get to make the trip.

Before we left Hawaii for our coming battle, those who wished were granted shore leave in Honolulu. I started out to go there alone, but at the dock soon met some guys I knew and discussed plans for a good time. We all decided that we would like a good meal (spell that "steak") at a nice restaurant. After being up in the hills for a while with no place to spend our pay, we had enough bucks for a fine time on the town. We were in general agreement on the plan and hailed a taxi. We told the driver we wanted to go to the best restaurant in town, and we got what we asked for. Boy, what a beautiful place! This was Lai Chai. If I haven't spelled it right, it's close, and I absolutely agree with the driver's judgment that it was the very best.

The restaurant was one of the classiest I had ever seen, either in person, or in the movies, or even in my fantastic imagination. It was spacious and partly open-air with many rooms joined by graceful archways. The decor was some manner of elegant Chinese, with tropical plants and works of oriental art; the whole atmosphere of the most tasteful thought and design for men and women of quality. (It isn't that we lacked any neatness in our military dress; we wouldn't have been allowed off the ship had we been deficient in deportment or attire. Still, as proud we were to be fine Marines, gentlemen all, from upstanding middle-class families, we could almost consider ourselves to be a bit out of our customary element.)

We were escorted to a fine table by a most professional maitre d' whose polish was underscored by his gentle and understanding treatment of his four gentlemen a bit awash in another society. The table had exotic flowers and table decoration soon to be put to shame by our server, the most beautiful Chinese woman in the world. She wore a flowered skirt, memorable for its sole flaw: a three-foot slit. We were treated as royalty, and even the large bill of fare handed to each of us was as tastefully designed as all the rest of our surroundings.

My three friends, Gus, "Big Red," and "Shifty," were from the motor pool. The only one whose full name I recall was Gus Midthun, a wonderful down-home guy from Illinois with a wife and two kids. I do remember that Shifty's moniker referred more to vehicle gears than to evasive eyeballs.

We four were in one of the finest restaurants around, really looking for the biggest steak in the islands but trying to decipher the descriptions in our hands. Gus finally zeroed in on the most expensive item, "sumthin', sumthin', sumthin' with beef." He figured that for the (considerable) price, this must be the steak he craved. The rest of us, likewise befuddled by the strange items, took a stab at ordering whatever in the Chinese description seemed to strike our fancy.

"Fancy" is the word to describe what came from the chef; nothing like we had ever seen before. What Gus received was a beautiful huge bowl of exotic herbs, fancy leaves, and flowers, with a light dressing of understated elegance, delicately redolent of eastern spices with fine little nuts—and several small pieces of select beef!

Gus was fit to be tied. This poor guy had been prepared to spend a month's pay on the biggest steak around, and got only a very fancy disappointment. But we were all pretty much in the same boat; we looked at each other, laughed, and made the best of it. After all, we were very truly in the very best place in town, maybe the whole Pacific. The folks back home would never believe this.

Chapter 4

THE CRUISE TO THE ISLAND

The time came when we were told to pack our seabags again and we went down to the docks in Hilo to board a ship. This time, we were sure, it was serious business. Our accommodations down below were bunks about two feet above or below one another. We got resigned to new surroundings and perhaps most important of all, found out where we were headed: Iwo Jima, which means "Sulphur Island." There were numerous "schools" up on deck with maps and models of the island, plus photos of the beaches and our landing areas.

We were told about our country's need for this island, about its rugged defenses and about our own strategies of attack. We needed this island, 800 miles from the Japanese homeland, as a base for fighter planes to escort our bombers on missions. Heretofore, the bombers had had no fighter protection for their all-important destructive attacks on the enemy's home. In addition, Iwo Jima would be a much nearer place for damaged bombers to land if they could not make it back to their bases on Tinian or other islands.

Knowing where we were bound and having more details as to our specific mission there made us all feel better, I guess, even if not a little more nervous and anxious. We were told that the eight-square-mile island, rather dumbbell-shaped, had been two volcanoes joined by a narrow waist a few hundred yards wide. The smaller southern end of the island was the extinct volcano, Suribachi, over 500 feet high, while the older, much larger northernmost part of the island was worn and weathered to be flatter with some rugged rocky terrain and some hills.

Suribachi had many caves, lookout posts and buried gun emplacements. The northern part of the island had two airfields and a third under construction. There were many cliffs surrounding Iwo and two beaches at the narrow part, the "waist" between north and south. The beach facing east was short and narrow and steep. It was volcanic sand, a fine sand with which we would deal later.

The west beach was longer, broad and gently-sloped—a much easier landscape for our beach party. We learned later that they expected us on the west beach and probably had all sorts of underwater obstacles waiting to tear the bottoms out of our assault boats and snag troops wading ashore.

Two Marine divisions would assault the island, with one division in floating reserve. (One Marine division, ready for combat with attached units, is over 20,000 men. A reinforced regiment would be over 5,000). The plan was to gain control in three days. With another seven days of mopping-up, the Army would land and take over. That was the announced plan. Our regiment, the 28th Marines, was to land on the steeper east beach at a narrow part of the island, proceed inland a few hundred yards straight west and establish its position more or less midway across the island.

The strategy was to split the island in two, with the 28th Marines attacking Suribachi, the high ground with many caves and guns—a most advantageous view of the whole island allowing the enemy to pinpoint gunfire wherever they pleased, as long as they held the mountain. The remainder of the Fifth Division, the Fourth Division, and soon after, the Third Division, would press to the north along the coastline and up through the airfields. That was very tough and bloody going for them. Although our bombardment had rendered the two airfields useless, the plan was to gain control and repair them for our own use.

It was nice to know the plan. Our officers did all they could to describe and explain the situation so we knew what we had to do and why. This was a most important operation both strategically and psychologically.

The Japanese considered this island to be part of their homeland and were dedicated to defend it to the last man. We were told that they had been fortifying this place for some years with thick reinforced concrete gun emplacements, machine gun nests, mortars deep in pits for their own defense and hundreds of caves, a few of them five or six floors down. There were over twenty thousand troops there to greet us and we were led to believe that they would put up one hell of a fight. We had learned from many news reports that the Japanese were dedicated and tenacious soldiers who would fight to the last man. These were our hosts.

For our part of the grand plan, Air Force bombers had been visiting the island daily for a month lacing it with high explosives to do what damage they could to the strong fortifications as well as letting on that we had strength and were going to be doing something important there soon. As the big day approached, our battleships and cruisers spent three days of heavy shelling of known defenses to further "soften up" this important fortress.

While we were being brought up to date on the plan, our growing convoy was steaming full speed ahead. We had been conditioned and trained and psychologically readied for what was about to happen.

Early in the morning of D-Day, February 19, 1945, we were roused from a short fitful slumber. Methodically we rolled out and went to as great a breakfast as you would ever get on a troop ship. We mused that this would be for many "The Last Supper." But we had work to do and were almost eager to get on with it, whatever it might hold. We gathered our gear and went up on deck.

The First Look At War—Boy!

As we appeared on deck hundreds of eyes swung to the west to see where we were. This sight clings to my memory as clear as my mother's face or my first look at my first-born. There it lay, a few thousand yards to the west, looking like the photographs and the 3-D model we had seen—but not "just like."

The island lay there out in front of all of us—not peaceful and quiet, but shivering and smoking from dust of explosions, smoking from naval bombardment, smoking from fires set by napalm. It almost seemed to rock now and then as big explosions shook both the island and us.

With both fear and excitement each Marine must have said to himself, "Holy shit!" or his equivalent. We could see Higgins boats, the smaller landing craft, near us circling as they assembled themselves into their waves to scoot to the beach when ordered. We saw wave after wave of landing craft hit the beach to discharge their human and steel cargo. We saw disabled boats and stuff in the water and we saw trucks blown up on the beach. We saw hell and consternation as men, weapons, tanks and supplies struggled onto the beach.

Prior to the first waves, the naval guns and planes pounded the hell out of the beach to soften it up as well as they could. As an ironic twist, the first few waves, including tanks, met little resistance on the beach. As they slowly moved inland the naval gunfire provided a rolling barrage ahead of them to quiet the enemy as much as possible. But the Japanese had hundreds of gun and mortar positions all over the place and had the coordinates of any place on the island so they could provide fire most anywhere, especially with wonderful lookout positions on Suribachi.

After the first few waves that beach got hot. The chirps of scores of bullets never left us. Fire seemed to come from everywhere. Bodies, wounded and dead, shared the beach with equipment disabled and busy. Explosions and smoke were everywhere. And our wave loaded up to get into the game.

In our boat we were told to keep our heads down, beneath the gunwales. Except for an occasional dangerous peek out, we saw only the guys we were with and maybe even felt the firm hand of our Lord on our shoulder. As if we didn't have enough on our plate, the diesel fumes tended to make us all a little sick. My friend Virg puked all over, but probably wasn't the only one. After a nervous century, we stopped circling and headed for the shore. There was no backing out of this one. Duty and curiosity reigned over fear and ignorance now. We wanted to get there and get on with the job.

The first waves hit the beach around 9:00 a.m. As the beach heated up, so I'm told, the waves around the 8th and 9th just about disappeared from massive enemy gunfire. Then, our generals found more distinctly where that fire was coming from and directed attacks against at least some of it.

We were in the 18th wave (of many) and landed around 12:30 p.m. If that sounds as if we landed along with the USO, the Stage Door Canteen and the Bob Hope Show—not so! We were greeted by a hail of bullets and mortar shells and maybe some rockets. We felt the LCVP crunch up on the sand; the ramp dropped, the beach was there. The war began for me.

Chapter 5

THE LANDING

Two dozen men rolled out of that boat as one and headed for the midway point of the island as we had seen on the map. Some of us made it only a few feet. I scrambled forward wishing I were much less heavily laden. (And for a moment perhaps, wishing I were elsewhere.)

Where the sand was wet, down by the water, it had some consistency, and was a bit solid, but where it was dry, this stuff was like talcum powder. Trying to run, or even walk, was really tough going; especially when "going" was the way to stay alive. And, to make it worse, the beach went up! I would grow up a lot in the next hours. By sheer fear, I plunged forward through this stuff; about fifty feet away I saw a shell hole about eight feet deep and dove into it.

Bullets were knocking off the sand on one edge of this 20-foot wide hole and lining the other side with lead, but if you stayed low in the hole you had a chance of being missed. There was already an occupant, I saw—none other than our company gunnery sergeant Joe Whalen, affectionately called "Gunny," who likewise wanted to stay alive. This man had many years in the Corps and several battles under his belt. He was going to be my ticket to old age. For all the training we had with live ammo and training films and all that, I still had nothing to compare this with.

Help was not only on the way; help was here! This man knew the ropes and I was eager to listen. He could have put things in perspective for me by saying something like, "You know, Miller, this is a walk in the park compared to Pelican Island last year." Even with all the shit that was happening, that would have made me feel better.

But that was not what he said. The Gunny knew what he was doing and he was going to get both of us out of there alive. He told me to look up and notice our planes coming down the island strafing areas near the base of Suribachi. They also dropped napalm bombs (liquid fire) on gun emplacements there, and every time the Japanese saw them approaching they would withdraw into their caves. Then, much of the gunfire stopped for 10 or 15 seconds, and that was the time to leg it to the next hole or other cover. So I watched, and he watched, and sure enough, when the planes began their run, the firing let up (didn't stop, mind you, but let up) and we made a dash for the next cover—however well you could "dash" in that powdery stuff. But we had the highest possible motivation.

It took a while, but we finally got to the solid ground above the beach, keeping covered as much as we could, and made our way to the company rendezvous point. At the company headquarters fox-hole, the first sergeant was very glad to see the Gunny as they were old buddies from way back. And I guess he was glad to see me too, so he could cross me off his "missing" list.

Now our company troops who had survived the beach were gathering and we were getting ready to consolidate our position according to the plan.

The Thicket

I may be the only one to call this place "the thicket," but that describes it to me. Just south of us, a thousand yards away, was the base of Suribachi. Between us and the base was a wilderness of brush and blown-up junk. We were getting a fair amount of distress from that area and some tanks rolled in there shooting and squirting fiery napalm at enemy positions.

I saw Tom, from Milwaukee, crouching by the side of a tank for some protection and recalled him saying back in camp that he liked pain. That's what he said. As I watched, a spray of bullets hit him and ricocheted off the tank, painfully tearing up his body.

Our company's position for the next couple of days was in a fairly clear area just north of the thicket, near the remains of a couple of coastal guns that had been pounded by air or naval bombardment. Busted hunks of concrete were all around, as well as lengths of steel reinforcing rods and what was left of canvas gun covers. We were here for about three days as elements of our forces continued to work on the enemy's positions in the thicket and on the mountain.

The word was that our regiment would be mounting an assault on Suribachi once we had better cleaned out the thicket and silenced some of the caves and gun positions on the mountain. Many of the caves on the mountain had guns mounted on rails, so that the Japanese could roll them out to fire and roll them back inside for protection when we concentrated return fire of some sort on the cave mouths.

Early in the war, when I was a boot and getting trained on the firing range, the rifles issued were Springfield '03s (bolt-action single-shot weapons loaded with a clip of five 30-caliber bullets). They were well-made, dependable, accurate rifles that had served well in WWI, and I'm sure our factories still had tooling to build them in quantity. The Springfield couldn't shoot as fast as more modern weapons, though, and the U.S. War Department decided that for this war we needed more individual firepower, especially for close combat. We had some B.A.R.s (Browning Automatic Rifles), but they were heavy and somewhat cumbersome—not what the men on the line needed to cope with an enemy like the Japanese, who among other things had many light machine guns.

The powers that be eventually chose, as the new official rifle of the Army and the Marine Corps, a gas-operated semiautomatic rifle invented by a Canadian-born engineer named Garand. (A semiautomatic weapon fires a shot for each pull of the trigger, without the shooter having to work the bolt to load another cartridge.) I don't know the details of how the Garand design was chosen over any competitors, but I'm sure that factory production speed was no less important than bullets per minute: We needed lots of rifles fast. What all this has to do with me is that the new M-1 (the U.S. military name for the Garand rifle) was reaching Camp Pendleton just about the time I got out of boot camp and started coaching at the rifle range. As a result I was instructing boots in the firing and operation of a new weapon that wasn't the same one on which I had learned to shoot.

In the field, that is, in the dirt and the grime of practice maneuvers as well as the battlefield, it was my personal experience that this new weapon had the weak spot of not reloading well if it was dirty or the atmosphere dusty. I had more faith in the '03. It was used by snipers, and I felt it was more accurate at a distance. Newly arrived on Iwo Jima, I wasn't in any close-quarters fighting where a gun that squirted bullets would be an advantage. There were weapons of all kinds lying about abandoned by their wounded or dead owners, so getting a new "piece" was pretty easy, and I picked up a Springfield. It and I became good friends.

In the three or four days we looked at Suribachi with the gunfire coming from many spots there, I had occasion to limber up my '03, and with the help of some tracer bullets to know just where I was firing at several hundreds yard range, I took pot shots at where some of these muzzle flashes appeared on the mountain. I felt I was adding to the general effort.

Home Away From Home

One night, it may have been on the second or third night while we held our position there looking at Suribachi, we experienced a light rain. Now, this was February, but we were also in the Pacific Ocean at about 26 degrees north latitude (about the same latitude as Havana), and that's semi-tropical at least. I would bet they never saw snow on Iwo. On this rainy night, three of us—"Sergeant Bill," Corporal Means and I—got ready to dig in for the night. Foxholes were the accepted procedure. Some of Iwo was hard volcanic rock, but there was a lot of sand and rubble about, too. We were beginning to get some shelling and aerial bombing in our area, so a deepish hole would be good. The digging with our shovels was pretty easy and we got down at least three feet in a good sized area six or seven feet long to be comfortable and reasonably safe. Now here is where Yankee ingenuity, desire for personal comfort, and what's available came in. Remember the steel reinforcing rods and the canvas gun covers? Well, bending the rods into arches and putting the canvas overhead made some pretty comfy quarters.

We really did get some shelling that night, and if I'm not mistaken, some planes came over to bomb us too. I witnessed a pyrotechnic display the likes of which no city's Fourth of July celebrations could possibly match. There were thousands of guns on ships out there all pumping out anti-aircraft fire. It wasn't until after we had left the island that I saw photos of the armada of ships we had there. I don't know the number, but at least hundreds of ships were there around the island. And when enemy planes came out to bomb us there were all those white streaks of tracers heading up from ships to answer the boldness of those bombing planes. Yes, I can now recall seeing photos of that night barrage. What a picture! More than I can tell in words, and more than you can imagine if you weren't there!

"Sergeant Bill" succumbed to the stress of it all and went a bit berserk; by way of the battalion aid station, he went out to a hospital ship and from there maybe headed back to the States. And that's not all that happened that night around our cozy hotel. As we looked out in the light drizzle, we saw a jeep about twenty-five feet away, with its driver looking for some shelter from the rain. He decided to climb under the jeep to get out of the elements. A while later, we heard a shell hit real close and looked out to see a ball of smoke where the jeep had just been. The war was getting closer.

Chapter 6

QUIETING THE MONSTER

Another Big Day was coming soon. The word circulated that some unit of our regiment would be assaulting Suribachi the next day. We, including the Air Force and the Navy, had really been doing quite a number on that mountain, and it was now somewhat quieter than before, but still a real (and psychological) threat.

It was always there! It was ever a cause for concern that they could see us easily. Each morning when we woke up, it was there staring at us and dangerous. (Even after we had quieted it, we could see it from any spot on the island, and the same shivers of fear echoed again in my body.)

I would have been pleased and honored if our company had been chosen to make the hike up those slopes, but that wasn't the way the ball bounced. Another unit of the 28th started up the next day and reported very light resistance. We kept watching the goings-on and could see our guys trudging up the east side of the mountain, with only occasional gunfire punctuating their ascent. We saw men reach the top, and I think I saw several of them waving to us down below.

Shortly thereafter, we saw men struggling up there doing something; then saw our flag go up with our men in their now memorable pose. Thousands of us cheered, even though neither the battle nor the war was over. I'm pleased to have been there for that moving and historic moment. Suribachi, threat to us that it had been, was a threat no more. But we had lots of acres to claim yet and lots of friends and buddies to lose before we could whip up a real cheer.

The Road North

After we took Suribachi, I assumed that the southern part of the island was reasonably secure except for possibly a few rat-holes we hadn't found and flushed out yet. It was time for our company to move on; that meant to start moving north with just about everyone else. What we had taken was very important, but only a small percentage of the total acreage. There was much left to do.

We started north by finishing the trip west, going a few hundred more yards to the west beach. This was the broad smooth beach with the gentle grade. It would have been great for swimming and a picnic under other circumstances.

We found an abandoned gun emplacement, an impressive edifice with very thick concrete walls buried under several feet of earth. Inside, we saw a large gun, about 88mm, I guess, mounted in an aperture (slit) that allowed a broad view of the beach. From that vantage point, they could have knocked out many landing craft and vehicles as they approached or rode on the beach. There were many other similar guns and emplacements guarding the beach where we had chosen not to land.

We had crossed the island at its narrowest and now headed north up this only somewhat safer beach.

I don't know what happened next, but I stepped on something that threw me up ass over teakettle into the air. I got up, checked limbs and digits and brushed myself off to get back in the game. Aside from being a bit dizzy, and my left leg feeling funny, I thought I was OK. A couple of buddies ran over to check on me. They offered to help me to the battalion aid station, but I didn't see the need of it. I still don't know what it was, but I went on.

Walking up that beach with little cover wasn't the greatest idea in the world, but that's where we were for a while. Then someone shouted and pointed up in the air. A couple of hundred feet up there was a cylindrical object, several feet long, sailing toward us. We scrambled from where it looked like it might land. I had just seen my first Japanese rocket; not some scientifically streamlined design with fins, but for all the world like a large water tank tumbling ungracefully end over end. It landed with a lot of racket behind us up the beach. That is when our little beach stroll ended. We headed a bit more inland to continue north. Further up the island later on, I was to see some miniature railroad rails and a couple of little dollies with wheels to fit the tracks—likely some of the rocket launching gear.

As we proceeded north on the western side of the island, we had cover of sorts at times. At other times, gunfire started in our area and we scrambled for whatever protection we could find in a hurry. At all times there was gunfire everywhere. We could hear sporadic, then intense gunfire to our right in the vicinity of airfield number one. Our guys advancing over on the airfield had better terrain for running than those of us in the sand or in the rubble that was everywhere.

But many guns were aimed at the airfield. When Marines tried to cross, machine guns came to life; and when men hit the deck to "flatten out," the Japs would throw in "daisy cutters" with their mortars. This unique military implement was a mortar shell with an attached rod projecting forward from the nose. When the shell came down (almost vertically—mortars fired in a high trajectory), the rod set off the charge a fraction of a second early, spreading shrapnel in all directions about a foot above the ground. Men nearby, even lying flat, would get a strong dose of steel.

Some days we would get a couple of hundred yards ahead, then get orders to "hold" until necessary to move out again. Other units were also heading north and spreading out as necessary to gain a few more acres of land for us. At times we ran into a lot of enemy resistance and had fire fights to clean them out and move forward. Other times we were the target of artillery or mortar fire and we'd need to move fast or seek cover until our counter-battery fire zeroed in on them. We would move slowly at times and wait, or consolidate our position and hold there for a few hours, or perhaps days, as other units moved forward when they could.

There were a few times when there was less going on in our sector, while we sure could hear a great deal of war going on elsewhere. The enemy was not giving up a square foot without a fight. We would lose men to wounds or to the grim reaper every day. We paid for the acreage in blood. This was the way it went—some days were busier than others. I had a chance at times to reflect on how different this was from getting across (and up) the beach. Many times I trembled thinking how I would really not want to cross that beach again.

Chapter 7

HOW IT FELT INSIDE TO BE IN THE BATTLE THAT WAS OUTSIDE

The fear and uncertainty we all knew, and the ways we kept ourselves "together," would certainly vary from man to man, but I am sure that how I felt can't have been too different from the emotions of other Marines there. This was a feeling nothing like anything I had ever known back home, or even back in the places we trained. None of the times I waited for my father to give me hell for some misbehavior, none of the times when a teacher (or boss, or policeman) was about to rain on me, did I ever feel anything but faintly like this. I can't say I felt "scared," in a normal sense of the term, but there was a tension that was always there.

I almost chuckle now because I have reread that last sentence to myself several times and each time I "hear" a different voice declare, "And those were his last words!"

Death was no stranger to us. You could literally smell death. We didn't breathe air; we breathed death and gun smoke and burning flesh. Death was all around, for at any moment a noise could ring out and someone would drop. This happened all the time. Death was a way of life here and we had to find ways within ourselves to handle that.

We had become used to that gnawing feeling of fear and anxiety, if those are the real terms for this. It was as though our emotions had "shifted gears." We had a new idea of what "normal" was. Different guys handled this in different ways, but I have never heard any veteran of combat say he was at ease about the whole thing. Bullshit! Some handled this mental state better than others. Some sought solace in a bible or prayer, be it spoken out loud or just quietly within. Some seemed at times to rise above it all with a "what the hell" attitude, but I saw little of that. So I don't even know if "fear" is the word. I had not known this feeling before, nor have I known it since.

Women are said to tell their husbands, "You'll never know what it's like to have a baby." It's just as true for us who have been in battle to say, "Baby, you'll never know how it feels to be scared so shitless you can't even feel scared any more!" Speaking for myself, and maybe for a few more, I'm sure that we entered a different "inside world," where feeling this way was "normal," and that we wouldn't know of any other way to feel until we were miles and months away from Iwo.

Stories are rife of veterans who never did rid themselves of ghosts or nightmares or other hangers-on of the horror of war. Somehow it can seem more horrible years later when you find out how real people live and think.

Millions of fighters have felt something like this over the centuries. And I've heard grizzled veterans of many campaigns repeat similar responses to the challenges of battle. I must admit, however, that at least a few of these disclosures were eased out of the vet's psyche by Jack Daniels or a few beers. Without beating the patriotic drum too loudly or getting too psychoanalytical, I would point out that the Marines' pride and esprit de corps (not to disparage the esprit of any other corps) have a constructive role to play in this, gluing the group together so that there is no feeling of, "I gotta do this all alone."

Consider, also, the maxim that "Marines don't leave their wounded"—here again there is a higher calling at work. In all the time training together, you not only learn and practice the "plays," you learn from experience that those other guys are there to help you, and you are all there to get the job done—together. This is an important cog in the wheel of an important total effort together. It is powerful stuff. And this is some of the stuff that helps keep a man from drowning out there in a sea of bullets and artillery shells.

The Road North, Continued

For a while we followed a "road" that was no more than wheel ruts worn in grass. I had seen the name of a village on a map and I thought this road led through it. When we got there, there was no village. If it had ever been there at all, nothing remained of it but rubble. A month of aerial bombardment and naval shelling had turned concrete gun emplacements to big and small chunks of concrete and busted up the rock hills and landscape into golfball- and football-sized rubble—and all other sizes too.

Even though Suribachi was ours and no longer a great observation spot for them to see what we were up to, there were some hills yet in the northern part of the island, particularly Hill 362. (Who measures these things?) From there the enemy had a great point of vantage on us at the moment our H Company was on the move up this road. We were in two somewhat "casual" columns so as to make less of a target than neat files of men.

After we had walked for a while, the company first sergeant halted us and called, "Fall out." This meant we could sit or find something at the side of the road to lean back against and relax a bit. I looked at the rocks, wires, trees and other junk at the side of the road and said to myself, "Boy, I'd hate to have to make my way through all that mess." Somehow I found a place to make myself comfortable, but just as I was beginning to enjoy this little break, I heard mortar rounds whistle on their way. The enemy, on the higher ground ahead, must have seen our column advancing; now they were firing at us, possibly aiming for a little knot of leaders who were conferring just ahead of me. Without a moment's delay, I headed for the spot I thought "impenetrable" minutes before, and I wasn't the only one. I'm not sure how any of us did it, but I sailed over it as explosions behind urged me to do what I thought one couldn't do. Another "experience."

After the first few mortar rounds hit, our counter-battery fire, coming from a bit to the rear, zeroed in on the location of the enemy's guns and had a quieting effect on the barrage. Or it could have been one of our great rocket trucks.

When the barrage had calmed, we went back to where our company had been, where some of ours were now lying dead and wounded. One of the dead was our first sergeant, whose head and brains were in his helmet in one place and his body in another. He had never been one of my favorite people, as he could be irascible at times, but I never wanted to see him this way. We lost a good leader.

The company gunnery sergeant, the same one who helped me get off the beach and was now the leading NCO in our company, came to me. "Miller," he asked, "Will you collect the first sergeant's personal items, especially his little notebook and that fountain pen that meant so much to him?" I said I would.

I didn't feel all that good about rummaging about in a dead man's things—this man who had been alive and guiding us a few minutes before. He was a good man and did his job of running things very well. I felt badly that I ever had any thoughts but respect for this man. I gathered all I had been charged to find and gave them to the gunny, and tried in my own way to tell him that I was sorry his friend was dead. I believe our company commander, Captain Carl Bachman, a fine leader, was killed at the same time.

Our officers were, for the most part, very good men who had been to college and were responsible for understanding the "grand plan." But it was the sergeants and other NCOs who really ran things—right up there where the bullets were and the men were.

From that spot we moved further north, regrouped and began to set our line for the night, not as exposed as we had been on the road.

A Field of Rocks

Later during our advance (only once during these days did we move back) we came upon another field of rubble, relatively flat, about the size of three baseball diamonds. There was no brush, no big hunks of rubble, but there were lots of jagged rocks the size of bricks and footballs. With no cover there, we needed to move quickly, but still carefully. However, this field didn't turn out to be so easy. We had to cross it, and we knew this offered a nice clean shot for machine guns.

The only good answer was to run as fast as we could with pack and rifle, trying to sail over the rocks and make it quickly to the other side where there was cover.

Several of us, one after another, so as not to bunch up into easy targets, started running across this field. Grass would have been real great, but it wasn't going to be that way. About halfway across, waiting machine guns began their rapid chatter. Without a moment's thought, I did what was by now automatic: I hit the deck.

The ground was about as un-soft a place to dive as you could imagine—the same bunch of unfriendly rocks I had deemed hazardous to cross carefully. I didn't injure anything important and was somehow close enough to earth not to catch a bullet, or several. With several men pinned down like this, our mortars soon lobbed shells at the machine gun positions, after which we got the hell out of there. I believe we all made it to cover on the other side without a drop of blood lost.

Napoleon Was Right

Napoleon is credited with the principle that, "An army travels on its stomach." (He said it in French, of course.) It is good for morale as well as for healthy nutrition that the troops be properly fed. Now that doesn't mean sumptuous meals with flagons of ale, topped off with brandy and cigars. As Sherman said, "War is hell," implying that the food may not be too great either. But our food in this invasion was sufficient in quantity and appropriate in quality.

At the beginning of the war, three years before I got to Iwo, the War Department was supplying the troops with K-rations. When I first saw these "Crackerjack box" meals, they held a small can of cheese or meat, a nutritious food bar that probably had some fruit in it, a little packet of dried coffee powder, some hard candies, and maybe something else.

Although I believe they had lots of proper nutrition handily packaged for men in the field, they were not all that delectable, and often even the hungry were not too inclined to eat them. Then the food scientists must have gotten together with the psychologists to come up with a better formula that was convenient and nutritious, would last forever, and was somewhat more appealing than the old K-rations.

I don't recall if they changed the package somewhat or mounted an ad campaign to tell the troops that the "new, improved" K-rations were not the same as the old ones and ask them to at least give their new stuff an honest try. Whatever they did, it seemed to work. The new K-rations caught on and were better than the old ones. They could be easily delivered to the front, and a man could carry several in his pack or in his large dungaree pockets. They would still probably last as long as the war, if not forever, and they tasted better, so the guys would eat them.

Problem solved.

Staying alive and knowing you were doing your job were probably more important aspects of the daily routine than great chow that you would likely eat in a hurry anyway. As long as the men were not suffering from malnutrition or attendant diseases, food was not usually the top item on their agenda.

As handy and improved as the new K-rations were, they were to be surpassed by the work of the good folks who think about these things for a living. Somewhere along the line, at least before February 1945, the dandy little olive drab cans of C-rations began to appear on the military scene. These made meal time, when you could arrange it, even more a pleasure.

As I recall, these little three-inch-high canned meals were available in several flavors, probably the result of further intense effort on the part of the food scientists and the psychologists' testing groups. I think I remember Bacon (or was it Pork?) and Beans, Beef Stew, Ham and Lima Beans (a favorite of mine), and maybe a couple of others. Now this was progress, unless you expected gourmet cuisine on the field of battle. I believe a lot of our down-home boys rarely had anything better than this back on the farm.

C-ration cans always found room in your pack, were easy to open, and could be eaten cold if you had no time or opportunity to heat them up. Vaguely I recall that, now and then, a bit to the rear, cauldrons of boiling water were set up to warm up the C-rations for delivery to the hungry at the front when they had the time to eat and enjoy. And, oh yes, I believe there were crackers or hard bread to go along with our meals-in-a-can. Sometimes it was eat fast and get going; at other times there was maybe enough time for a piece of candy, some coffee (on your own), and a pleasant after-dinner cigarette. Boy, this was livin'!

Back at the rear, only a couple hundred yards away but really a busy other world, they often had field kitchens and hot chow. Once, around the third week on the island, the word came that we would get a hot meal that day. I believe this turned out to be some warm meat, lukewarm potatoes, peas, and some peaches. It was a nice gesture and at least a change, but not quite the rousing banquet we may have imagined from the term "hot meal." We ate and enjoyed, but it still was not like back home.

Even more progress on the "food for hungry fighters" front: Something new, again, had come out of the laboratory in time to improve our life on Iwo Jima. They kept on thinking of us. This time it was "10-in-1" rations. I never quite figured this out—was it ten meals for one man, one meal for ten men, or some reasonable combination of those numbers? But it was an advance in feeding the troops on the field. It came in a box about a foot and a half long, a foot wide and about nine inches high. (All estimates.) These packages were intended to provide more variety and more quantity for situations when there was more time to prepare and enjoy than we had been having while manning the front lines.

As I remember (all this was 60 years ago, you know), "10-in-1" rations included larger cans of ham and lima beans (my favorite), other great entrees like spaghetti and meat balls, some canned butter and bread of some sort, and other goodies. Maybe even some dessert. These were really neat. But I don't think we got them more than once on the line at Iwo.

Keep in mind that just about everyone had feelings of fear or anxiety or that "buzzing inside," and they affected our appetite. Although there were times we just "held" or waited, much of the time we were busy doing what we were paid to do. Getting the job done—right—as best we could—was not quite what it took to make us hearty eaters.

We all lost weight; we just weren't all that hungry.

Chapter 8

HARD LUCK HANK
AND OTHER STORIES

He was a really good guy. Hank had been in the paratroops, seen action down in the islands, Guadalcanal and maybe some others. I don't know if he was wounded there, but he came to Camp Pendleton to help us form the Fifth Marine Division.

Hank joined us at our tent camp in Las Pulgas ("The Fleas") Canyon at Pendleton. He became part of the demolition squad, working as a flame-thrower man. While out on a field exercise, he was either thrown to the ground or hit the deck for some very good reason. Hitting the deck with a 70 pound tank of napalm (jellied gasoline) on his back caused some broken ribs or even worse damage to his body, putting him in the hospital. Well, they patched him up and healed him and sent him back to our company. That was the beginning.

In the canyon we lived in rows of pyramidal tents on 12 by 12 foot (I guess) wooden platforms, with an opening door flap facing the company street, on the other side of which was another row of similar tents. On one memorable day two of the guys were throwing a baseball back and forth in the company street. One of them may have been practicing his fast ball when Hank walked out of his tent into the street catching the hard pitch in his temple. So back to the hospital again.

That was back then. Fast forward to Iwo Jima where Hank is back in action again with his demolition squad. We got word that he was hit in the ankle by a bullet and went out onto the hospital ship. He was on the mend, so I'm told, when a blood clot moved up through his body and did him in for good. Three times and out? We missed him; he was a pleasure to have around and a genuine good guy.

Lunch with the Officers

Our food, as I've said, was not haute cuisine, but very serviceable. One day I pulled out a can of C-rations for lunch and began looking for a place to enjoy it. It would be more comfortable—and more American—to be seated for lunch than to squat, Japanese style, but there were no rocks or tree stumps to sit on. What to do?

Looking around, I found the solution to the problem right behind me: a dead Japanese—a captain, at that—cold and stiff with rigor mortis, lying there on his side for my comfort. I ate my lunch with as much nonchalance as at a picnic bench in the park. Some things you take more seriously than others!

We were accustomed to events there on the island you don't usually accept back home.

Ingenious "Ishiwara"

Things may never be as organized in battle as we would like, but events did often move along as if guided by unseen hands. Moving northward on the island—we intended to push the enemy to the sea in an enveloping maneuver—two or three of us came upon one of our own food dumps. These were strategically placed here and there by the quartermasters from the rear for distribution to the troops as necessary. This pile of boxes was the size of a one-car garage back home and very likely contained the same K- and C-rations I've spoken about above, as well as other necessary stuff awaiting parceling out to the outfits nearby.

One other relevant background fact: Although the Japanese had been continually fortifying this critically important island for many years, and although our recent forceful attention had alerted them that we would be coming soon, their supplies had run low. They had caves within caves and caves beneath caves, but the Japanese prisoners told us, by their appearance as well as their own spoken admissions, that their food and water were running out. (There was no source of water on the island.)

Enter "Ishiwara." (Not his real name, of course; I've coined it to give him the dignity of an identity during his brief appearance in this story.)

Atop this sizeable cache of food—atop, mind you—sat "Ishy" excitedly opening cans of our food and munching away eagerly. Imagine our surprise at finding him there, actually behind our lines. We watched him eagerly devouring America's gifts to him as if he hadn't eaten for days. (Likely true). To a man, we all had the same thought: "Let him have a couple of more happy minutes before we send him to his ancestors."

Which we did.

The Coffee Club

Most of us were coffee hounds. Navy coffee, even if its flavor left much to be desired, did have caffeine, and all in all, it was far superior to nothing. I don't recall that this beautiful brown nectar was regularly served to the troops. The ground beans were available, but you were on your own for the rest of it. There were several solutions to this problem; here was ours.

As a "spare part," I was available for a variety of missions, but I was usually a rifleman, filling in where a body was needed. Consequently, I often traveled with the same two or three guys. This allowed us to take a cooperative and organized approach to the problem of having "joe" when we needed it. When our coffee club lost a man, we would replace him with another willing member. To say this brings back sad thoughts; we lost many good men.

I'm not sure whose idea the club was, but it worked just fine. Here's how: By common agreement, each of us took on one job. One would carry (in addition to his regular pack and stuff) a large container of ground coffee. Another would carry one or more extra water canteens. A third man was responsible, possibly along with a fourth, for finding three fist-sized rocks and arranging them as a small triangle on the ground with a golfball-sized piece of C2 in the middle. (C2 is a plastic explosive, also known as RDX. It is useful for demolition work, as it can be molded to shape. If hit by a bullet, it does not explode. If it is in your pack, this is a comfort.)

Once the rocks and the C2 are in place, one man sets his steel helmet (NOT the fiberglass helmet liner, please) on the rocks; the water man pours a pint or so of water into the helmet, and the coffee man adds a fistful of coffee to the water. The flame man uses a match or a cigarette lighter to ignite the fuel (after, repeat after, the water is added, or else bye-bye helmet). C2 burns fiercely with a white heat, so in less than twenty seconds the water is at a rolling boil, working its wonders on the grounds. At just the right moment the water man deftly adds a splash of cold, settling the grounds—and coffee is served. Faster than your favorite restaurant.

News from the Other Side

By the third or fourth week into the campaign, our outfit was making its way slowly forward on the western side of a sharp, steep-walled ridge. While we were slugging it out in some slow going on our side of the ridge, we could hear the racket of all hell breaking loose on the other side. Our forces there must have run into something big; I could hear our artillery and mortars, and maybe even our rocket trucks, weighing in from the rear on the battle over there. This was knock-down, drag-out, serious noisy stuff. We were occupied with problems of our own, but we were most curious about all the happenings hardly more than a couple of hundred feet to our right.

Our curiosity got satisfied in a roundabout way.

There were hundreds of our ships of all kinds out there just off the island. Men-of-war directed fire from their guns as necessary and as called for by the colonels and generals. Hospital ships patched up and cared for the wounded. Cargo ships and "lighters" (smaller ship-to-shore carriers) buzzed back and forth bringing in all manner of supplies to feed the needs of aggressive land warfare. Many of these ships would pick up the radio war news for their own information, and one particular supply ship occasionally printed its own little "newspaper" for the enlightenment of the ship's personnel.

Thanks to that huge flotilla of ships, we continued to receive needed supplies on our side of the ridge even while all the busy racket was going on the other side. From one of the sailors who were bravely carrying ammo, or whatever, up to our line, we were fortunate enough to acquire a copy of the latest edition of his ship's newspaper. I would love to tell you all the details that may have been in that rag, but I really don't remember. I do remember, though, that we finally learned all about the raucous action of our buddies, literally a stone's throw away on the other side of the ridge. Their reports to their battalion headquarters were being relayed on to the generals, to the news folks, onto American radio, back to the radioman at the supply ship, thence to the publisher of the shipboard newspaper, and finally winding up after thousands of miles in our dirty, sweaty hands.

The "New Hand"

Since the Marine Corps is an arm of the U.S. Navy, Marine talk includes many naval terms, like "deck" (ground or floor), "bulkhead" (wall), and "head" (latrine). Another word, "hand," as in "deckhand," is a common term for a man, used in both services. I like this term; it has a friendly yet respectful tone to it. I enjoy the feeling of being one of the many "hands" involved in a "gung ho" (a borrowed Chinese expression meaning "work together") operation. This is part of the heritage of the naval service and spirit of the Corps.

On one particular day I was with members of our mortar squad. Somehow I don't think I was assigned to them. They were a well-drilled, efficient crew, to whom I would have been of little use. I may well have been bringing up supplies or even just shooting the breeze with buddies there. From time to time there were moments in the action when we could be real persons, rather than cogs in the well-oiled military wheel, the way we needed to be most of the time. This was that kind of a visit, and something happened that will help put several details of our "special life" in clearer perspective.

There was a new body in the mortar squad area that day, a clean-shaven, youngish-looking man wearing clean new dungarees and clean new boots, too, if I remember right. (I repeat "clean" on purpose—it has an important bearing on the story.)

I greeted John Nehme, the corporal in charge in this mortar emplacement, and asked him, "Who's the new hand?" Nehme respectfully replied, "Corporal Miller, this is Lieutenant Johnson." He looked so young! I had sized him up as a "boot" fresh from the States, there to help fill our depleted ranks. I regained my composure and respectful deportment and gave the new guy a bit of a salute with my index finger. (Big official salutes in battle zones are often a kiss of death for the officer saluted, for obvious reasons.) He acknowledged the salute after a fashion and I shook his hand.

"Welcome aboard, Lieutenant." Almost chagrined by this formality, he replied, "Just call me 'Candy'; that's what everybody calls me." "Yessir, Candy," is what I said. Some guys just look younger than others, of course. He told me that back in the States he had been a cartoonist or illustrator.

He looked so clean and young. Nehme and I weren't old men—I was twenty years old—and "Candy" must have been to college, at least for a while, but he looked so fresh and clean. I know I keep saying that—it's just that my memory of him is so vivid, in his brand new right-off-the-shelf green dungarees that looked as though they had never been worn before.

What this is all about is that after three or four weeks on the island, all our dungarees were the color of the local dirt—all the tougher to distinguish from the landscape. All our more or less bearded faces were tan from sunshine and brown from dirt. We never washed our faces; if they were clean they would have shown like beacons—great targets. I don't remember seeing "Candy" again. I hope he fared well, but in his get-up, life expectancy could have been pretty short.

So much for hygiene. Oh yes, the other stuff. Maybe there were latrines way back in the rear, but I never saw one. On the front line you just wandered off somewhere a bit away from others and did your business. You had a short shovel; foxholes were one use, "number two" was another. If, in your life back home, you had been a hunter, hiker or woodsman, you knew all about this already.

Incidentally, the flares our artillery and ships sent up to light the night sky drifted down lazily suspended by little silk parachutes. These hankies were all around and found many uses.

Into The Canyon

The landscape of Iwo varied from place to place. If you have ever seen the Grand Canyon, or the Badlands of South Dakota, we had lots of places like that. There were places where weather and water may have washed or blown away softer rock and left a pillar standing twenty feet high. And there were many places where "cliffs" four feet or forty feet high would sharply rise from the prevailing terrain.

Continuing our northward progress, we found a place where two of these cliffs, starting a couple of hundred feet apart, gradually converged to form a dead-end canyon. We swung around the open end and began to make our way in. We didn't like it. If we went in we would be trapping Japs, not good for them, and they would be trapping us, not good for us either. A lot of our guys were thinking, "Let's get some guns or flamethrower tanks in here to do this place up." But our wishes were not what ran things. Our orders were to go in and "get 'em."

We went beyond the open end and started back into the canyon. We could see, farther on, lots of enemy soldiers scurrying around, in and out of caves and all over. Suddenly, just a few yards ahead, a Jap popped up out of nowhere and banged a grenade on his helmet. (Japanese hand grenades were stubby, fist-sized cylinders with a button on a stem sticking out a bit on one end. Unlike a U.S. grenade, whose time fuse you started by yanking out a restraining pin before throwing, a Japanese grenade was armed by striking the button sharply against a hard object—often the grenadier's helmet. After listening for a moment to be sure that the fuse was hissing, the grenadier would fling the device in the direction of his target, where it would explode a few seconds later with a very loud bang.)

Our man, after hitting the grenade on his helmet and listening, hit it again, listened again, hit it a third time—still no luck—then frantically shook it and looked at it, appearing almost like a perplexed monkey in a comedy. Still not hearing the expected hissing, and getting very nervous with us confronting him, he banged the grenade on a nearby rock two or three times in desperation.

This unintentionally comic scene had us almost on the point of laughing, but then we ended it—and the grenadier's consternation— with a few well placed shots. We did have other serious work to do.

Those shots seemed to stir up more action in the canyon. The surprised, disorganized Japanese ran around and fired at us now and then as we fired at them. One of the many men advancing into the canyon was Paul Idoux (of St. Louis, I believe). He carried a B.A.R. (Browning Automatic Rifle, sort of a one-man light machine gun) and couldn't pass up such a chance to knock off many enemy soldiers at once. By climbing about ten feet up one of the rock pillars rising from the canyon floor, he got a very good look at swarms of them— and shot many before he became their target. Score: Idoux, a dozen; Japs, one. I felt sad for him, but acknowledged that his bravery had shortened the war just a bit more.

Then we got a lot busier. We bagged our limit before dusk fell and the canyon was quiet.

Chapter 9

ASSORTED NEWS ITEMS

"Grenades for the Cookies"

Our company cooks were spare parts like me, and in battle they often served as riflemen on the line. (That's why they went to the rifle range like everybody else.) At one point a cook I knew named Tolliver, along with another cook whose name I have forgotten, was posted at the base of one of those four-foot "cliffs" I have mentioned. They were looking onto a field almost at their eye level when an unseen Jap threw or rolled a grenade in their direction. It spilled over the edge and landed at the cookies' feet, where it exploded. Now, it would be wrong to imply that Jap grenades were not capable of causing death or grave physical damage, but for some reason they didn't scatter as much shrapnel as U.S. grenades did. Sometimes their only effect was concussion—a very loud bang.

That is what happened this time. Neither man was hurt by the explosion, but the expression on both of their faces—sort of a stupid, dumbfounded, bewildered look of surprise—was rather humorous to see. I don't know if they lived to cook another day, but I sure remember that sight. Bon appétit!

"My Little Nick"

We continued trudging up the "road"—I use the word loosely—to the north. Most of the time we traveled over whatever terrain led to our next objective. The rest of the Fifth Division was off to our right. Like us, they were trying to get north, rooting out caves and well-designed gun emplacements along the way. Other outfits were heading over and around the treacherous airfields, while still others came up the east coast. Slowly we were closing in on and trapping the enemy in a smaller and smaller pocket on the north end of the island.

Iwo Jima was an outpost, to be sure, 800 miles from the main islands of Japan, but it was considered part of the "homeland" and served as one of the first lines of national defense. Enemy forces had been here for years, improving a well-designed system of sturdily built interlocking fortifications and steadily preparing to defend the place. An important part of the system was a large number of mortar emplacements. These were like deep wells in the ground, each protecting one or more mortars, which fire up at a steeper angle than other types of artillery. Each mortar's crew had previously calculated the elevation and azimuth (direction) required to hit any desired target within a couple of miles. This allowed them to lay shells on us with ease wherever we went, until we dug them out, which was very difficult.

On one of our advances over a field some mortars hit ahead of us and as we hit the deck, a shard of shrapnel hit my shin. It didn't go in very far, just broke the skin and stuck in the bone. A nameless (my fault) Corpsman was nearby, came over, pulled out the steel, sprinkled on some of his magic powder and wrapped a bandage around my leg. He directed me to go back to the battalion aid station, but I felt fine and continued on with my unit.

"Non-Hit"

I was not officially wounded on the island. I never got back to the aid station to get my name on the list. But at another point, while advancing with one of our platoons, I heard the sharp crack of a shot aimed near me. Did I feel something hit? I wasn't sure, but later, during a break in the advance, I checked my pack and found two small new bullet holes, one entry and one exit. I guess I did feel something after all—mark up "one wounded pack." You'll recall me mentioning that C2 explosive, so vital to our "coffee club," had the handy feature of not being ignited by the strike of a bullet; if that weren't the case, you might not be reading this.

Another interesting non-hit I experienced struck my buddies as humorous. Several of us were taking a rest (we weren't always running over rocks). I was wearing several layers of clothing, and my sitting position caused the fly of my trousers to bunch up a bit. As we talked we heard another of those rifle reports that sounded as if it were aimed awful close (you get to know from experience how to tell these important things), and a bullet zipped through the folded cloth at that spot. No contact with my person, but a wise guy among the witnesses remarked dryly that I was lucky I wasn't reading a letter from my girlfriend! This brought forth a few earthy chuckles from the rest.

The Lucky Helmet

I believe that I was back at Camp Tarawa in Hawaii after Iwo when one of my fellow Marines told me this story. I'll call him "Marty" because I don't remember his name. But I remember his face, and I sure remember the story.

The helmets we wore in battle were steel, with a composition liner inside held on the head by webbing. They were good at stopping shrapnel, but were not expected to stop a rifle bullet if it hit squarely. Marty proudly showed me a bullet "meant for him" that he had felt and heard as it hit his helmet. The bullet had hit the helmet at an angle, but still pierced it and whizzed round and round inside until it had spent its energy. The Corps let him keep his lucky helmet and bullet as souvenirs.

Even Luckier Stevenson

His first name was Stan, but Marines, even talking with very close friends, mostly called each other by their last name or a nickname. That's the way it was. Stevenson was in our second platoon, and a friend of my real good buddy Hal Wolfe. He was quite young, like just about all of us; a quiet, pleasant, likeable guy.

During the battle Stevenson disappeared. This happened to a lot of Marines, and lots of times we found out only later, if ever, what had happened to them. We would ask and sometimes get the answer that so-and-so was "hit," meaning that he was wounded; other times we would hear that someone had "got it," which meant that he had been killed. I don't know if this was the lingo only in our particular outfit or if it was in more general use.

We were all happy to see Stevenson again when we returned to Hawaii for R&R (rest and recuperation) and plenty of replacements. He had one hell of a story to tell. He had been shot through the head! A bullet had entered one temple and exited the other, with no noticeable damage or disability resulting. He said he had medical records and X-rays to back up his story. "Lucky Stevenson" immediately became his nickname for life.

Since he was "as good as new," or at least had no apparent impairment to his military functioning, the hospital sent Lucky Stevenson back to us. The only evident thing different about him was that his eyes appeared a little bit sunken in his head (this could have been my imagination, or some psychological effect of his experience on the island).

Upon close examination there was a pink pimple-like spot on one temple and a similar but larger spot on the other side. My guess, from what little I know about anatomy, is was that the projectile whipped through his head behind the eyes but did not hit anything he couldn't do without, mentally speaking.

Stevenson wanted to return to his outfit, but we told him jokingly that he should complain of terrific headaches (who would question that?) and get himself sent back home in a hurry. I don't know if he followed our advice.

Chapter 10

GUS & ME, AND OTHER STORIES

Gus from the motor pool was a "spare part" like me. In battle, we always needed riflemen, runners, and "gofers" much more than truck-drivin' men. One day the company position was set up on the edge of an open area about baseball stadium size, with lots of brush. Off to the right was one of those cliffs standing about five feet high. Although the brush afforded some concealment, there were a few gaps that looked like paths running down away from us. Very likely some of these were machine gun lanes where anyone seen down the lane would draw bursts of gunfire. All in all, not a great place to be.

Our company leaders had news that some of our wounded might be out in that field. They sent Gus and me out there to search for people and get them to the battalion aid station. At the far end of the field, just past the cliff, he and I could see several men and a jeep marked with a red cross. We hustled out in that general direction, running stooped over and low so as to be hard to see through the brush, scooting across the open lanes as quickly as possible, and keeping our eyes and ears open for any sign of wounded Marines. Three or four times we stopped to listen.

We were all getting better at recognizing the sounds of different kinds of gunfire and reacting appropriately. As I have said, when you're in somebody's rifle sights, the sound of his shot at you is a very sharp "crack"; if the rifle is aimed "over there some place," the report is duller and less distinct. Gus and I had covered fifty or sixty yards in short runs, hearing occasional fire but confident that it was aimed away from us, when we made another of our brief listening stops. As we hunkered down, his left shoulder touching my right shoulder, there came a telling "crack." In the time it took me to turn to Gus

255

and say, "Boy, that was sure close," he lunged forward, then slumped to the ground. He had been hit in the left shoulder, inches from me.

I put my hand on him and said, "I'll get help." He did not move or say anything. I took off like an Olympic runner for that ambulance jeep, which by now was not too far away. I got back to Gus quickly with stretcher bearers and a Corpsman, who checked Gus and said, "He's dead."

Later, I found out that because he was bending forward, the bullet that hit his shoulder had gone down into his body and cut up his insides, bringing swift death. That sure was close for me; much closer for him. Somehow death brought us even closer to each other. The feelings I had at that moment I still have, and tears want to come to my eyes thinking about him, and his wife and his children.

The Cold Beer

Another thing we learned about as we gained experience was the rules and regulations of combat and of war. These were all for our own good, of course, and to make everything run better. Before we left Hawaii for the island, for example, we were told to turn in any money we had. Food, ammo and cigarettes were furnished, we were told, so why would we need any money? Not everybody obeyed this rule to the letter. For myself, if I had any cash, it was only a couple of bucks.

One day one of the sailors brought supplies from one of the ships up to the line. Along with the "official" provisions, whatever they may have been, this enterprising soul had also brought along a can of beer—on ice, even! He let it be known to everybody within earshot that any of them could own the can by outbidding the rest, and all hearers who happened to have any (illicit) cash joined the auction. Eighteen dollars finally got the lucky guy a drink of cold beer, with envious eyes helping him drink it.

If I'd had nineteen bucks, I could have happily slaked my thirst.

Home Sweet Home—Kinda

In boot camp we were issued collapsible shovels and had a bit of practice with them. In our field training exercises at Camp Pendleton, we sometimes dug drainage ditches around our tents at bivouacs. At Iwo, we really put our shovels to work, usually in making a home for the night.

Most of the time two or three of us would share a foxhole. We liked to dig them about a foot and a half deep and wide enough for a couple of tired bodies to sleep. The holes wanted to be deep enough so that we were below ground level if possible, and we would sometimes care to be deeper than that.

We were fortunate that much of the surface was sand. It was generally easy to dig in; and as an added benefit for cool nights, a little below the surface one would find some volcanic heat and maybe even some steam. Some parts of the island, though, were made of undiggable rock. In those places we would need to build "foxholes" above ground by arranging rocks in a rough circle—much like the snow forts that we (those of us from up north) had made as kids. In any case, we had blankets and ponchos to roll up in at night.

We would usually halt our advance (if we had advanced) toward late afternoon. Our company would set up its line for the night, tied in with other outfits on our right and left flanks. This usually meant that foxholes would be spaced a few yards apart across the width of our company's area—close enough to "see" each other at night. We would get dug in before dark, receive any special orders we needed to hold our line, talk for a while, and have some chow and maybe "joe" and a cigarette if it wasn't too dark. (Matches or lit cigarettes in the dark were absolutely verboten, for the obvious reasons of keeping our position unknown to the enemy.) Sometimes we would have the same hole for two or three nights as we ran operations in the neighborhood, or just held our position. As simple and temporary as the hole was, it soon became familiar as "home."

I have heard and read stories of some of the other Pacific operations where the almost worst part of the whole thing was swamp, heat, jungle, insects, and other environmental aspects. As history has recorded, Iwo was one bloody and difficult battle. The enemy was smart in building very elaborate and effective interlocking and buried defenses. These little monkeys we care to ridicule at times were first class fighters—real marksmen, with good weapons and a will to fight. Iwo was no picnic, but we did have decent weather and less troublesome terrain than some I have heard of.

Night Time Protocol

The most important thing to be sure of in bedding down was having someone standing watch all night. We would take turns, but at least one man must be awake in the foxhole. I don't know if this was the rule way back in the rear, but it sure was up on the line.

There are stories from many wars about men on watch falling asleep, leaving a hole in the line. In fact, I have heard stories from "my" war in which a watchman caught sleeping was done in by his comrades for gross negligence that could jeopardize the whole outfit. The Japanese were notorious for patrolling at night and infiltrating where they found weaknesses in our line. We needed to anticipate a variety of enemy ingenuities.

You may have seen movies or heard stories, as I have, about our troops using secret "passwords" and "countersigns" (such as, "What's the capital of South Dakota?")[1] in order to move around among our positions at night without being mistaken for clever Japanese impostors. Those are interesting stories, and I am sure orders and practices differed from place to place and situation to situation; but I saw little or nothing like that on the island. As far as I know, there was one

---

[1] Answer: Pierre—pronounced "peer." How many Americans could answer that correctly?

simple rule: If you were out of your foxhole at night, you were liable to be shot. Period. In my own company, I was told, one of our mortar men left his hole to get some information from a sergeant in a nearby hole but was shot before he could ask his question. I have heard similar accounts from Marines in other outfits.

The Price of Pineapple Dessert

Ever been in one of those fixes where you say, "Someday we'll look back on this and laugh?" This story is like that. But even after sixty years, I still don't laugh too loud!

About the fourth week on the island we set up on a line that placed my little team on a rocky ridge sticking up maybe eight or ten feet above the surrounding grade. No digging foxholes here—this was solid rock, a place to gather stones and build ourselves a little fort.

To make it a particularly nice day, a friend from "back there" at the rear showed up while we were settling in; he brought a number ten can of crushed pineapple and offered me half. Yum! I had never been great on sweets and candy and all that, but this was such a nice change to our diet that I gladly accepted and I ate it for supper. This was delicious. How good to taste fruit again; such refreshing sweetness.

But wait! I was about to get a hard lesson in the physiology of pineapple digestion.

Things had settled down for the night, and as usual, our artillery was whooshing shells over our heads. I am sure the trajectories were at least a hundred feet above us, but up on this ridge they sounded like freight trains—so awfully close and fast that we would duck a little each time one went by. There was occasional and sporadic gunfire out there in the dark, but all in all, it was a relatively uneventful night.

Just as I was getting comfortable in a corner of our stony home, my insides began to rumble. I had made my daily deposit satisfactorily that morning, but now it was looking like I would have to schedule a special evening "extra." I didn't like that idea, but soon internal events brought pressures for a change of plan. That thought grew swiftly as abdominal action got serious. The urgency built with each passing minute. I was facing grave alternatives here:

Plan A: I could perform the "extra" in my pants, to my great chagrin, resulting in days of soreness and yards of stink; or

Plan B: I could pull down my skivvies and let 'er rip in my foxhole, shared with two comrades who had a right to better treatment than that; or,

Plan C: I could slither with all deliberate speed over the wall of our fort (exposing myself to the artillery shells whooshing by close above, and to the harsh "shoot first, ask-questions later" nighttime protocol); relieve the increasingly painful pressure out there, and scramble back in.

I paused little to debate the practical and moral questions of the dilemma. Sensing that hesitation was the worst alternative, I slithered over the rock wall fast, pulled 'em down fast, and added my own contribution to the chorus of the artillery. I slithered back over the wall fast and pensively added my name to the list of the other few lucky ones.

I ate no pineapple again for forty years.

Chapter 11

THE PROPHECY AND OTHER STORIES

I was only twenty years old when I came to Iwo Jima, but many times in my short life I had received "information" from mysterious sources. I am not talking about random thoughts or associations that can come at most any time. These "messages" or "viewings" or "connections" could come in dreams, in half-sleep or during a busy day, but they were urgent and purposeful, not casual, and I learned that the information was always accurate. Well, almost always.

I still now and then have premonitions that come true, and I have even learned how to make some sense of the connections. I have also talked with many others who have had similarly unexplained experiences. You don't need to have had experiences like this, nor do you need to understand or explain them. I will tell you what happened and you can take it from there.

Once I was talking with some friends in high school about what we would like to do with our lives—what we would do when we grew up. Some of them had pretty definite life and career goals, but I couldn't say that I had given it a lot of thought. When my turn came to reveal my plans, a powerful and frightening feeling came over me, and it seemed someone else's voice came out of my mouth saying, "I won't live to see my twenty-first birthday." They all smiled politely or smirked and that was the end of that. This was a very serious moment for me, but in time I forgot about the strange message and went back to having fun in my life.

I was twenty, and my birthday was coming up on March 16th. On March 15th, the platoon to which I was assigned was beginning to set up for the night. You know, pick a spot, dig a hole, get the latest orders and settle in for what was to come. We were on a sort of plain but not exactly flat area about the size of a baseball stadium with us near home plate with some small ridges behind us and higher ridges encircling the field out there at the fence.

It was not an ideal location for us. A nice straight line is probably the easiest to manage and defend, but you can't always get it like the book says. Because of the higher terrain behind us, our line had to bulge out toward the "pitcher's mound," leaving us more exposed than we would like. But then, if everything were perfect, we would all be back home drinking beer.

The chance for night infiltration of our lines was always present. Unfortunately, our exposure here was almost an invitation to the enemy, many of whom we knew were most likely out there in the rocks and ridges that were a few hundred feet in front of us. Our leaders must have had some apprehension of this.

The Japs were in fact out there, and later that night all hell broke loose. They unleashed a bit of mortar fire to soften us up, then came at us in swarms with rifles and flamethrowers. I don't recall bayonets, but there was one hell of a lot of gunfire. In minutes, and before we could get artillery or other support from the rear, they were all over us.

They did not break through the line, but we took an awful hit. My two foxhole mates were killed in the hole as they exposed themselves to shoot. You could barely see out there, but there was enough light to be killed by.

The light of morning shone on a field of carnage worse than I had seen on the beach. There were dead bodies all over the field, both theirs and ours.

This was the morning of my twenty-first birthday. Everyone around me had been killed.

So much for prophecies.

The Marine Statue

In the morning after that night attack, Marines' bodies were being carried off the field and dead Japanese pushed aside. We had lost at least a couple of dozen men. Someone said thirty-four dead. I can't imagine or recall a stronger feeling of sickness and sorrow and longing for my comrades in my whole life than what I felt all alone on that field. On that quiet battlefield there was a sight as sharp in my mind today as it was sixty years ago: One of our Marines was still there half-kneeling with right arm raised to throw a grenade. He was frozen there by a Jap flamethrower, skin blackened, burnt to a crisp, with a scream of pain you could almost hear, still on his scorched face.

You don't forget things like that. You don't ever forget things like that.

I still hurt from that scene.

A Visitation by Wilson Grounds

On the ship from our camp in Hawaii to Iwo, we had had several days of "schools" on the coming operation, but there had also been time to relax. Standing on deck looking out at the sea, I met one of the guys from our company whom I had seen before but never really knew.

His name was Wilson B. Grounds. We struck up a conversation and found each other interesting persons. We spoke of our homes (Texas was his) and families and interests. He enjoyed duck hunting and told me some great stories of this pastime. I had other friends but it was nice to have such an interesting new buddy. We chatted on several occasions, and talked of getting together to talk more when "the operation" was over. I liked him. He was a tall, good-looking, well-built guy with a rather distinctive large head. Somehow that head made him look smarter than the average guy. Maybe he was.

Some time during the night of the devastating enemy attack I just described, I clearly saw before my eyes an apparition—the head of

Wilson Grounds, larger than life and glowing green. His eyes were open but gazing off in an emotionless stare. There was a distinct spot above the bridge of his nose. A green hand with extended index finger swung in and out of the picture pointing to the spot on his forehead. That's what I saw, unmistakably.

The next morning, along with clearing away the bodies and getting our company back together, we who survived exchanged impassioned information about the night and what had become of our friends and buddies. I was saddened to learn that many of those I felt close were gone, including Grounds. I asked the guy who reported him dead, "Did you see him?" "Yes," he said. I asked where he was hit. The answer: "Right between the eyes."

Rocket Trucks

I have talked earlier about how useful napalm (jellied gasoline, or liquid fire) was to our side. Our planes dropped it in bombs to clear out guns and emplacements that were giving us trouble; and flame-throwers (tank-mounted or man-carried) were handy in burning out enemy positions in caves and brush that would take the riflemen days (and many men lost) to destroy without them.

We had another dandy weapon that really did a number on the enemy and earned enough of their respect for them to respond fiercely to its use. This weapon was the rocket trucks, 3/4 ton rugged trucks fitted with rocket racks on their beds. The racks were 6 x 6 arrays of 4.5-inch rockets that could be aimed together and fired in a salvo, all of them very quickly—almost instantaneously.

I am not sure of how many of these trucks the Division had (maybe sixty-four or more), but they sure did a job. They would kind of "carpet bomb" an area about the size of a football field, cleaning out just about anything above ground, and maybe some of the stuff below.

Here's how it worked. After the leaders had determined the

target—often requested by the companies on the line—the truck would roll up to a point of vantage and aim the rack. I am told they used the windshield wipers to fix the direction and hoisted the front of the rack to get the right elevation for distance. Then they hit the switch that set them off.

At once the rockets would whoosh out with smoke and roar to their target, and the driver would get that truck out of there as fast as he could.

Almost before the truck's dust had settled, the enemy mortars would blast the place where that truck had been. You never saw anything happen so fast. The moment the Nips saw that truck pull into place, or at least no later than the moment the first rocket hit its target, those mortar crews had to be cranking their guns into swift retaliation.

They hated those trucks. We loved 'em.

Chapter 12

RICK AND THE PRISONERS

Rick Sharp was the intelligence guy we saw the most of in our area. He wasn't an officer, just a plain Marine, but one sharp cookie. He helped gather information from various sources, including enemy equipment and prisoners.

As the campaign progressed, the enemy was getting low on supplies and their soldiers were poorly fed. They were getting mighty hungry. It may be that for a Japanese soldier to surrender was the ultimate dishonor, but basic needs like hunger and thirst can be strong motivation. Some of their gaunt and tired men capitulated more easily as time and food supplies dwindled.

I ran into Rick once as he herded a few hands-up prisoners back to intelligence HQ. Seeing their emaciated rag-tag appearance, I felt we were getting our job done. Rick told me that he had found them while searching one of their caves—maybe an important headquarters—for useful information. In addition to the prisoners and some papers, he had come out with a stack of Japanese currency (which came in various sizes, the larger the denomination the larger the bill). Rick showed me a wad of Japanese 10,000-yen bills several inches thick. He handed the fistful in my direction, and asked, "Here, do you want them?" Not being much of a souvenir collector, I declined—it was just that much more stuff to carry.

This snap decision came back to haunt me a few months later, when I was transferred to serve with the Occupation forces in Japan. Such forces often, as a way of controlling black marketeering, issue their own currency to replace that of the occupied country. This Occupation, though, did not do that. Japanese yen continued to be legal tender in the local economy, and we American troops were paid in this same currency. In my innocence I had turned down a small fortune. So much for my knowledge of money.

Chapter 13

THE RADIO BATTERY

"Spare parts" could lead interesting lives with a steady variety of challenging new missions. One of these assignments that I had for quite a while was to carry with me a spare "B" battery for our company commander's radioman, Delmar Rambo. I think the captain's name was Howe.

While most other communicators employed "walkie-talkies," the captain's radio link with battalion HQ and other places needed a much larger battery in a pack-sized unit on the radioman's back. This more powerful unit needed lots more than some flashlight cells to make it work. Its larger "B" battery was about the size of three bricks atop each other, and rather heavy. So that the captain had this important communication tool operative at all times, a spare battery was needed nearby when the other one went out—or the captain was without ears to the major. So, I was asked to carry this (in addition to the all-important C2 for our coffee) and all the other stuff Marines carried in their packs.

Ever since I joined headquarters platoon as company armorer, I had frequent business with our battalion quartermaster personnel, with goods going back and forth and all that. I often worked with them and helped their general effort in one way or another.

Each day as we advanced, or sometimes merely held our ground, toward the latter part of the afternoon, a couple of hours before darkness, we would set up our line for the night. This is the line of foxholes described earlier. Conditions of the terrain, locations of outfits to our right or left flank as well as the disposition of the enemy ahead all helped determine how and when the line was set up.

This particular evening of this event we had begun to set up our line across a "road" that ran forward through a shallow gully. One of the battalion quartermaster men came by in a jeep, told me to bring my battery, jump in the jeep and help him put some stuff in a small supply dump he was setting up in a shallow depression just to the right of the road. Then we piled the supplies in this spot that was right behind our line. Then he thanked me and drove off. So far, so good.

We were just starting to dig our foxholes to establish the line for the night when the sergeants passed the word that we would be quickly setting up a couple of hundred yards back from where we were. The officers didn't consult the troops on such matters—they just did what was ordered. If it were necessary because of tactics, security, new information, or whatever, for us to move, we did it. Officers understood the "grand plan," sergeants saw that it happened, and the troops did what they were told.

According to the needs of the change, we dug in, figured who did which watch, maybe had some chow and settled in for the night, as always hoping it would be "quiet." (It was never quiet; there was always gunfire several places on the island at any time. If we had known absolute quiet it would be too spooky and we would really get scared.)

I had stood my watch earlier, so when I was aroused around 2:00 a.m., I was pretty foggy. Someone gave me a firm shake and said, "Miller, Miller. Where's the radio battery? Rambo's radio is dying; where's the battery?" I shook my head and rubbed my eyes to come out of it.

In a few long moments it started to become clear to old sleepyhead here what he was talking about. I said, "Ya, ya, O.K.," while searching my foggy mind for where my pack and constant companion (the battery) could be. Then the voice in my head said, "Oh-oh," and it came to me that the battery was not with me in my pack, but in that dump out there somewhere. "I'll get it and bring it to Rambo," I said. That made my visitor happy and he left. Well, wasn't I in the soup? It didn't take me long to figure out who was going to get the battery to the captain. It took a little longer to figure out how.

I have described night-time protocol and included most ominous warnings against leaving the foxhole at night. Regardless of the pass-words and secret countersigns used in some places, and almost always in the movies, we still religiously believed in: "Shoot anything that moves out there" at night. And we knew of too many cases of this being a deadly truth.

With this vividly in mind, I pondered my alternatives.

There really weren't any. Our company's communication with bat-talion was absolutely vital to "the plan" and of grave importance to the swift and sure function of our military machine. That communica-tion depended on the CO's radio man having a workable battery. My life may have been short, but my choice was clear.

Looking out into the dark, very much awake now, I oriented my self to set a path from here to the dump, wherever that was—we had moved everything so quickly. I was lucky that where I lay was near that little road, and so was the dump. Otherwise I would still be lost out there. I know what it was I needed to do! For the second time on the island I slithered out of my foxhole at night—a bold move, as you know. I left behind my pack, my trusty '03 rifle, and everything else except for my Smith & Wesson .38 special in my pocket.

I became as one with the earth. When I headed out, I remembered that one of our foxholes was a few yards to the right. I knew the guys there, and stage-whispered the names of two of them, hoping that they could still recognize my faint voice.

I got a friendly reply instead of a bullet, and I confirmed my vital mission to get the spare battery to Rambo. I told them that I would be back later and said, "Don't shoot." I knew that if I got by them safely, I wouldn't come across any more of our guys; out in front of our lines I would be "in the clear." I didn't want to think that I was likely behind the enemy's lines as well. It was quite dark but I could make out some of the landscape and the road in front of me. I probably wouldn't "see" any Jap positions until I was right on top of them. "Moshi-moshi, tomodachi!" ("Hello, buddy.")

I had acquired my .38 special in Alaska and had used it a few times on targets and shooting rabbits. It was an excellent piece and instilled great confidence. I felt it in my pocket as I made this 6-foot, 200-pound frame as low to the ground and invisible as I could. I forgot everything except staying low and moving smoothly forward. I felt kinda snakelike, and that felt good. As foot after foot was behind me (it seemed like a hundred miles) I began to believe I would make it without suddenly hearing rifle fire.

I knew I was headed in the right direction. But as we had relocated our lines so fast and I was so busy with my battalion quartermaster buddy and the jeep, I wasn't really sure how far down the road that dump could be. I pictured our C.O. asking Rambo if he had the battery yet, and guilt helped me move a bit faster. But I was still alive, very much sensitively alert to everything and believing in every reptilian inch of me that I was doing it right.

I kept moving silently (oh, boy, was I quiet!) and cautiously down the road keeping an eye peeled to the right of the road for that pile of stuff that had gotten overlooked in the fast shuffle. I don't know how many minutes or hours later I finally came upon a bend in the road that I recalled was near the dump. Around the bend I made out a small hill that looked familiar—like one near where we had stopped. I was feeling a lot better now. At least some signs of success appeared. Somehow I knew I was going to make it. Then I saw the dump.

It took a little time to dig and unstack stuff quietly. I knew just about where we had put the battery, but in the dark and with the fear of making noise (and being shot, or worse, captured) if some boxes tumbled over—boy, was I careful! Digging further into the pile, my fingers felt just what I was looking for. Hot dog! My old friend the battery, my ticket back to an honorable life.

Things were different now. I felt elated enough to make even better time back to our lines. I used my recent experience in invisible snaking to slither along even quicker. Knowing that our guys at the near roadside foxhole already expected me made life even easier. I got back faster than when I went out because I knew more of what I was doing.

Nearing the friendly foxhole, I called out my buddy's name again and got a friendly reply. Not only that, but he told me that they had relayed the situation back through the lines to the company HQ and everybody was expecting me to come through—with the goods, of course. Getting back to the captain was easy. He and Rambo were there. The radio was there awaiting its fresh supply of juice. Rambo was relieved and the captain said something like, "Nice work, corporal."

I replied proudly, "Just doing my job, sir."

Chapter 14

THE NON-SING

This is about an event that didn't happen. It was planned to be happy and fun, but it didn't happen.

After some time on the island I got to see my old singing buddy Hal Wolfe long enough to talk to. We recalled the plans we and the other members of our quartet—tenor Tom Dahldorf and bass Ted Pyle—had made back when we were on the ship to get together for a "sing" once things quieted down on the island. Now, we remarked sadly, the sing would not come to pass, because Tom had been killed on the beach and we hadn't seen Ted, a Medical Corpsman, for some time.

My get-together with Hal could have been a chance to sing, had the other two been there, but it would have been short, for there still was a really serious battle going on. Before the battle, while we were still on the ship, the four of us had joked among ourselves that I should be especially careful not to get killed, because baritones are hard to find. But as it happened it was Tom we lost. Tenors are hard to find, too.

The Kid

This is one of the saddest memories I have.

In our H Company was Private J.J. O'Connor. He was as close as you could come to everyone's kid brother, a good-looking blond fellow who looked even younger than his true tender years. He was the kind of guy everyone wanted to be nice to and help. If you were a friend of his, you felt so good. He would read letters to, and write letters for, one of the real tough (but nice) guys who was not so good at reading and writing. I'm sure that J.J. was on everyone's list as the

last they would want to see get hurt. Always smiling and good na-
tured, by his very honest unassuming pleasantness and friendship he
gave much to us all.

We used three or four different kinds of grenades. The fragmentation grenades—the "pineapples" you've seen in the movies—usually
came in a wooden box with separators and layers of grenades in rows
this way and that. As I recall, they were not individually boxed. There
were also phosphorous grenades (for burning things up and illuminat-
ing), and smoke grenades, and maybe even some others. These were
individually encased in telescoping cardboard boxes and wrapped at
the seam with heavy-duty yellow plastic tape identifying the type of
grenade in big letters.

I hope I'm right about all this; I made no notes at the time. If I had
to pass a test on all this stuff now, I could be drummed out of the
regiment. But memories of many things are clear, and the feelings will
be there to my last breath.

We all wore dungaree trousers (and dungaree jackets). The trousers
were loose at the bottom and could get caught on brush and other
stuff; an annoyance. Maybe that's why they had leggings in the WWI
uniforms. J.J. made life a bit more comfortable for himself by taking
some of that yellow tape from grenade boxes and wrapping his
dungarees down there by the ankles. He was resourceful enough to
put two and two together to solve this problem. He was the only one
to do this, as far as I know.

Battle can be busy and messy. We piled things where we needed to,
including bodies of our own dead to be taken care of by the grave
registration crew when they got to it. They were busy too. Sometimes
death came too fast to be taken care of "right now."

Two or three of us came around a bend where we now saw a
garage-sized pile of our own dead Marines, not yet processed by the
appropriate personnel. Near the bottom, sticking out of the pile were
two legs with yellow wrappings about the ankles and boots. We were
stunned.

If no tears showed, we cried inside anyway.

War Movies

The United States Marine Corps is not without its faults, but as a fighting outfit, from what I have seen and heard, it is first class. This must also be said: The Japanese military showed many signs of being a highly organized, well-disciplined and dedicated force also. Their layout of guns, fortifications, caves and brilliantly engineered interlocking lines of defense and very adequate weapons made our assaults on their islands most costly endeavors.

Not to be lost is the horrid truth that Japanese tortured prisoners and mutilated bodies of dead Marines. In giving the Marines well-deserved accolades, our enemy must be given honest accounting as well.

Our Marines are a superior fighting force because of their superb training, the discipline that lets each man know he is supported by the other men and allows each of them to know that all will put forth maximum effort and skill to get the job done. The esprit comes from knowing what you are doing and knowing that all the rest of them know what they are doing too. The job gets done at whatever cost, with little concern for self and dedicated concern for one's fellow Marines.

I have seen movies where combat scenes seem to exaggerate blown-up bodies, severed limbs and protruding viscera. Not that such things don't happen, but movies seem to include them "for effect" rather than to tell the story of what the men actually did all this time in battle.

Then there's the other kind of war movie scene, where groups of soldiers in a foxhole or trench sit around smoking cigarettes and chatting about the girl back home, mom's blueberry pie, their favorite dog—all this kind of like soda-fountain chatter, more bullshit than reality, and pointedly meant for consumption on the home front.

My observation in six weeks of battle with Marines is that the overwhelming amount of time in conversation was spent on the very serious business of getting the job done. Not that there weren't lighter moments, and not to deny that home was often on the men's minds, but these were highly trained, well-disciplined and intensely motivated fighters who lived with indescribable personal fears, most inhumane conditions and grinding fatigue—and still got the job done with pride, alive or dead.

What I just wrote is the most important paragraph in the book. I wish I were articulate enough to do the job right of telling it how it was. But the folks back home don't know, and without having these experiences they will never know how it was, no matter how many stories are written by very able writers who do know. The folks just don't know. That's the saddest part of all.

Chapter 15

GAS ATTACK

I didn't get back to battalion HQ too often, but I happened to be there one day (maybe sent, as a "spare part," to deliver a message or get something) when the battalion commander got some hot poop (information, more or less official) on his phone: The Japs were now using poison gas! The major was shocked but elated. He almost shouted, "If they're using gas, we can just get everybody the hell off this island and bury 'em with gas shells."

That sounded like a great idea to me; I was ready to go.

But it didn't happen. (You have never heard of such a mass exodus, have you?) Follow-up investigation of the report showed that a substance called picric acid (I think) was an ingredient in some Jap ammunition. If one of their shells exploded when the air was heavy and with little breeze, the resulting smoke was a thick green vapor that moved slowly over the ground in a way that resembled, but wasn't, a release of illegal poison gas. I saw this sometimes myself.

So we remained on the island for some time more. I'm no chemist, so that's the best I can tell of what happened.

The Night of the Sore Arm

This one was almost fun at times, but with a price.

We were setting up our line for the night just in front of some low ridges. Out in front was a large broad field a couple of hundred yards across and about as deep. It was fairly flat and fairly open except for a semicircular stone wall, three or four feet high, that curved toward the company position and had a ten-foot gap in the middle, near where our foxhole would be. I wondered what function the wall had served, but couldn't come to any sensible conclusion.

About twenty feet behind the wall and a bit to the right of the gap was a small Jap tank. We may have knocked it out, and it didn't seem to be manned. It looked intact, though, and besides, the Nips were sneaky. Could it be a Trojan horse? We didn't know.

The lieutenant wasn't too worried about the tank. His great concern was the gap in the wall. At night, Japanese could sneak toward us from the far end of the field, crouch behind the wall, and make their way, undetected, to the gap. Then what happens? We didn't know either, but the lieutenant had a plan to deter them from using that route to approach our line.

The plan was simple: The two occupants of the "front and center" foxhole, nearest the opening in the wall, would pitch fragmentation and illumination grenades just over the wall all night long. They would be re-supplied with more boxes of grenades throughout the night; Marines in nearby holes were let in on the scheme and alerted to expect (and not shoot) the delivery men treading their way past them in the dark.

The lieutenant reviewed grenade pitching procedure with the two chosen night grenadiers (my buddy Sanders and me). Throwing a hand grenade isn't like pitching a baseball, with a bent elbow that straightens out as your arm extends to the release point. It is more like making a hook shot in basketball, with a straight arm that acts as a catapult.

The lieutenant told us that the launches should be frequent, forty to fifty or more an hour, but at irregular intervals, so that any "wall sneakers" couldn't predict when there would be a lull in the explosions. "Mix 'em up to cross 'em up," was the big idea here. He also told us to mix fragmentation and illumination grenades irregularly so we had chances both to "blow 'em up" and to "light 'em up."

That was the plan; I think it was the looie's idea. He was quite proud of his ingenuity, and he had a right to be.

With "Fireball Miller" and his bull-pen sidekick "Smokey Sanders" both on the mound for the "Company H Hornets," the night was relatively quiet except for distant sporadic rifle fire and some artillery stuff. "Relatively quiet" meant not too much was happening in your part of the front. We were the noisy ones. Serious as our mission was, it was the kind of fun kids would have—except that it went on all night long. We paid the price with sore arms the next day even though we did what we could to avoid straining ourselves.

By doing our flinging in shifts, we both got at least some sleep. We found it an interesting challenge to pitch a grenade as accurately as possible at some particular target point, or to get real tricky and bounce it off the top of the wall to fall and explode just beyond. I must say it was something different and helped relieve the tedium of pretty much the "same old thing" each day.

We never did see any Japs that night, nor any signs that our efforts had thwarted any infiltration attempt. None came through that gate that night, I can tell you. We did see the lieutenant a couple of times before morning, probably checking on the success of his brainchild. And we did see the haulers doing their job to keep us well supplied with grenades. We were happy when daylight came and we resumed our usual routine. I think what made us happiest, aside from the obvious success of the mission, was to see the mountain, repeat, mountain of grenade boxes behind us. They did not haul away the boxes that night, and we laughed proudly at the pile we had made.

It was fun to have something new to talk about, and to clutch our pitching arms in exaggerated pain as the guys came up to ask us about our big night.

362 Boom

We had seen "Hill 362" on the map and occasionally spotted it off to our right on the island. We were told that besides being a good observation and fire control post for the enemy it was probably their main defense headquarters on the island, with caves going down five or six stories. Our planes and artillery did a pretty good job of ruining the above-ground parts of it, but from what we heard, our attempts to hurt the Japs under ground there were not so successful—they were pretty well dug in. After all, they had been fortifying this place for years and regarded it as important to defense of the homeland.

I got only bits and pieces of all the hot poop on Hill 362. One day, though, we were all told that we had a loudspeaker truck over there broadcasting speeches at the main entrance to the caves, trying to talk the occupants into surrendering while they still had the chance— before we sent them all to their ancestors. (Recalling the emaciated looks of some of the few prisoners we saw, and knowing that their food supplies must be very low, we wondered if our truck might have succeeded better with big fans blowing aromas of steak and onions into the cave.)

I would like to believe that by around the fifth week, even though this enemy HQ was holding out, we pretty much had this Iwo operation licked. That doesn't mean that no more of us would be killed and that it would be a picnic, but the Japs must have known that the bell was tolling for them by now. (Thank you, John Donne and Ernest Hemingway.) Maybe there was a chance we could wind this up right now and everybody go home.

But the enemy was reluctant to accept our generous offers of continued life on planet Earth, so plan B swung into action: Big trucks of explosives were backed up in front of the caves on 362— BIG trucks of explosives—and we were told to be prepared for a mighty bang when we lit that baby. The object of this big bang was not to blow up the mountain (unlikely), but to close up one or several of the entrances as best we could, reducing this hill as an effective force, and to send a strong message to the Japanese headquarters command that we had muscle.

We had been warned, and so had the Japanese. The whole island shook according to plan, and 362 became a less potent number.

Chapter 16

WHAT YOU SEE ISN'T WHAT YOU GET

We were in the last few days of the operation, slowly putting the squeeze on the Japs in a shrinking pocket at the north end of the island. (I learned much later that the press had christened this area, with its rocky ravines, "Bloody Gorge.") Again our company set up a line looking out on a large field with some low ridges behind us. We often set up in front of ridges like that—probably not by accident, more likely smart tactics. We would be harder to see with the dark ridges behind us than if we were on higher ground, outlined against the sky. I liked that idea.

This was another of those places where foxholes could not be dug, so we got rocks and built little forts for ourselves. The field out in front was broad and flat, maybe five or six hundred yards across and at least that deep, ending in cliffs that fell quite a distance to a beach of some sort below. Our job was to push the enemy down toward the water, where gunboats offshore would use flares and searchlights to spot them and fire at them. The Japs could try to escape up a couple of steep ravines that led from the shore back up to this field, but we had riflemen posted near the top of the ravines to cut them off.

In case the would-be escapers somehow managed to make it past those riflemen to the top, we had rifles at the ready waiting for them at our end of the flat field. In addition, we had the plain crisscrossed with dozens of ankle-high wires that would set off explosives and flares if anybody—even a good-sized mouse—bumped into them in the darkness. Most of the action, though, seemed to be taking place in the ravines, from which we heard heavy rifle fire all night.

As we sat and listened to all of this action, happy in knowing that we just about had this whole thing whipped, our ships were intermittently sending up tons of star shells that lit things up as much as several full moons for minutes at a time. In between these near-daylight periods came spells of at least a few minutes when it was very dark again and we had to really strain our eyeballs for signs of enemy. It wasn't long before we saw things moving out there. We could even put arms and legs on them. But why didn't the trip flares go off?

I was not the only one seeing these night figures on the plain. Several times my foxhole buddy had one in his sights; but then some of those illumination shells would burst, lighting up the whole field, and instead of seeing our encroachers more clearly we would see nobody out there at all! When darkness returned we would strain our eyes anxiously in hopes of bagging a couple of intruders and getting ourselves on the scoreboard in this turkey shoot. Both of us "saw" those figures often that night, and I would have bet the farm that they were really there, but again and again they would vanish when the lights came on again. I wouldn't blame you for thinking, "These guys were ready for a Section 8" (the looney bin).

It was a very busy and interesting night. In the morning light we could see piles of Jap bodies at the tops of those ravines. It's a wonder our guys there didn't run out of ammo.

The Cemetery

Finally there were no more Japanese to shoot.

There may have been a few still holed up in caves. But it was quiet on the island. Down somewhere near where we had spent the first couple of nights were the graves of the forever fallen. What a sad sight—all those white crosses that once were men. How sad I was.

I really had only one purpose to go there. I wanted to see my singing buddy Tom. (As I sit here comfortably typing on a beautiful summer day in Maine, I cry.) I found his cross and stood there quietly, almost unemotional; then a flood of tears came that I could not stop.

My body shook with pain as I thought of him. I had no control of my acts. Fortunately, a chaplain was nearby. He came over to me, put his arm around my shoulder, and muttered whatever the hell a man can mutter to console another. I appreciated his arm and strength. I pulled myself together again—but never completely.

Chapter 17

LEAVING THE ISLAND, LEAVING FRIENDS, LEAVING MEMORIES

As I left the cemetery, where a cloak of sadness covered me, I began to feel a difference on the island. There were busy sounds of trucks moving about and other busy noises of things being done. Even so, the island where I was seemed quieter somehow. I think I heard an occasional shot from mopping up in caves where enemy soldiers still didn't know the battle was over—for them. The hum on the island was no longer of the threatening sounds that could kill. Even in the sorrow that befell me at Tom's grave, I began to feel a bit more free. I could stand upright out there in a field, pretty sure that no one would shoot me or that no mortars would come my way. Much of the life-saving apprehension that had been my life for weeks began to lift a bit—a bit. Now and then a P-51 would take off from the airfield and then shoot straight up! I was impressed. "Ours," said the voice in my head.

There was talk of leaving the island soon. "About time," I figured. We had done our job—which, as I recall, had been to take control of the island in three days (ho, ho, ho!), then spend seven days mopping up, then turn it over to the Army, which would move in to occupy it for Uncle Sam. As you now know, it didn't quite go that way. Later, I heard scuttlebutt (a rumor) that even just before we were to land, some of the high brass had argued that the assault should be put off for at least a few days. The naval bombardment and some of the air attacks had concentrated mostly on the beach defenses, and latest intelligence indicated that enemy positions in the interior needed further softening up before we sent flesh and blood against them.

I guess you can't do everything. If we could make the island ours by bombing and shelling, why would we need the Marines to make their assault? The Japanese were smart military men, had good equipment and years to build very well-designed and effective defenses. They were ready for us and made it tough.

Although we had bombed and shelled the place considerably and this certainly did some damage, they were so well dug in that much of the explosive effort only moved dirt from one place to another, pretty much leaving their elaborate defenses operative. So much for: "Get in, hit 'em hard and get out."

Things were quieter now. After thirty-eight or so days on the island it looked as if what was left of our company would be leaving. We had lost a lot of men. Of the 230 or 240 we had when we landed, only a dozen or two of the originals were still here to leave. I don't know the exact figures.

When I left the cemetery, I took with me forever the picture of those thousands of crosses and stars of David.

I notice that in recalling these stories, I have written little about combat death and wounds. I certainly saw and heard about plenty of tragic and gory things. I have read about them and I have seen them in movies—sometimes well presented, sometimes not so well—but I don't seem to write much about them myself, not in detail. I don't know why not. Things like that don't seem to be what I naturally focus on, and I feel better telling you the stories in my own way.

Let me pursue this line of thought a little further.

Many writers have been deeply concerned that the American citizenry during the war did not really know what very brave men were giving for them out there, and could not understand why, even if they did know. Writers like these wrote so that those innocent folks back home could not ignore the pain and tragedy out there. They wrote to help people understand the strong and noble feelings of brotherhood that led men to give up their lives for those who fought beside them.

I couldn't agree more that these things needed to be said, and I almost believe that I owe it to my readers to tell more about the killing and carnage—almost. I want to be forthright and honest, as your reporter, and I haven't forgotten about the blood and gore and broken bodies and torn limbs and cries in the night—they were around all the time. But there are other things that need telling, too, and that is the job I have chosen for myself, perhaps as a matter of emotion rather than an intellectual decision. Different people act differently and see things differently; I see these contrasts as interesting and compellingly important. They make life fuller for each of us, and I believe that acknowledging and discussing them helps us know each other, and ourselves, better.

My thoughts keep returning to the cemetery. That picture remains vivid in my mind. But more than a sea of markers, I see fathers holding mothers, parents who will never again hold their sons. I see wives whose tears cannot drown their loneliness and pain, especially when the kids ask, "Where's Daddy?"

Even more sorrowful is the thought that so many of the folks back home, in spite of all the reporting, still know nothing and care little for the sacrifice of others on their behalf, in World War II or any of our other wars. This "What war?" view bothers me and I don't know what to do about it. I write this to tell you what I saw, but I can't make you know how it feels to have a "brother" blown up in front of you. I can't make you imagine how it felt when the lights went out for you and you became only a white cross in a distant field. But such thoughts lead only to torment and bitterness. I am not bitter. I am blessedly lucky. I have been to the valley of despair and returned, I think, a better man.

Chapter 18

ALL ABOARD, AGAIN

We went about the tasks of assembling the remains of our company—and what little gear we had—to get aboard the ship. This was definitely something to look forward to. It may have been just a carbon copy of the ship we came on (thousands were built), but this ship was different. It was a peaceful place, and headed on a peaceful mission, or at least not taking us to another war.

We all knew there was a war going on but were not thinking that far ahead yet; just glad to have gotten clear of the last one. There would be time later to think about what challenging plans our leaders had for us. We didn't know about the April invasion of Okinawa that was in progress as we sailed away from Iwo. But knowing that the war was still on and that we would be called upon again, we did wonder if our next act would be another of those little dots on the map of the Pacific—or the "big one," Japan itself.

In time they would tell us. Right now, they were giving us a chance to lick our wounds, so to speak—get some R&R, some replacement troops and weapons, and some training for "the new plan." All this was originally supposed to happen on Guam, I was told, but because of the heavy losses we had taken, the leadership decided to send the division all the way back to its home base, Camp Tarawa in Hawaii, for "repairs." The Fifth Marine Division had suffered 8,770 men killed or wounded—well over 40 percent.

The ship we boarded to leave Iwo contrasted interestingly with the one that had delivered us there a few weeks earlier. That ship, the USS *Lubbock*, had been full to the gunwales and beyond with troops (packed like sardines), materials and machines of war. This "get-outa-here" ship had plenty of room aboard for our sadly smaller number. One of the first things I wanted to do, and I'm sure it was the same for the rest of the men, was to get cleaned up! I mentioned earlier that on the island, it was good for our health and longevity to blend in with the soil, so we had all gotten very dirty. The thought of a shower and a shave and some clean duds loomed very big for us now. Our leaders and hosts were happy to oblige. I went to the showers, threw away my many-weeks-seasoned dungarees, stepped in and did the soap and hot-water thing. Worth a million, soap and hot water. (Thinking back now, I wish I had kept those clothes, dirt and all.)

Oh, that shower! They usually say it only about women, but I "luxuriated" in my bath. And didn't I hear the happy sound of others doing the same. Great!

I dried off, then went to the "wash up" to shave. Who was that gaunt, bearded, very sun-tanned young man looking out at me from the mirror? Not I! My mother would not have known her boy! (It's just an expression; even through six weeks of beard, my mother would have known.) After some struggle, I finally figured out how to scrape the whiskers off a little at a time, and there was the new me.

I was given some fresh dungarees, a size smaller than I used to wear (I was twenty pounds lighter), and now in my new life and with my new body my stomach had messages for me. Especially as we lined up for chow and could smell real food, eager anticipation reigned. Each of us picked up one of those big, shiny, compartmented steel trays and plodded too slowly through the line that led to the source of the succulent smells. I piled on steak, ham, turkey, potatoes and gravy, sweet potatoes, peas and other veggies, bread, pie and ice cream—really! And, to top it off for heroes and gentlemen, a cigar. I forgot all about the island and death and hunger and cans of beans, and even forgot some of the fear. That indestructible steel tray held as much joy for me as a toy store would for a kid.

I found a place at a table (a table!) with my messmates, and dove in. I devoured a forkful of steak, had a taste of the ham (great ham!), a spoonful of sweet potato and a pea, got a bit of the pie down—and the gate closed! My stomach must have been about the size of a golf ball by now. The food was delicious, but no more would go down.

One of the saddest things I ever did in my life was to empty that feast into the garbage. How I would have eaten it all and gone back for seconds. Everybody else had itty-bitty stomachs, too. One of the prices we pay for war. To salve my despair (I hated my small stomach right then), I went topside, lit the cigar and said, "This is hard to beat," or something like that. Life was different again.

This was no cruise ship, but there were fewer of us than there had been on the way over. On that trip we had been crammed into canvas stretchers laced, two feet apart, onto pipes in the bowels of the ship. We had comfortable bunks this time, much nicer. There were six or eight of us in a 12-foot by 14-foot (or so) compartment; really plenty of room for all us gentlemen passengers. Some previous occupant had cut a flap in an air duct by the wall, allowing a fresh breeze to gush in. Life was good.

There was little thought of what lay ahead of us in the war, or at least little talk of it. This was a bit of well-earned R&R. As I recall, there were very few if any "formations" or any other organized activity for the guys. As a matter of fact, we became quite lazy, and enjoyed doing nothing. This was in sharp contrast to combat on the island, where we felt constantly "busy" even if we weren't moving (remember all that mental stuff I told you about earlier).

Lying about aboard ship, not having to be constantly concerned with "the job" any more, was quite a pleasure. The sea was calm, the air was fresh and we had plenty of time to shoot the breeze and get acquainted again with things of the outside world; time to swap stories about home and catch up on some of what had happened on Iwo to guys we hadn't seen much the past six weeks. This was great. I didn't get the chance I had looked forward to for more interesting talks with Wilson B. Grounds, but there were new friends to make and old ones to catch up with.

The meals they served during the rest of the trip to Hawaii didn't measure up to that wonderful welcome feast, but as our stomachs rose to the challenge of real food we became able to eat more and enjoy it. I had some weight to regain as did many others.

Right after lunch on about our third day after leaving Iwo, a bunch of us were out on deck, standing and sitting and lazing in the sunshine. The atmosphere was carefree, insouciant, resort-like. You could feel the guys beginning to let go and relax some, breathing easy. The web of tension that had held us together for weeks was loosening. I was sunning myself on the after deck near the fantail, leaning back against some of the aft superstructure, contentedly breathing in the sea air, maybe even smiling.

Then it happened: WHAM!—the loudest noise I ever heard bristled all my nerves and sent some men to the gunwales ready to jump overboard, while others frantically began trying to claw foxholes in the steel deck or scrambling for a hatchway in the superstructure.

I grew instantly older. I shook, not so much from fright as from shock. My nervous system went back to "high alarm"—the tense feeling that I'd had to live with on the island and that had only recently started to fade.

The ship's public address system could have announced, "Now hear this: There will be target practice for the ship's aft five-inch gun at 1300 hours." But they didn't.

Days later, we were still a bit edgy, especially when we went near the aft gun tub, but we were getting closer to our destination, where there would be new things to do. We saw the big island of Hawaii getting larger. There it was, green in the sea, waiting for us, friendly-like. Not at all the same as approaching Sulphur Island weeks before. The people who do these things brought the ship into port. Before long we grabbed our gear and gladly marched from the docks over to a pleasant nearby park, just across the street from the clean and beautiful city of Hilo. There our leaders halted the battalion and gave us the "at rest" command, meaning that we would stay leisurely in place in our marching formation while we waited for the trucks that would take us up in the hills to Camp Tarawa.

The people of Hilo welcomed us as heroes. They had set up a stage there in the park, where a Hawaiian band played for us and pretty Hawaiian dancers in grass costumery artfully shuffled and writhed in the rhythms of their native music. We were red-blooded American males, and the girls smiled and swayed seductively, but hundreds of eyes focused elsewhere. The object of this mass gaze was a sign in the window of a place of public refreshment across the street: "BEER."

Chapter 19

BACK AT CAMP TARAWA

In time the trucks came. We loaded up and rode through the streets of Hilo, where to our great surprise, many of the local people turned out as on a parade route, waving flowers and signs welcoming us back as heroes. On Iwo, we had been buried in the push of "getting the job done," and except for our royal reception aboard ship, it had been months since we had gotten an "attaboy" from anyone. This was kinda like being back home kinda. I was deeply moved by these appreciative and affectionate greetings. Thank you, people of Hilo. We noticed!

Emerging from the city, we took the long ride over the desolate, moonscape-like lava fields back to Camp Tarawa, our Division's old familiar "home" up on that vast plateau. We few remaining "originals" were tickled to death to find some of our old buddies waiting there for us. Many men who had left the island wounded came back to their old outfit. How good it was to see them! It was like getting together with "the old gang" again—like welcoming back lost brothers. The reunion was saddened only by the thoughts of those we would never see again.

The Division granted the returning troops a few days of R&R, trucking them to a beach somewhere and providing barbeques and other refreshments. I went on one of these beach getaways and found men in swim trunks (no girls) showing off the scars, stitches and missing body parts resulting from wounds and surgery—kind of a military version of an elementary-school show-and-tell. They all seemed to be glad to be back with their old outfit again.

I went on only one of these excursions; not because I didn't like beaches or barbecues, but because I had work to do. I was still the company armorer, charged with storage and care of company weapons and related items. I had to find a suitable facility to set up shop, get workbenches and lockers installed, and start keeping records of what we had and what we needed. So while my buddies played, I was focused on "getting the job done." My father was that kind of man, so I guess I came by those traits honestly.

After most of the troops had spent a few days on this relaxed schedule, orders went out that the Division would return to its usual training routine. I was so busy that I didn't learn about this until it had already happened. "Where's *my* R&R?" I asked, shaking my head. I guess it had passed by while I was building my own little empire. "Tough stuff," as they say in the business.

I eventually got my reward, a third stripe for my sleeve (as a corporal I had worn two)—I was a sergeant now! I was happy to get the extra prestige and the pay raise, and I'm sure the folks back home celebrated in their own way. I can see my father passing out cigars or buying his buddies a round of beers to honor his son's leap up in the military structure.

A note here about sergeants. I enjoyed being a sergeant and felt greatly honored, but there was an important difference between me and the "line" sergeants, whose job was to provide leadership, in combat and elsewhere. Sergeants like me won our rank through technical expertise (like the Ordnance specialty I had picked up in Alaska and was following now). I greatly respected the line sergeants I worked with during my service, and my praise of them in these pages is in no way intended to reflect glory on myself. My job was different.

The officers knew and understood the "grand plan"; it was the line sergeants who got the job done by seeing that the troops carried the plan out. Should the truth be known, the line sergeants made it all work. Many an officer, especially the newer ones, found his sergeants to be the source of important information, experience and ability. These officers would have been much less effective without the sergeants, many of whom had the years of battle and leadership experience. Ya gotta love the sergeants, even if you hate 'em.

I respected the line sergeants for what they accomplished with their men, and one H Company sergeant in particular sticks in my memory. Paul Meredith was a bright, good-looking, companionable sort, whose easy demeanor did not fit the popular image of "Marine Sergeant." He was an exceptional leader of men, though, and because of his outstanding qualities and deeds he was commissioned a Second Lieutenant on the field of battle. We were all proud of him.

Following this ringing encomium for the sergeants, God bless 'em, let me state a sincere commendation for us "spare parts." We were the cooks, clerks, quartermasters, and even the Field Musics (buglers) who performed our own indispensable functions when in camp and in training. But we were still riflemen, because that's the way the Marine Corps does things—we were all part of a professional military team. It is tough enough for a thoroughly trained rifleman on the line to do his job well after months or years of training and combat have made it second nature for him. But please consider the difficulty and threat to the man who spent those months or years cooking or clerking or bugle-blowing. At a moment's notice he may be called on to step up to the line, fill another's job and fill it well, in order to save his own life and those of others. This happened constantly on Iwo: Marines whose "real" jobs were to drive trucks (or to make spaghetti or to make sure salaries got paid) had to fill in on the line for the many men who were wiped out. They all fought the war!

It was good to be back in the familiar surroundings of Camp Tarawa—great to see old friends and interesting to meet the new men who were arriving to replace the many we had lost. I can't say I was an "old salt," or even felt like one. (I was twenty-one, you remember.) But I was "experienced," and it was good for my pride to be able to give the new guys some of the lowdown on how it's done. It was also fortunate that my duties as an armorer didn't take all my time, so I got to do field training with the guys on the line—running the plays, just like in football. This gave us all a better feeling, me especially.

From time to time at Camp Tarawa I would get together with Hal.

We couldn't re-create the "Tune Timers"—it would never be the same without Tom and Ted—but we found some other fellows to sing with. There was a tenor whose name I forget, who looked a bit like the 1930s child movie star Freddie Bartholomew; and a rugged, raw-boned gem of a guy with a real bass voice, Ogle Lemon (real name) from somewhere in Tennessee. These two left after a while for God knows where, but fate was kind and we found a couple of artillery guys, named "Buggsy" and "Frenchie," who could sing. (If they can sing, who cares what their names are?)

We rang some chords and had some fun. Then, in time, they too slipped away to other pursuits. Much to my sorrow, the old Tune Timers with Ted and Tom had never made any recordings or even had photos taken, but I still have a picture of Hal and Buggsy and Frenchie and me. I treasure that.

Now that I had my third stripe, I became a member of the newly organized Sergeants Club. The staff sergeants (four stripes), gunnery sergeants (five stripes), and first sergeants (six stripes) were considered non-commissioned officers and had long had a facility of their own, the NCO Club). Now there was a place where we "just plain sergeants" could meet for a beer in the evening. Not only that, our club had its own separate mess hall. When we didn't feel like partaking of what the general mess was serving, we could go to our Club, pay a little extra, and get gourmet meals—served by our own chefs on real plates instead of the durable stainless steel platters the troops used.

As I recall, there was a fair amount of lamb available from New Zealand. This was neat, but not everyone loves lamb, and even lamb-lovers want a break now and then, so a couple of resourceful sergeants put two and two together and came up with a winner of a plan. The mastermind of this scheme was a hot-rock sergeant who in real life was a reporter for the St. Louis Post-Dispatch (as I recall—his name shouldn't escape me, but it does). Camp Tarawa was situated on a broad plateau (roughly the size of Rhode Island) which was also the location of one of the largest cattle ranches in the world. The reporter and two buddies grabbed a jeep and a rifle and returned with a sizeable cow that must have happened into the path of a stray bullet. The sergeants now had a fine change of menu.

Back to work. With our company now augmented by several of our returned wounded, as well as our bright new fresh replacements, we turned to the task of training for our next assignment. We took this even more seriously than we had before Iwo. With at least that campaign under our belts—more in some cases—we were seasoned veterans, and we knew we had a war to win.

The company's exercises in the field "clicked" better than before Iwo, with the troops running the plays like the best of the NFL. It was encouraging to see how eager the Marines who had been in battle were to help the replacements, some of them only raw recruits, learn exactly what to do and how to do it when ordered. For their part, the new men were glad to be coached by the guys who had "been there." This worked well. We had a "team."

Having lived through Iwo, I was experienced, but I appreciated the chance to improve my skills and understanding. I was still the company armorer, but I had the armorer's tent running smoothly, so I got to work in the field exercises as a rifleman on the line, as a part of the demolition squad, and as part of the mortar section, where I mostly handled ammunition. I was also sent by H Company to some of the "schools" run elsewhere in the Division, where I acquired new know-how and brought it back to convey to our the troops in small-group training presentations. Just another job for the "swing man."

I enjoyed my several specialties and welcomed the challenges of doing them—playing my part in running the plays well. We were getting good, but we also wondered where we were going. Where were we to use this ability we were working so hard to get?

We began to narrow down the answers to this question when we were assigned some new training exercises: throwing three-pronged grappling hooks up the side of a cliff and pulling ourselves to the top with rifles in hand and full gear on our backs. This was tough work, and dangerous.

Chapter 20

CHANGE OF PLAN

As our training progressed into the summer we got in real good shape and the team worked well together. Some ideas of what we would do with all this ability began to appear in our orientation sessions. We had kept up on world news—of grave importance to us and we didn't need a crystal ball to come up with a good guess for the next major target to be hit: the Japanese homeland!

It was only the staunch confidence in our team and our commanders that kept us from fear of such a daunting task. How can I say this more strongly? We had even heard estimates of the cost in American lives of a direct assault on the home islands. Very Big Numbers! One report estimated 100,000 casualties and suggested the loss of a whole division of the Marines who were first in. There were no written orders for this division after their landing. It was assumed they would be gone. Us??

Then throw this into the mix: The Japanese military was smart, resourceful, well equipped, and determined to fight to the last man. And how much harder would be their effort and resolve when it was mother and children and home they were fighting for? On top of that, add those many millions of Japanese not in the military—even the grandmothers and women and children who would fight us with rocks and sharp sticks in village after village.

And the cliffs: They could throw rocks down at us throughout our rugged climb, before we even reached level ground to fight on. Would we need to kill millions (while losing tens of thousands of our own) to make 'em give up? Not a happy prospect.

AND THEN:

In early August our company was on maneuvers about seven miles out of camp. Word came over the captain's radio that there was

important news and that we should return to Camp "on the double."
("Double time" marching means trotting in step.) The word was that
our Air Force had just dropped the biggest bomb ever made on the
Japanese city of Hiroshima.

I won't say we ran back seven miles to the camp, but we did do it
at a "forced march" pace (a little bit like Olympic race walking) with
hopeful anticipation that maybe, just maybe, this could help wind up
this war without the United States having to invade their homeland,
and we wouldn't need to climb those cliffs.

Corporal John Nehme, the mortar section leader, and I had our
bunks in the armorer's tent. We returned there now to wait with
cautious hope for more hot poop (news) on the situation. Having
worked up a sweat on the march back, we decided that a cooling
drink was in order. We had stashed a case of beer in a hole in the
ground beneath the tent's wooden floor to keep it a bit cooler (the
beer, not the floor), and we invited Nehme's lieutenant to join our
vigil and quench his thirst at our gracious expense. I think the three
of us killed that case in about twenty minutes.

After two long days of anxious waiting, we received news. It
seemed that the obliteration of Hiroshima had not been enough to
make the enemy call it quits, so our planes had dropped a second
unimaginably huge bomb, this one on Nagasaki. Rumors, later confirmed, indicated that the Japanese were suing for peace.

I can't tell you how deeply I felt at hearing this news, but I'll try.

Imagine you are in the electric chair (and you are innocent). The
countdown has almost reached midnight, the executioner is about to
throw the switch, and suddenly the statewide power grid fails. Moments later, the governor is on the phone with his order for your
release.

We didn't know what would happen to us, and neither did the big
brass, I guess. Things were a lot different now. Would they ship us all
right home?—somewhere else? Maybe to Japan for occupation? We
didn't know, but we were jubilantly happy with this turn of events.

While the brass was figuring out the next move after this surprising change in the grand plan, we troops were kept busy getting "organized" while awaiting "the word." We didn't need to wait long. A few days later, the unconditional surrender of the Japanese leaders was accepted by General of the Army (five stars) Douglas MacArthur aboard the USS *Missouri*.

Many Marines never cared too much for this general, and often spoke of him in derision. I don't necessarily begrudge him this moment of glory, but for me the real hero was Harry S. Truman. The president was in on the atomic bomb during the final stags of its development and testing. It was "Give-'Em-Hell Harry" who weighed the world's possible moral response to the bomb against the saving of countless of our lives in an assault on the Japanese islands, and came down on the side of the troops.

This invasion was to be a battle of thousands and thousands of men, not just some faraway "assault," as abstract as a chess move. I was scheduled to be one of the "assaulters" and very likely one of the numbers in those "thousands and thousands." Harry was talking about me! Most of the other guys knew this, too. Who was going to pay the price for this war somebody else had started? My buddies and I had paid quite a bit already, and we all had known many men who paid much more. I voted for Harry when he ran for president again. He had guts!

Chapter 21

NEW ASSIGNMENT, NEW SCENERY

Eventually "the word" came: The Fifth Division was going to board ships again and sail to Japan as an occupation force. This was by far a better way of getting there than fighting our way in. Even at this distance in time, I shudder at the almost inconceivably costly assault that might have been required, and that could have been the final act of many thousands of us.

The prospect of occupying Japan was exciting and greatly preferable to the invasion that might have been, but it offered its own risks. I had heard about military occupation forces in the past having their day-to-day mission made miserable and deadly by attacks, direct as well as surreptitious, from the local populace. Large troop assemblies could be hurt by a grenade suddenly going off in their midst; troops patrolling the streets could become targets for snipers; and an off-duty soldier walking by himself could be grabbed, dragged into an alley and knifed.

We had every reason to expect a sullen, hostile populace in view of the fierce, determined military attitude we had encountered in their armed forces.

But that was something to worry about later. Somewhere along the line we had been issued Japanese phrase books. I had always been interested in language and languages, so poring over my phrase book was time happily spent as we steamed to our new destination. I learned some words and phrases that would come in handy later.

I recall us trying out our newfound language on each other, passing back and forth the usual phrase-book questions and answers. I learned to say, in halting Japanese, "I am an American Marine sergeant" (for whatever they cared), or ask, "Where is the toilet?" And of course, one of the first vocabulary items of interest to many of us was the Japanese word for "beer." It turned out (what a surprise!) to be *biiru* (pronounced "bee-ee-ru"—three syllables, with accent on the first). Some of our guys turned this into "beer-oo," which was probably close enough for practical purposes.

Before our trip to Japan I had lamented that the Schlitz beer shipped from the states was "green" (probably not properly aged) and weak (only 3.2 per cent alcohol), and I expected Japanese beer to be some thin watery stuff with rice hulls floating on top. Not so, by a long shot! Happy testing later revealed the local product to be full, rich and sufficient in alcohol to make a one-liter bottle a great flavorful beginning to a happy buzz. Downing three bottles of it would get to the best of us veteran beer drinkers. This Japanese brew was made from old German recipes (a fortuitous result of the Berlin-Tokyo axis?) I was so wrong about the beer, and it was so-o-o good!

Our trip from Hawaii to Japan was not all fun and games. We were headed for a most important mission that would demand discipline and skills we already had, plus new modes of operation that we were being taught while still afloat. As the big brass worked on their plans for a successful occupation (and our role in it), we troops were repeatedly warned to stay together, to stay within areas designated for us, such as our own compounds, and to be ever watchful for signs of local resistance or hostility.

We kept rolling along westward, and finally we could begin to see the green coast of Japan's southernmost island, Kyushu. We were told that our destination was Sasebo, a Kyushu city of 250,000 people, with a large enclosed harbor that was the home of an excellent, extensive, and well-protected naval base. To get to the harbor we had to negotiate several miles of rather narrow channels defined by many high cliffs. As we slowly made our way through these channels, it began to dawn on the troops that these cliffs looked familiar—we had studied maps and photos of them as we trained for the assault that we had, thankfully, not had to carry out. This was to have been our beachhead, and these were the cliffs we had been expected to scale in order to launch attacks against the Japanese defenders at the top.

All the Marines aboard stood at the gunwales, silently staring at this hostile terrain as it slid past. The words were written on every face: "Holy shit! We would never have made it!"

Chapter 22

NEW LAND, NEW PEOPLE, NEW JOB

As we emerged from the channels, the whole of Sasebo Harbor opened up for us. On the far side of it (several miles away, it seemed to us) lay the naval base. Slowly still, we made our way toward it.

There was plenty to look at and ponder in these foreign waters. Of especial interest, we saw a man rowing a little boat out to a harbor island barely the size of a large living room. Back home, we would have overlooked a spot so small except maybe for the "adventure" of rowing out to it. This man was farming it! He had crops growing on every square inch of soil there, and he commuted by rowboat to cultivate them. As we were to see, feeding the Japanese people in wartime required all manner of highly intensive land use.

I still didn't feel comfortable about the whole operation. Would there be renegade forces making desperate forays against us? Would fanatical loyalists risk their lives to kill a Marine?

How likely was it that all these millions who had been schooled for so long to hate and fear us would suddenly lay down their arms and cease to include that hatred among life's concerns?

The Japanese had been told that no man was allowed to join the Marines unless he could prove that he had killed his mother and his father! This painted a mean, heartless and fearsome picture of us. We and our leaders didn't really know what to expect—and, I guess, neither did the Japanese. They seemed to be an inscrutable people.

Our main job in Japan was to "be there"—to maintain a governing presence. The division would begin by dispatching teams, in all deliberate haste, to gather any Japanese weapons and render them useless. Once we had taken this step to dispel hopes and means of insurgent activity, we were to be prepared to follow any new orders the diplomatic and military powers upstairs found necessary to maintain order and command of the populace and general situation.

We docked in the harbor not far from the city and "debarked" (got off the ship). As per the plan, we marched away from the dock to the downtown area, where we assembled and organized our outfit for further movement.

We marched through what had been a busy city of a quarter-million, many of them likely employed at the naval base and ship-building areas. But we saw no people! There were only the downtown buildings, little damaged by our air raids, and a few Japanese policemen with their swords as badges of authority. The buildings were there, but where could the people have disappeared to?

At one point, still downtown, our outfit halted for a break. Not knowing whether it was "legal" (or wise), I went over to one of the uniformed police officers, eager to try out my skills with the new language. I asked, "*Benjo wa doko des' ka?*" (Where is the toilet?)

He smiled politely and pointed to a door in a low building that could have been a railroad station. As I approached the doorway, a lone Japanese woman came out of it. "Oops—this isn't right," I said to myself and quickly reviewed my Japanese phrases in my mind. "Yup, right phrase," I said silently, returned to the same smiling policeman, and repeated the question.

He smiled more broadly, showing even more teeth, and pointed again to the same door. Although I could read none of the Kanji writing (ideographic characters) above the doorway, I went in, figuring that he knew what he was talking about. Inside, I looked around and concluded that this was communal, rather than separate as a public restroom back home would have been. I did my business and departed, a bit chagrined, but wiser in the local customs.

As we marched on, through the outskirts of the city, we could see window curtains pulled aside and curious slant-eyed faces staring at us with wonder. That answered one question. The rest of the folks had fled to the countryside. Whether they had been ordered to do so or not, I don't know, but the city was mostly deserted.

The main street we had been following northward became a country road which took us a few miles (past more curious peeks from the locals) to our new home, an area of very suitable barracks and parade grounds that had been a training station for Japanese naval officers. Here we would stay for a while, maintaining our "presence" as we awaiting more detailed orders for our occupying mission.

Our leaders used our time well, schooling us on aspects of military occupation and keeping us up to date on what was going on elsewhere in Japan and the world. They also scheduled daily formations and some drill to keep us military.

We had reveille, morning chow and the morning report, a daily parade-ground formation at which the sergeants reported to the officers that all hands in their units were "present or accounted for." We also had the evening formation, when those in authority reported to higher echelons, including the battalion commander, that we were all there. After this formation ("recall"); which happened about 4:30 p.m. every day, we were "free" for the evening. We were well fed, curious about our future—and, at least some of us, a bit bored.

Gunnery Sergeant Sparacino was one of those whose official functions included receiving and passing on reports at the evening formation. On our third or fourth day at Sasebo, right after recall, the "gunny" and I were looking out over the countryside and heard the whistle of a train. We could also hear it "chug-chugging" slowly as if it was going up a grade or around a sharp bend.

We looked at each other and without a word each of us asked, "I wonder where that train is going?" It seemed only a couple of miles away, so we started wandering over the hills in the direction of that whistle, following paths that linked acre-sized plots of land with the homesteads that cultivated them. With a sense of high adventure, we forgot any warnings given us about our physical welfare and threw ourselves into the pursuit of our quest.

Reaching the railroad right of way, we sought out some locals who could tell us how to get around. We found a couple of elderly Japanese gentlemen and learned, via halting Japanese, even more halting English, and many gestures, some of the information we sought. Yes, what we had heard was a passenger train; it went by here every afternoon at this time (around 4:50 p.m.), slowed greatly because of the grade and sharp curve; it stopped at the next village, Koura, a few miles north.

And yes (also pretty important), there was a train coming back south through here around five o'clock in the morning.

We looked at each other. We forgot about the war, the formations, the occupation, and our important daytime duties; vague visions of adventure danced in our heads. We had little concern for protocol or the possible dire consequences if "things went wrong." We had been to hell and back and maybe had a right to a bit of lighthearted joy, wherever we might find it. And what could be worse than being on Sulphur Island?

We returned to camp and did some strategizing. We picked up another buddy, Red, to join our adventure, and not many days later, armed with coin of the realm (chocolate bars and cigarettes), we made the first of what would be several trips to Koura.

The first time we boarded this train with its three small wooden passenger cars, the other riders, mostly old people and children, were so astonished that they sat like statues, wondering what was going to happen. Soon, though, our casual demeanor and our lack of weapons seemed to put them somewhat at ease.

When the conductor came through collecting tickets, he almost had kittens, but quickly regained his professional composure. He too noticed that we had no weapons, and after an exchange of American cigarettes, he was our ally. This would be very handy on our downhill trip coming back.

I like the epigram, "Good things happen to good people." Things couldn't have gone better. When we first arrived in Koura (a village with very little "downtown") we made prudent inquiry of the astounded villagers and soon located some young women for companionship.

These ladies were Korean; that makes a lot of difference! A few years before, the Japanese army had invaded Korea and sent many of its people back to Japan as "laborers"—pretty much slaves, really. The Koreans burned with hatred of the Japanese, so can you imagine the welcome we "liberators" received from our hostesses? These girls thought we were the cat's meow. They just couldn't treat these three nice guys any better. There was a lot of partying, including some drinking, dancing (yes, these girls could dance), singing, and general frivolity. We had it made. We had fallen into a pot of jam, and we knew it.

Alarm clocks got us up in the morning to catch the southbound local, following a cup of tea apiece and several hugs.

A few miles out of Sasebo the engineer, who liked American cigarettes as much as the conductor did, kindly brought the train to an almost dead halt in the wilderness, allowing three weary Marines to jump to the ground and make their way back to camp.

After a few trips, and small gifts to the regular passengers, we became the stuff of little local legends. And we made it every morning for roll call, so we were present (as well as accounted for).

From time to time our comrades back in camp would ask things like, "Haven't seen you around, where were you last night?" We would point generally northward—a direction that included some nearby barracks as well as Koura—and tell them we'd been visiting friends "over there." We considered that an honest answer.

Chapter 23

NORTH TO THE PITTSBURGH OF JAPAN

It came almost as a relief for our poor party-weary bodies when our battalion was pulled together again for a new assignment. This time we would be "maintaining a presence" in Shimonoseki, one of a trio of large cities (the others were Kokura and Yawata) at the northern tip of Kyushu. I don't remember whether we traveled there by trains or trucks, but I know we didn't march those hundred-plus miles.

This area, not far from Honshu, the main island, was called "The Pittsburgh of Japan" for all the heavy industry there, especially steel work. Because these three cities manufactured much of the heavy equipment for war, they received particular attention from our air force. As a result, if you had a big truck with large tires, I believe you could have driven in a straight line anywhere you wished over the mortar and concrete fragments that had once been buildings.

Something like thirty blocks of downtown Shimonoseki was naught but rubble, except for three buildings that our flyers had been given special orders not to destroy. They sure showed their skill, because those three came through with hardly a scratch: the depot from which ferries departed for Honshu, a certain bank building, and an office building upon the front of which was an enameled sign that read (in English) "Greater East Asia Co-Prosperity Sphere."

The GEACPS was the Japanese government's euphemism for the empire they had created by taking over half the islands and nations of the Pacific basin—in the "best interests" of all the conquered people, of course. They had a saying something like, "We need to hang together with all our brown brothers." I doubt that many of the overrun people bought that idea.

Beyond the downtown were the remains of large factories. Huge sheds that may have contained heavy equipment and ships under construction had been pulverized, along with railroad tracks that ran through them, but machine shops and engineering offices situated in caves in the mountains were relatively undamaged.

We had quarters in a set of buildings that may have been offices or apartments before we got there. Substantial by local standards, they were neat and served our purposes of billeting quite nicely. Around the whole compound was a six- or seven-foot wall made of ten-inch boards, and we were more or less expected to stay inside it. The wall was not particularly easy to climb, but part of one board was missing, allowing us to peek at the "outside world." One day while peeking out I saw a Japanese man peeking in.

I was curious and so was he. Haltingly, assisted by gestures, we conversed to our mutual delight in smatterings of two languages. I sprang my, "I am an American Marine sergeant" phrase on him; he said his name was Hisashi Takahashi, and managed to communicate to me that he had been a radio operator on a ship (maybe in the Indian Ocean).

On a later mutual visit to the hole in the wall he brought along a brother to meet me. I asked Hisashi his brother's name; and he replied, "Ani." So, trying out my Japanese language and Japanese politeness, I greeted the brother with something like, "Good afternoon, Ani." This generated curious chuckles from the two of them, who explained to me (politely) that "Ani" was not his name, but the Japanese word for "older brother." We all had a good laugh.

On another occasion I was at the hole in the wall when a pretty young Japanese girl showed up to get a look at the strangers inside. Doing the best I could, phrase book in hand, I politely asked her name. She replied, "Leiko Oonishi" (long 'o', like "oh-oh"). We had a dignified but pleasant chat, and met again the next day at the "hole." I said I would like to visit her; she pointed to her house nearby and indicated that I would be welcome to call that afternoon.

When the time came, I got over the fence and knocked at her door. My knock was soon answered by a dignified, smiling older gentleman, obviously her father. Between the two of us, we worked out that he was indeed the father of the pretty Leiko (three syllables—her name had a very liquid sound). He was a superintendent of some sort at a nearby power plant, so I could tell I was in respectable company.

He invited me in, just in time for me to see Leiko disappearing into a back room with her mother. Now and then she peeped through a curtain while her dad and I knocked off a few thimbles full of sake or plum brandy or whatever it was. Smiling and bowing, we toasted our two countries and wished them everlasting peace and good will. I was getting the hang of people-to-people diplomacy here, but I'm not sure I made any time with the daughter.

Things got a bit livelier in Shimonoseki and on a few occasions we got out at night to visit a "downtown" of sorts that was developing in one of the neighborhoods. We had received our pay in yen and it burned a hole in my pocket until I could find a place to buy some beer.

I wished I could forget my having turned down a basketful of Japanese currency a few months earlier—many tens of thousands of yen—because I hadn't been able to believe that we would be paid in that same "funny money" if we went to Japan. (So much for being considered, at times, a bright student!) There was a bright spot, though: We found a brewery in Shimonoseki that charged us a few sen (hundredths of a yen—I calculated about 43 cents U.S.) for a case of 12 one-liter bottles. And this was the good stuff! Not everything went wrong!

It was slowly dawning on me that we had run into no "resistance," none of the attacks on our persons that we had expected, no insurrections or other trouble anywhere around. The more I thought about this the less I could figure it out. I found it difficult to believe that all these people were as friendly as they seemed. They should have been scared shitless of us, and at least a few patriotic radicals could be expected to "kamikaze" themselves for the emperor.

The only explanation I could come up with was that this nation was traditionally obedient to authority and that the emperor must have told them, "These Americans are now the bosses of this country. The Sun of Heaven has spoken."

That may not be completely right, but it helps make sense for me.

I'm not sure if we ever really had permission from our battalion commander, Major Smoak, to be out and about the town on other than official occupation business, but we did get to see a few things. A couple of us were wandering around down by some small docks where fishermen came in. Some people lived on small boats there, too, and my musical friend Hal was with me in spirit when we heard music coming from that direction.

Believe it or not, the boat dwellers had cranked up a record player from which came the strains of "My Blue Heaven" (in English). Several of them were sitting around singing (in English) along with the victrola, and we joined them—in English, of course, and even with a bit of harmony. They were amazed—probably for several reasons. We were surprised as well.

In Shimonoseki, as in many other Japanese cities full of wooden structures, there were many swimming pool-sized concrete reservoirs scattered about through the neighborhoods to serve as sources of water for fighting fires. A small local boy fell into one of these reservoirs while we were stationed there and would have drowned had a Marine, named Bill Callahan, not been nearby to jump in and save him. This made the local newspapers, one of which printed a large photograph of Bill and the boy on the front page. I didn't know until somebody showed me that picture that Bill had been a minor celebrity before joining the Marines—a pitcher for one of the Red Sox farm teams.

I never did see Leiko again, but I never forgot her (and her ambassador of a father).

Chapter 24

GOOD DUTY BY THE HARBOR

The time came to leave Shimonoseki. For about two dozen of us, what came next was a new kind of assignment, from which we didn't know what to expect. We would be returning to Sasebo (not near that favorite railroad line of mine, unfortunately) to form a "Provisional Detachment." We would be under the command of a Marine lieutenant answerable only to some big guy higher than our division commander, maybe someone in Corps HQ. Didn't we feel like hot stuff! We packed our gear and took off for good old Sasebo Harbor.

The Detachment's responsibility was to patrol about a thousand yards of docks, which had been taken over by the U.S. Navy to provide repair and re-supply services for its ships in the area. We were also responsible for guarding an access road that led from the docks to a large warehouse about half a mile inland. That huge building was a repository of Japanese personal weapons, and our lieutenant was specifically directed to post a twenty-four-hour sentry on the access road to keep souvenir hunters out unless they had written authorization from someone very high up in the chain of command.

I was never much of a souvenir hunter myself, but there were many who lusted for samurai swords and/or Japanese small arms to take home as prizes of war—or proof that they were there.

I *know* I was there.

As it all worked out, I wound up with a job that I thought was much better pickin's than sentry duty. The lieutenant called us all together at the outset, explained what the unit's mission would be, and asked for our suggestions as to how to divide up the necessary work among us. This worked out just great. Some of us chose to man the wharfside patrols, others opted for sentry shifts on the "thou shalt not pass" road, and still others volunteered to keep the home fires burning at our unit headquarters (not all that bad a building). This last group included me and two or three others who elected to share cooking duties; also some men who took on cleanup and housekeeping responsibilities (they probably made good husbands in later life); and a couple of able clerical hands who helped the lieutenant keep needed administrative paperwork up to date.

We were a happy crew, and we admired this young officer (whose name I've unfortunately forgotten) for his faith in the troops who must get the job done. We looked forward to a smooth-running and cozy job free from some of the chickenshit interference one runs into sometimes with officers unsure of their abilities.

I don't know what our building had been used for in the past, but suitable as it was for our housing, it lacked a kitchen. Luckily, our unit included some pretty good scroungers, with an entrepreneurial bent. We were ready to innovate when necessary, and open to solving problems in "fun" ways (a concept usually absent from the military lexicon). In that spirit, we "chefs" began searching for potential cookery stuff.

Living in a shipyard, we found many interesting items at hand. For example, seagoing vessels need ventilation shafts that circulate air from the great out-of-doors to the dank and dark caverns below decks. To keep sailors from accidentally falling into them, such shafts have safety caps installed. We found several of these caps—open-bottomed steel or cast-iron boxes about four feet on a side (big ships require wide shafts!) and a foot or so deep, with steel gratings across the top. Propped up on bricks we found lying around, these boxes made dandy barbecue grills—there was plenty of charcoal, too. The foodstuffs to feed our two dozen mouths were provided by the supply folks, who kept big trucks rolling our way. We were in the cooking business.

Soon, various "ships of the line" (important firepower providers of the fleet) began arriving to dock in our unit's area of command. (I liked that phrase: "area of command." We had suddenly become important cogs in the wheel!)

It wasn't long before, to our surprise, the captains of these ships began appearing at our door with something on their mind other than repairs and resupply. Somehow they seemed to have heard that our unit controlled access to a huge stockpile of rifles, pistols, and samurai swords that the Japanese wouldn't be needing any more, and they asked to see our commanding officer. Whether interested in souvenirs for themselves or for their men, they were extremely interested in building good will with us. Even if they had the necessary high-level authorization to visit the warehouse, they wanted to make sure there would be no problem getting past our sentry.

It was tough for us troops to hold back a smile when we saw these very senior officers, veterans of many sea campaigns, showing up with gold-bedecked hat in hand (metaphorically), trying to be casually buddy-buddy with our lieutenant. Able as he was, he was a lowly officer, junior to them by three, four, or more ranks. (It also amused us to wonder why a sailor would want a samurai sword, and how he would explain having acquired it. Did he wrest it from the grip of a ferocious Japanese admiral in hand-to-hand combat on the open sea?)

Gentlemen and men of the world that the captains were, they did not ask favors from their newfound friend the Marine lieutenant without being prepared to grant favors of their own to smooth the way. Into his office came bottles of pain-killer—the good stuff, names highly born men would recognize as gracing their own cabinet. And the appreciation of the aristocracy of the sea did not stop with the lieutenant: cases of beer arrived for his worthy troops as well. Nor was that all. Before long came cases of eggs, frozen vegetables, boxes of frozen steaks and anything else to ease the hunger of troops far from home. I don't recall apple pie, but these guys were certainly trying to do it right.

How the naval brass overall did booty-wise, I'm not sure. I know some of them came back with the goods and kept a happy ship. I know that we ate very well, often needing to beg our troops coming through the chow line to have another steak so we could start on the next case before the disaster of thaw. As one of the "chefs" it was a pleasure to feed these guys as well as they had ever eaten in their lives, if not better. We had a happy ship, too.

Other good things happened. We were fortunate enough to have a slab of concrete in our area that was just right for a basketball court. Where we got the hoops and balls, I don't know, maybe some go-getter recreation officer found them for us. The exercise was welcome; we had been settling into an indolent life. Soon after our games began, some athletic young Japanese men began hanging around, and before long we had some pretty good games going with them. They weren't too tall (neither were we), but they were quick and agile. Even better, some nearby young ladies showed up to watch their boyfriends. Needless to say, we watched the girls.

As much fun as all this was, we were still doing our job, and very well, I believe. But things were changing in the grand plan, and our delightful duty at the harbor was coming to a close, leaving us with some most pleasant memories.

My only regret is that I don't remember the name of our fine commander. He held the rank of lieutenant, but he was a general in our book.

Chapter 25

THE BIG SHIFT—AND THE CASE OF THE MISSING WEAPONS

We soon got word about some very important happenin's. Many of the men here had enlisted in the regular Marine Corps early in the war, and their four-year hitches were due to expire soon. Others, who had joined the Marine Corps Reserve instead, were enlisted "for the duration"; but under a "point" system established as the war was ending, many of them, too, were becoming eligible to return home soon.

The Occupation seemed to be going peaceably, so we probably didn't need all those troops there any more. If every man eligible to leave went home right away, though, the two divisions (the Fifth and the Second) that were USMC's main contribution to the Occupation of Japan would be left severely undermanned and weak. What to do? Someone upstairs came up with one of the world's greatest ideas: transfer all the "short-timers" into the Fifth Division and send it back to the States, and put those whose obligations were not completed yet into the Second Division, which would remain in Asia for awhile. Great solution. It took a bit of doing, but we all set about to accomplish it.

I was taken from my beloved Provisional Detachment and sent back to the barracks at Sasebo, where I resumed my job as armorer of H Company, 3rd battalion, 28th Marines. I had my work cut out for me as we prepared for the Fifth Division's return to the United States: In addition to swapping our newer guys for the Second Division's short-timers, the plan called for all our weapons and equipment to be turned over to the Sixth Division, which had some units in Japan and some in China.

I was told to organize a working party, collect all company weapons, pack them in Cosmoline (grease), and deliver them by truck to our battalion quartermaster for onward delivery. We did all this as ordered.

The quartermaster's collection point was an open field full of piles of equipment. Trucks aplenty were driving in and out, loading and unloading, and the quartermaster's men were up to their necks in work.

I spotted Corporal Pilkington, a member of the quartermaster section with whom I had often transacted company and battalion business, and asked him where he wanted our company stuff. He pointed to a vacant area in the midst of all this madhouse and I had my party unload our company weapons there.

Per standard procedure, I had brought along a sheaf of paperwork to be signed by whoever accepted my delivery, documenting that responsibility for the goods had been transferred. I handed these papers to "Pilk," but he was busy handling the rush of other traffic, so he stuffed them in his jacket and said, "I'll get them back to you." He and I had been doing business for two years with no problems, so I felt that my mission was all taken care of. End of story?—No, sir!

All of us short-timers were only a couple of days from getting on some boat and heading back east. There was no duty for us but to wait impatiently for the ship and get going. One thing we could do, we could go over to the "slop chute" (enlisted men's beer hall) and hoist a few. I was enjoying this pleasant pastime when an aide entered the door and barked, "TEN-HUT!" We jumped to attention, and a captain strode in.

He immediately put us, "at ease," but this visit was a highly irregular event. We wouldn't wander into Officers' Country without specific summoning, and the officers in turn had respect for our humble territory. I can't recall any other officer ever coming into an enlisted men's beer hall uninvited and unannounced. I don't remember what this officer's name was, but for the sake of the telling I'll call him "Captain Hardnose". I had never seen him before; he was probably from the now resident 6th Division.

We had just settled down from the shock when he spoke. Very businesslike, looking around, looking for someone in particular. "Sergeant Miller?"

I rose respectfully. "I'm Sergeant Miller," I said, not thinking that there may have been more than one of those in the room. (No one else responded, in any case.)

The captain, wearing a most officer-like unfriendly gaze, spoke again. "Would you be in my office at 0900 hours tomorrow." It was not a question. Mustering my respect and personal resolve, I replied, "Yessir!" in a brisk, but gentlemanly, manner. Everyone looked at me as if I had committed some heinous crime. I tried to look innocent of anything, but really I was most surprised, and not just a little bit puzzled. I had *no* idea what this was all about.

I didn't sleep well. Had someone squealed about the trips to Koura? Innocent enough!

Needless to say, I was in Captain Hardnose's office at 0900. He had a lieutenant at his side, as if he were not fearsome enough all by himself. At least, my curiosity was about to be satisfied. I saluted, saying, "Good morning, sir," almost as if we were about to go off for a game of tennis.

My attempts at a bit of easy demeanor did little to raise the temperature above absolute zero in the room. I was scared, but didn't want to show it. I was as good a man as he was, I thought—maybe better—and I was going to get my chance to prove it.

Not a glint of compassion in his eye as he began. "Miller," he said as if it were a dirty word. "Where are the Company H weapons?"

I would have liked to be able to respond, in my breeziest manner, "Oh, that—here they are, sir, right here in my pocket." I decided that it would be more prudent to come clean and tell him all I knew.

"I delivered them to Corporal Pilkington at the quartermaster assembly station as I was ordered, sir." (Not as cool as my first thought, but at least a straightforward response. Is this all it's about?

Huh? Huh? Huh?)

"There is no record of your committing the weaponry to the regimental quartermaster, Sergeant." (He wasn't loosening up a bit. So much for straightforwardness.)

"I delivered the weapons to Corporal Pilkington, with the paperwork. He said he would get back to me. We could ask him—he would have the papers and confirm my story, sir."

"Corporal Pilkington is in China, Sergeant." (Very cool, this guy. My knees were feeling weak; maybe I should fall on the mercy of the court? No, now was the time for a dazzling offense—hey, it works in football, why not in tennis? I paused to gather my wits and my corpuscles.)

"To my knowledge, Captain, those weapons are all still in a warehouse nearby. They are probably no longer laid out by company, but I have a complete duplicate list of serial numbers of all the weapons we had in Company H, sir, and I believe I can locate all those we turned in."

This was a pretty good response. I was beginning to think I had a chance to win our morning tennis match. But Captain Hardnose wasn't through with me. He said, in his sternest military manner, "Those weapons are worth 287 thousand dollars [or some such huge number] on the market. How do we know you haven't...." His voice trailed off, menacingly.

My knees got weak again. Did he know what he was talking about? Did he think I looked like the kind of guy who would sell our weapons to a hostile power? Was he just trying to scare me? If so, he was succeeding—if he didn't buy my story, I might be facing years in Portsmouth Naval Prison.

It was time to pull myself together for a supreme effort. Look at this through the captain's eyes, I told myself. He needs to get off the hook too. He probably works for some colonel with a nose even harder than his, a boss with questions the captain has to come up with satisfactory answers for. He needs my help—I will help him.

(Pretty good composure for a twenty-one-year-old, eh?)

"Captain," I began (authoritarian officers always like it when you acknowledge their superior rank). "I will get my copy of the records, descriptions and serial numbers. I have always been most meticulous about that."(I *hate* detail and was just lucky that I had a copy of the records.) "I can go immediately to the warehouse and find the weapons I turned in to Corporal Pilkington. I know you need to clear this whole thing up. Would you care to send a couple of your people along to verify that we have identified the weapons in question?" (Notice the "we." Thanks to my Oscar-worthy performance, the captain and I are on the same side now. And if he provides men to get some of the work done, we'll get the whole bloody mess over a lot sooner.)

To help your heart, I can tell you that we found enough of the Company H weapons by serial number to put Captain Hardnose's mind at ease (and, I hope, the minds of his boss, the boss's boss, and so on). My mind was more at ease also.

End of story. I came out of this one without a scratch. In a few days, I was not in the brig, but on a ship back to the States, headed for discharge at the end of my enlistment.

Chapter 26

WHAT HAPPENED AFTERWARDS

I left Iwo Jima wearing both my dog tags. (Each Marine wore a chain around his neck with two metal tags, similar to the ones you get for Fido. The tags were stamped with your name, serial number—mine was 356706—and other administrative information. If you were killed, the Graves Registration people took one of them off for the records. The other, I guess, stayed with your remains. Keeping both dog tags was good.)

When I got back to the U.S. I was offered a fourth stripe for my sleeve (a promotion from Sergeant to Staff Sergeant) if I would "ship over" for another four-year hitch in the Marine Corps. Instead I chose the unknown perils (and freedom) of civilian life, and returned home to Oshkosh, Wisconsin.

I got back on a Saturday, had a job on Monday, and enrolled in a nearby college on Tuesday. I have been busy ever since.

I worked in machine shops, mostly on product development after I had acquired some skills. Later, I enjoyed the challenges of building new things, working for several different inventors. More stories there.

The opportunities of industry were not enough to keep me from pursuing studies in psychology, in which I earned a degree and did graduate work. I also got more experience in music—singing a lot, studying and writing and becoming active in music education. Oh yes, I got married a couple of times and raised children whom I love more and more.

Friendships have always been important to me. My buddy Hal, like me, was sent from Camp Tarawa to Japan after the war to take part in the Occupation. We were in different outfits, in different places, but we resumed contact afterwards. When we both came home, I went from Wisconsin down to Illinois to visit him for a few days. How nice! I am still in touch with him from time to time and have told him about this book. He says he will send me some experiences of his own to add if this all works out. He is older, but is still around. It is great to talk to him now and then.

My various musical and other interests all got put to work after I moved to Maine. There I met Pete Mickelson, and with him invented a device called "HearFones" to help singers sing better. The two of us have gone on from there to do further serious research in science, music, and education. So much for "retirement."

I live now in the quiet town of Paris, Maine, so as to get more work done. I spend pleasurable times with (very good friend) Miss Smith nearby. Very pleasurable times.

Chapter 27

FINAL THOUGHTS—FOR NOW

Everyone's life is different—how unbearably dull it would be if it were otherwise!) In my own life I have done much serious thinking, read a lot and loved to learn, have been most curious and always wondered how and why people meet so many different fates.

When I enlisted in the Corps, I was looking for challenges. I have sought interesting new goals all my life—that's the way I am. I had many different duties in my time as a "spare part"—I enjoyed doing new things and I appreciated the respect my superiors had for me to give me these varied assignments. Beyond just coming back with both my dog tags, I think I usually did my job well.

My four-year stint with the U.S. Marine Corps gave me a million-dollar education and an unforgettable experience. I appreciate how all of that helped to mold a better person of me. I appreciate all that so many men gave for others. I appreciate being alive to watch each new morning blossom. I appreciate your reading what I have to say.

That "million dollar education" was worth even more if you lived through it! And I *did* live through it. So many who went to Iwo Jima did not. No words can describe my sorrow for the many men lost—boys who would never have a chance to grow up, men whose children would never see their daddy again, wives with never again a loving hug from the man they chose, parents who sent away a boy who never returned. I cannot think of this without tears coming to my eyes and a strong pain in my body for all the loss to so many families. But I did live through the battle and it changed my life.

I believe there are great lessons to be learned here. I know that the tribulation I (like many others) experienced in those six weeks on Iwo Jima truly registered with me and changed my life for the better. I am bold enough to believe that what I saw and felt and learned can give some strength, hope and comfort to many who stumble through their days with little appreciation of how precious life can be. It could be a matter of life-building importance for them if they care to listen.

I digress briefly. I circulated the first draft of this memoir in the Marine Corps community and was pleasantly surprised to hear from retired General Fred Haynes, who had read my account with some interest. He had been on Iwo, too—as a major, with far greater duties than mine—and had also written a book about his experiences there published in 2008 as *The Lions of Iwo Jima.* Now majors don't usually get too chummy with sergeants, but he seemed very interested in what I had done after the war. It was his interest that started me thinking that my Iwo impressions were all part of a much larger picture. I really can't guess what my life might have been from 1947 on had I not joined the Marines and experienced Iwo, but I'm sure it would have been vastly different. I went off to the war directly from high school, and must admit that I enjoyed learning and singing and acting so much in my student years that I gave little thought to life after Oshkosh High. Thanks, General Haynes, for getting me to look more closely into what happened after world affairs stepped in to direct my activities. I don't always give that a lot of thought, but somehow, it really is one big picture.

What I have to tell covers decades, involves many other people, and includes widely varied experiences that I feel should be seen as a whole. There's a lot to tell, but in essence it's the simple story of a boy who became a man, a man who truly appreciates being alive. How did I gain that appreciation, and how can others do it? I don't think it's self-indulgent to say that to understand these things we must begin at the beginning—the cold March night when I was born on the far south side of Chicago—and learn about the path I took.

My father had begun his adult life as an engineer, but his lifelong career passion was in the field of recreation, which was beginning to become an important part of American culture. At various times in his life he competed as a professional and semi-pro athlete; taught boxing and wrestling in the army in World War I; served as a playground director in Chicago; and later served as a recreation director in three different cities. He came from a family of workers and brought a "get the job done" attitude to everything in his life. He had a ready smile and enjoyed people. He loved his son, but (in the time-honored Old World way) was reluctant to show him "too much" affection. His ability to organize activities for many people taught me about being organized; I also learned from him the joy of working.

My mother was raised in northwest Minnesota in an academic family. (Her father, another hard worker, was the founder and president of a small college; her mother, the valedictorian of her high school class, was one of his students when she won his heart and went on to marry him.) My mother became a schoolteacher to please her father, but she was always very active in sports, and after one year of teaching she moved to Chicago to attend a physical education school. The family she roomed with there introduced her to a friend of theirs who was later to become my father. Mother had a love of people, a light heart, a limitless imagination, a dear sense of drama, and she had me! (After being married, of course.)

I am happy to believe that I acquired, by way of genes, example, and learning, the better attributes of this great pair. Much of what I inherited from them helped me get into the routine and expectations of military life. My father's loving but rather controlling ways accustomed me to taking orders—sometimes softened by the lighter view of life that guided my mother, but always motivated by my father's get-the-job-done attitude.

All in all, I got along well in the Corps, surviving boot camp, the west coast rifle range, Camp Elliott, Alaska, Seattle, Fifth Marine Division forming and training in California and Hawaii, the Real Thing in Iwo Jima, Japan invasion training in Hawaii, and then (saved by the atom bomb!) Occupation duty in Japan.

Back in the (other) real world, after four years of life run by the USMC, I needed to set my own directions. Notwithstanding my father's organizational skills, I don't recall that we had ever talked about what I would be doing with my life after high school. I'm also quick to admit that I had given this very little serious thought. But I found myself enjoying learning interesting things, having fun and getting acquainted with friends in school—and working.

When I went over to enroll in the nearby Normal School (teachers' college) after the war they asked what line of study I wished to pursue. I really didn't know, but after some discussion I embarked on a "pre-professional" path and got going. I was a bit rusty in study habits, but a couple of the girls were kind enough to give me advice and encouragement. I spent a semester and a summer session at this college while working nights in a factory. When the union there started planning a strike that looked like it would put me out of a job for a while, I left school and went to Chicago, where my mother now lived, to work for another manufacturer.

I enjoyed making things and learning more about machine work, and I was beginning to find that I liked the challenge of new tasks. I was able to exercise my imagination and inventiveness enough to be good at working with inventors, and at some of the more interesting jobs in product development. I was now confident enough to look for challenging jobs, with rewards that were not just financial. I liked working and my employers liked my get-the-job-done attitude. My goal was not so much to amass a lot of money as it was to have a sense of accomplishment and to become more competent in my field. (I did enjoy some of the things money could buy to make life easier and more fun, but if I'd been bent on money for its own sake, I would have been doing other things.)

Now, with more skills and increased confidence, I was beginning to pick and choose jobs in tool making and experimental machining that interested me. My work and my life seemed to grow out of much the same philosophy. I usually saw my work as an important aspect of who I was, but also—equally important—as fun.

I left a second industrial job in Chicago, a well-paying one with a good future, to go back to school. I wanted to finish my four-year degree (maybe more) and get onto some more focused career path. I had always been interested in people, not only as friends, but as humans who do certain things for their own reasons, and I kept wondering how those reasons developed. So I went to Lawrence College in Appleton, Wisconsin, not far from my home grounds, and chose to major in psychology, with a minor in English.

I enjoyed these studies, and am glad I made the change. Shortly after starting the fall term, I got married and began a family. While finishing my last three years of school, I found myself usually working forty hours a week—not because I was a workaholic, I think, but because I just liked to do it. I almost always enjoyed the job I had chosen, and I tried to view my employment as some kind of adventure. Upon graduation I chose not to work in the field of psychology; instead, I looked for more interesting challenges in business and product development. I wanted to exercise my imagination and inventiveness, to satisfy both the boss's needs and my own desire to accomplish things in my own way.

At least a few times in my middle years others would ask me, as I often asked myself, "Where are you going, and what are your career goals?" I could never really answer that question. All in all, I enjoyed what I was doing. I enjoyed my family and I was spending more time in music, both singing and writing. Often in those years I felt deep inside that I was "preparing myself" for something with all this work. This may not answer some of those questions, but after taking some lengthy aptitudes test (to find out "who I really am") I discovered what I had kind of suspected: that I had strong aptitudes, or strong interests, in several different fields. There would come a stage of my life, I felt, when I would have the chance to put all of them to use. I'm happy to say that I've reached that stage now, as I work with my business partner Pete in a little research and development business where my aptitudes and interests all come in very handy.

Which brings me up to today—and to the "truths of success in life" that over time I've discovered work for me. I'm a happy guy. I still appreciate very much being alive, and making good use of my time on earth. I try to enjoy every day—not that I necessarily deserve it—but I'm certainly not going to throw it away!

I have come to believe that each of us has a "gift" (or several), and that when a person finds that gift, he should use it to begin contributing to his family and friends and as much of mankind as he can touch. The "gimme, gimme, gimme" folks lose out on the happiness giving to others can bring. When I help someone else, even if it's only a kind gesture, I feel good and am inspired to do more, so far as my abilities allow. This isn't complicated stuff. The golden rule has said it before me, and the world works better that way. If we all work together, just one little attempt at a time, we will improve things. This will be more rewarding than the self-centered person's efforts that benefit only himself, if anyone.

What has this sermon to do with my experience on Iwo Jima, the way it challenged and changed me and the ways similar experiences affected others? About as good an answer as I've come up with is that the experience made me get very serious about enjoying being alive. Here's a lighter-hearted expression of the same philosophy: Working hard to give to others, having purposes beyond yourself but also letting life be fun for you, will bring rewards beyond measure. You'll get so much more than the lost souls who focus on themselves, believing someone owes them joy and happiness. (No one does!)

Back to Iwo Jima and a world of contrasts and mixing thoughts: in reflection, I would have to say my mother and father gave me a good start in life, both in genes and in habits. Like any normal young man, I didn't always follow everything mom and dad said to do. I had a mind of my own, often to their consternation. My thanks to them and their "faith" in me or their faith in God or in themselves. In any case, I had a good solid start in living life successfully.

My life in the Marine Corps taught me (the independent thinker) the advantages of working together to achieve a demonstrated common goal. As I have said in my narrative, we trained to "work the plays" together to accomplish important results. This came from learning the basics of the Marine style of military life. A trust in those who gave the orders was necessary to doing what needed to be done. This was no democracy; the officers and sergeants knew, for the most part, what it took to get a job done, and we privates had to believe they knew what they were doing. They earned their rank and had to prove it by successful performance. We needed to believe in them and also believe that the buddies we worked with would do what they were supposed to do, in the smallest of activities as well as in the grand battle strategy. Trusting that all the other members of the team would do what they were trained to do would not only help us accomplish our objective of the moment but also tend to keep us alive. This didn't always work, as the death toll figures attest. We learned that every day.

The imminent threat of pain or death has been described in various ways—equally true, but not the same—by those who have "been there" in battles over the ages. Each soul has its own way of knowing it is present at the edge of death. That incessant "buzz" in your body—the ever-present vague feeling of fear—was your own personal fright, to be felt as your very own. The feeling was always there. It was now a part of your identity. It wouldn't go away, even in the short, fitful times we called sleep. At home you could simply stand in a field, enjoy the sky, and take a deep relaxed breath. The man who tried this on Iwo would likely be shot in seconds. Death could come any time from any direction; bang, just like that.

Now I am back home away from all the danger, but not at all forgetting it. Everything that happened to me in the six-week trial of fire on Iwo Jima helped to temper me into a better, happier man. Every day now, I am very glad to be alive! After leaving that island, I enjoyed being free to do pretty much what I pleased. I had developed a sense of purpose that stays with me today. I gained personal confidence that the man I became could do almost anything I wanted to do—within reason.

My imagination and my naturally curious nature have given me many new ideas that I've eagerly tried out. Not all of them succeed, but this doesn't affect my self-confidence. I don't mean the big-shot, blowhard bluster I hate so in other people, but the inner courage to at least take a shot at making my ideas work. Again the get-the-job-done habit was a lot of help. I enjoyed my confidence gained from learning about people and about life. I enjoyed doing things for people as persons and as a whole human race. I was idealistic enough to want to make a better world somehow, and in some ways I believe I did.

I feel sorry for folks who follow the path of wanting money and status and stuff, of desiring others to entertain them and make them feel important; rather than the path of doing good things in the world and enjoying the real satisfaction of personal accomplishment. Many folks wander about, apparently lost, who never got the idea of learning to feel better about themselves by becoming better people. I have enjoyed and still enjoy doing things for people because that's the way I am and I feel life is better because of it.

Ray

FROM THE VOLCANO TO THE GORGE
GETTING THE JOB DONE ON IWO JIMA

Howard McLaughlin was a Fifth Marine Division combat engineer. Because of heavy US casualties in the early hours of the Iwo Jima invasion, he came ashore on the first day as a member of a machine gun crew. For the next month he destroyed enemy fortifications to enable infantry units to conquer the island, yard by yard. Since the war McLaughlin has lived in California, where in addition to a forty-year career as a civil engineer in highway construction and fifteen years as the owner of a Fuchsia nursery, he was active for many years as a volunteer in community service.

Ray Miller was an armorer with the 28th Marine Regiment, Fifth Marine Division. He landed near Mount Suribachi on the first day of the invasion. After the summit was captured he took part as an infantryman throughout the grinding northward march to overcome bitter Japanese opposition and conquer the island. Miller lived in Wisconsin and Illinois after the war and eventually moved to Maine, his present home. He became a skilled machinist, tool designer, and inventor as well as earning a degree in Psychology. He is also a fine singer and has pursued a lifelong interest in music and music education.

CPSIA information can be obtained at www.ICGtesting.com
Printed in the USA
BVOW03s2039141214

379235BV00024B/396/P